P9-EJU-383

from Motorcycle Consumer News

Proficient Motorcycling

The Ultimate Guide to Riding Well

by
David L. Hough

BOWTIE
PRESS

A Division of BowTie, Inc.

Irvine, California

Also by David L. Hough,
Street Strategies: A Survival Guide for Motorcyclists.

Ruth Berman, editor-in-chief
Nick Clemente, special consultant
Amy Fox, editor
Michael Uyesugi, designer
Rachel Rice, indexer

Library of Congress Cataloging-in-Publication Data
Hough, David L., 1937-
Proficient motorcycling : the ultimate guide to riding well / by David L. Hough.
p. cm.
Includes bibliographical references and index.
ISBN 1-889540-53-6 (soft cover)
1. Motorcycling. I. Title.
TL440.5 .H67 2000
629.28'475--dc21
00-008873

BowTie™ Press
A Division of BowTie, Inc.
3 Burroughs
Irvine, California 92618

Printed and Bound in Singapore
10 9 8 7

Proficient Motorcycling

DEDICATION

While the contents of this book are really a collective wisdom gleaned from fellow motorcyclists and the school of hard knocks, two individuals were instrumental in allowing this book to come to life.

First, it was Bob Carpenter, the editor of *Road Rider*, who salvaged my first article back in 1972. Bob encouraged me to keep submitting, showed me by example how to write, and then suggested I tackle the "Proficient Motorcycling" series that eventually served as the basis for this book. Thanks, Bob. It's been quite a trip so far.

Second, my wife, Diana, has been tolerating my travels, travails, and tantrums since we got married. She has accompanied me on many long motorcycle journeys on a variety of motorcycles that weren't very comfortable; endured more than a few cold, wet, windy days; put up with my motorcycling fanaticism for the past thirty years; and kept me moving on this project even when I would rather have gone riding. We got married in a little country church on Bainbridge Island forty-three years ago, and we're still together. Pretty amazing, huh?

CONTENTS

Foreword

Like most motorcyclists, my initial rider training (if I dare call it that) came in the form of a salesman pushing a bike off the showroom floor into the parking lot and pointing out its control features to me. "This is the throttle and this is the clutch. Your left foot does the shifting—down to first gear, then up to each of the other four—and your right foot does the braking. There's a front wheel brake at your right hand, but try to avoid using that."

With that, he kick-started the little Kawasaki and held it for me to climb aboard. After about 15 minutes of wobbling around the parking lot, getting a feel for the strange beast, I went back into the dealership, wrote a check, and within a few minutes was out on my own, dicing my way through city traffic at rush hour.

I'm very lucky to be alive today.

I believe the year was 1973, and with my new-found interest in two-wheeling I immediately went to a newsstand and purchased every motorcycling magazine available. Luckily for me, one of those publications was a fairly new one called *Road Rider*, produced by a renegade publisher in California named Roger Hull. And within its pages I found, during the ensuing years, the wisdom that I credit with keeping me alive and riding to this day. Most of that wisdom came in the form of detailed instructions on how to ride a bike safely and efficiently, written by one David L. Hough.

I read David's semi-regular articles for the next fifteen years or so, often carrying a dog-eared copy of the magazine with me to a vacant parking lot, where I could practice the procedures he outlined. Then I would stop and read them again, then practice again, and on until I achieved the desired results in cornering, braking, obstacle avoidance, etc.

Eventually I discovered a professional motorcycle riding academy, and signed up for their training courses. I suppose I expected to learn something new and different but was surprised to find that the teaching texts and range exercises were nearly identical to those I had learned from Hough's "Proficient Motorcycling" magazine series. Many years later I would discover that nearly all of the private and state-run riding schools that sprang up during the great motorcycling boom of the seventies were based on David's prolific output in one way or another, whether they credited him with it or not. In fact, to this day I often find exact, word-for-word copies of David's nearly thirty-year-old writings being used and repeated on the Internet, in newsletters and magazines, and as training materials in schools around the world—without one word of credit as to their source. And I don't believe David has ever made a dime off of, or even complained about, this rampant plagiarism of his life's work.

My love of motorcycling eventually led me away from my engineering career and back into college for journalism training, after which I became a full-time writer and eventually the editor of a motorcycle club magazine called *Wing World* in Phoenix, Arizona. Then, several years later, through a series of odd twists of fate that would seem ludicrous if they were fiction, I came to California to accept the post of managing editor at *Road Rider*. Immediately, I set about attempting to resurrect "Proficient Motorcycling," which David had ceased writing, believing he, "had said all there was to say on the subject."

Through his mentor, *Road Rider's* editor, Bob Carpenter, I tracked David down in the wilds of northern Washington State, and began badgering him to revise and revive his much-copied series. He was reluctant at first, but I convinced him that there was a whole new crop of riders that had grown up since his initial series who were entitled to the same life-saving teachings that I myself and so many like me had benefited from.

Luckily for me, he eventually agreed, and the next generation of "Proficient Motorcycling" was born in January of 1991 in the pages of *Motorcycle Consumer News*, the offspring of *Road Rider*, which Bob Carpenter and I created that year.

In the nearly ten years since then, David has written over one hundred new "Proficient Motorcycling" articles, also contributing all of the photography and drawing all the detailed diagrams and sketches for the training exercises. "Proficient Motorcycling" has won several awards, not the least of which was the National Motorcycle Safety Association's award for "Excellence in Motorcycle Safety Journalism"—twice. In his spare time, David has produced the world's first comprehensive training system for sidecar operators. He has also served as a consultant on motorcycle safety and training issues for the Motorcycle Safety Foundation, the American Motorcyclist Association, the Motorcycle Riders Foundation, the State Motorcycle Safety Administrators Association, and too many other groups to mention, both here and abroad.

But beyond all the awards and accolades, I believe David received his greatest recognition in the summer of 1999. He came down from his Washington cabin to California for a week to participate in a "Meet the Staff" ride put on by *Motorcycle Consumer News*. On Saturday morning, nearly one hundred riders from all over the U.S. gathered at our offices, and we rode together through the Santa Rosa and San Bernardino Mountains to the Mojave Desert with David bringing up the rear. At our lunch stop, speaking to a group of the riders, David commented that the state of rider education in the country must be better than he had thought, judging by how well this diverse group had ridden through the mountains. He was impressed with their riding skills and told them so. Then one of the older riders spoke up. "Hell, Dave, we're just practicing what you been preachin' to us for all these years. I don't know about these other folks, but I ride well because I learned it from you!" He looked around himself, and suddenly everyone else began nodding their heads and adding their comments and thanks to what had been said.

I have known David Hough for many years, and he is not an emotional man, nor one to take undue pride in himself, or even take himself too seriously. But I guarantee I saw an extra bit of bounce in his step for the next couple of days.

Whether you are a novice to motorcycling or a seasoned old campaigner, I think I can safely promise that there's something in this book for you to learn. Something that will make you a better rider than you were before reading it. And afterwards, you'll join the thousands of other riders, like myself, who owe David Hough a debt of gratitude we can never hope to repay.

Fred Rau
Senior Editor
Motorcycle Consumer News

Preface

I've always been interested in how things work. I remember taking apart my new cap pistol when I was six years old, and then hiding it when I couldn't get all the springs back inside. After a few more years of dabbling in things mechanical, I could overhaul the planetary-geared hub on my bicycle and respoke wheels. I worked on outboard motors and built a few boats. In college, I took some mechanical engineering courses and learned about machining, casting, and welding before I switched over to industrial design. I started maintaining the family automobiles out of necessity, and when we needed a new house for a growing family, I learned concrete work, carpentry, plumbing, and electrical.

When I started riding motorcycles back in the 1960s as a way to get to work, it was natural for me to wonder about the curious behavior of two-wheelers. I realized that riding motorcycles involved not only mechanics but also the dynamics of how to control them. My commute to work by motorcycle eventually extended to a thirty-year passion. I absorbed more than a few lessons about motorcycle dynamics and experienced the joys and challenges of long-distance touring, group riding, foreign travel, three-wheeled motorcycling, off-pavement riding, fighting for motorcyclist rights, rider training, and, yes, writing about it all.

In the mid-1970s, I started putting down my thoughts on paper, contributing occasionally to *Road Rider*, a small southern California touring magazine with a fiercely loyal family of subscribers. I began to offer safety tips at the local motorcycle club meetings and taught several "road survival" courses. When the Motorcycle Safety Foundation (MSF) came into being, I became MSF certified.

The "Proficient Motorcycling" column sprang to life in the May 1984 issue of *Road Rider* after editor Bob Carpenter asked me to write a six-part skills series, which he intended to publish every other month for one year. I didn't want to call this a safety column because I didn't think people rode motorcycles to be safe. I figured readers might rise to the challenge of getting more proficient. So I named it "Proficient Motorcycling." Little did we realize at the time that "Proficient Motorcycling" would outlive *Road Rider*, capture a few awards from the motorcycle safety folks, stretch out another fifteen years, and start a trend toward the inclusion of riding skills articles in other enthusiast publications.

By 1991, *Road Rider* magazine had been purchased by Fancy Publications and was reborn as *Motorcycle Consumer News (MCN)*, a black-and white, advertisement-free, no-nonsense, quick-turnaround, product-oriented monthly. The "Proficient Motorcycling" column jumped the gap from *Road Rider* to *MCN* almost without skipping a beat, and seventeen years later it is still a popular feature of the magazine.

Over the years, since "Proficient Motorcycling" had become a staple of *MCN*, more than a few readers have asked two questions again and again: *How do you pronounce Hough?* and *When are you going to publish all the "Proficient Motorcycling" columns as a book?*

Hough is pronounced like "tough." And the book? Well, here it is.

—David L. Hough

Introduction

Begin at the Beginning

I've been trying for years to break the taboo about discussing the risks of motorcycling. Motorcyclists know instinctively that the risks of riding are higher than those associated with other vehicles, but there seems to be a general consensus that ignoring the risks will make them go away. Certainly, motorcycle salespeople tend to sidestep the safety issue for fear of squelching a sale. Most motorcycle magazines focus on the bike as a machine or a lifestyle or an addictive pursuit, but seldom will one find articles on how to control a bike or how to get through traffic unscathed. If a motorcyclist is still trying to convince his or her family that riding a two-wheeler is an acceptable mode of transportation, maybe it would be smart not to bring up the risks. In my opinion, it is possible to reduce the risks of motorcycling to an acceptable level.

In *Proficient Motorcycling*, the subject of risk is faced openly and honestly. Yes, motorcycles are potentially dangerous, but whoever is holding the handlebar grips can significantly change the odds. If you want to avoid pain and lost dollars, you need to understand what the risks are and take positive steps to control any situation to your advantage. The proficient motorcyclist knows what trouble looks like and has the skills to avoid whatever happens along. The big payoff is that becoming a proficient motorcyclist is immensely satisfying.

In the name of efficiency, I've often stacked up a lot of hazards in close order even though I know that can be a bit intimidating. A novice rider faced with all these hazards might consider just parking the bike and hanging up the key. In real life, however, one person is not likely to encounter hazards as frequently as I've tossed them out. The point is for you to be aware of hazards that have caused other riders grief. If you can learn from the mistakes of others, hopefully you won't have to learn it all through trial and error.

Every attempt has been made to keep discussions of motorcycle dynamics simple, but some people may still have difficulty understanding the concepts. Sometimes they won't become clear until you take the book out to the garage and experiment with your motorcycle, or until you take your machine for a spin and listen to what it's telling you. And if you don't feel comfortable with any of the riding exercises suggested in the book, perhaps you should be practicing under the watchful eye of an instructor at your local rider training site.

When experimenting on your bike or practicing a skill, please wear your best crash padding. The subject of protective riding gear alone can take up an entire book. In other words, I'll try to give you all the no-nonsense information

I can, but this is only a book, not a training course. So for the purposes of this book, appropriate protective gear includes abrasion and impact resistant full jacket and riding pants, tall leather riding boots and full-fingered gloves, a genuine Department of Transportation– (DOT–) approved helmet, and shatterproof eye protection.

This book is based closely on the "Proficient Motorcycling" column from *Road Rider* and *Motorcycle Consumer News*. It includes the core knowledge and skills that the proficient motorcyclist should possess. You can study this book in any sequence you choose, but the contents are arranged so that one subject leads to the next. It will probably make more sense to you if you start at the beginning and read through to the end.

Throughout *Proficient Motorcycling,* you'll meet characters such as Biker Bob, Rider Ralph, Cruiser Carla, and a few others who may seem familiar to you. Be aware that the characters in this book are fictitious, although most of the situations are based on real accidents and incidents. You may even recognize a bit of yourself in these fictional folks. Think of these tales of woe as myths, which may not be exactly true but have the potential to be learning experiences. In some cases I know I've played the part of "Bob" myself. Please do us both a favor and don't get hung up on the names or the gender.

You'll notice that once in a while a mysterious *we* offers advice. That's because I get a lot of feedback from veteran motorcyclists, rider training professionals, and other journalists, and the advice reflects this feedback. Even when I go out on a limb, most of my information is a collection of knowledge I've gleaned from a widespread family of motorcyclists.

Consider this book only the beginning of a journey toward becoming a proficient motorcyclist. Ten years ago I mentally added up the various bikes I'd ridden and figured I'd accumulated about 750,000 miles. I haven't bothered to keep a tally since then, because I'm more interested in the lessons than the miles. One thing I know: Over the horizon, there are many other lessons waiting to be learned.

CHAPTER 1

RISK!

Canyon Bites

August 23, 1998: A sunny Sunday morning in the Colorado mountains. Perfect weather. Light traffic. The pavement is clean and dry. Norman and Christine are motoring eastbound through scenic Boulder Canyon, enjoying the ride and the view. Both riders are wearing protective gear, including high-quality full-coverage helmets. Norman is paying attention to the curves, planning good cornering lines, and keeping his Suzuki well in control.

Notice where the rider is crossing the centerline. When you are approaching a blind curve, remember this image, and make a point of avoiding the critical area.

Westbound, Mark and three of his buddies on fast sportbikes are dicing with each other, enjoying their race-bred machines, the excellent road conditions, and the rush of friendly competition at the spirited pace, showing little regard for the speed limit or the double yellow lines. At the moment, Mark is slightly more willing than the others to jack up the risks, and his Honda is pulling ahead of the pack.

Just east of Hurricane Hill, Norman slows the Suzuki for the sharp blind turn through the rocks, and leans the bike over into a nice curving arc that should kiss the centerline just at the apex. At the same instant, Mark carves into the same turn westbound on his Honda, realizing too late that the curve through the rocks is tighter than he had assumed. There is nothing Mark can do to prevent the Honda from drifting wide across the double yellow lines, right into the path of the approaching Suzuki.

Frantically, Norman shoves his grips toward the right to swerve the Suzuki away from a 100 mph head-on collision, and Mark pushes so hard on his grips that the Honda low sides in a shower of sparks and plastic. The Honda's tires clip the Suzuki just hard enough to send the Suzuki cartwheeling into the rocks. Norman dies instantly, his helmeted head ripped from his body. Mark tumbles to a stop, bleeding profusely but alive. A second later, Mark's buddy carves around the corner and spins through the mess of wadded-up bikes and bodies. Norman's wife, Christine, dies an hour later at the hospital.

This is a true story, and we're not relating it just to gross you out. Similar accidents occur over and over again to weekend motorcyclists on various twisty highways across America. And, yes, there is a moral: If you want to survive those entertaining twisties, it's not enough just to cruise along minding your own business. You've got to plan for the stupidity and arrogance of other motorists, including other motorcyclists. Let's consider some practical tactics for avoiding such "canyon bites" on your weekend rides.

The Double Yellow

Years ago, road crews were more frugal with those double yellow lines. We could pretty well depend on the double yellow no-passing zones warning us of hazards such as dips where another vehicle might be hidden from view. These days, road engineers continue to extend the double yellow lines farther and farther, until some highways are double-yellowed from one end to the other. If you're riding a quick motorcycle, it's frustrating to hang back behind a creeper car when you can see the road is clear and you know you have plenty of zip to get around. More and more of us are giving in to the temptation to just ignore the yellow lines and get on with the ride.

Legally speaking, it's no more illegal to pass over a double yellow than to exceed the posted speed limit, but the laws of physics are self-enforcing. Being on the wrong side of the road at warp passing speeds is certainly an invitation to a head-on collision with a car that may suddenly appear from around a corner, or a farm truck chuffing out of a hidden side road. You'll have to decide for yourself when and where you are willing to risk passing over the double yellow. My advice is to never ever be out in the wrong lane while crossing a bridge, approaching the crest of a hill, or rounding a blind curve. But what about a long uphill sweeper, where you can see the road 8 or 10 seconds ahead? What about a wide intersection with no one in the left turn lane? And when you come up behind a vehicle waiting to turn left from a busy two-laner, is it smart to come to a sitting-duck stop, or should you swerve over onto the shoulder, pass on the right, and keep moving?

Regardless of the law, before you decide to zip around any slow-moving or stopped vehicle, take a good look at the situation and try to figure out what's happening and what's about to happen. It's not just you and the road out there. Is there a side road or driveway into which the other vehicle could turn? Is there a tree-shaded intersection ahead from which another vehicle could suddenly materialize? It's unwise to pass in any areas where there are roads or driveways along the highway, even if it isn't a no-passing zone. And before you pull around a stopped vehicle, take a good look behind you to ensure that someone else isn't in the process of zooming around you.

David L. Hough

Sight Distance

We often use the phrase, *adjust your speed to sight distance.* Let's be specific about what that means. At any given speed, a certain minimum distance is needed to stop a specific motorcycle. If you expect to avoid that wild deer or those motorcycles splattered on the pavement just around that next blind turn, your speed must be limited to your stopping distance. For example, let's say your machine is capable of coming to a stop from 60 mph in 120 feet. If you can't see any farther ahead than 120 feet, your speed shouldn't be any faster than 60 mph.

Of course in real world situations, it also takes a half-second or so to react, and another second of progressive front brake squeeze to get full on the stoppers. At 60 mph, 1.5 seconds will eat up an extra 132 feet. *Uh-oh!* That means that your actual stopping distance from 60 mph is more like 252 feet. If your sight distance is only 120 feet, your speed should really be no more than perhaps 40 or 45 mph.

While we're riding, very few of us can accurately judge distance in feet, yards, meters, or car lengths. The pavement goes by in a blur, too quickly to make a mental measurement of distance. The trick is to make time measurements. Pick out some fixed object ahead such as a signpost, and count the seconds it takes you to get there. Count out loud, *one-thousand-and-one, one-thousand-and-two. . . .* By taking an actual measurement of your sight distance and comparing it to your speed, you can make intelligent decisions about how far you are hanging it out.

I'll offer some guidelines:

SPEED	MINIMUM SIGHT DISTANCE
40 to 50 mph	4 sec.
50 to 60 mph	5 sec.
60 to 70 mph	6 sec.
70 to 80 mph	7 sec.

Give these numbers a try, and see if you agree with the minimums. If these minimums make you a little nervous, add a second. If your reflexes are really quick and you can make consistent hard stops without flipping or high siding, shave off a second. The point is that you arrive at a method of gauging honestly how your speed stacks up to you and your bike's stopping performance. If you consistently find that you are entering blind situations at speeds too fast to stop within your minimum sight distances, the message should be obvious: get on the binders and slow down quickly whenever sight distance closes up.

Ride Your Own Ride

When you are out riding with others, it's amazingly easy to get stampeded into doing things that you wouldn't do if riding by yourself. Speed is so intertwined with self-worth and motorcycling that most of us will risk an accident rather than risk being seen as a slow (unskilled) rider. When someone zips past me and cuts in too close, my natural reaction is to crank up the gas and show them some speed (skill, bravado, daring, etc.).

One of the hazards of riding in a fast group or following a big dog rider is that we tend to fixate on catching the taillight of the bike ahead. This usually means focusing on steering and throttle, while ignoring a whole bag of other cornering tactics that maximize traction and minimize risk. It's often the second or third rider in a group who takes the soil sample attempting to stay with the leader. On more than a few occasions, I've seen small groups of three to six riders pull out onto a busy highway, with the tail-end riders so fixated on catching the taillights ahead that they didn't even remember to look for approaching traffic as they roosted out of the parking lot.

When riding a twisty road with other riders, the smart tactic is to back off from the bike ahead until you can't see its taillight. Then you can ignore your position in the group and ride your own ride, choosing for yourself what line to follow, when to brake, when to roll on the gas, and what your maximum speed should be entering a blind turn. One advantage to this tactic is that you aren't challenging the guy or gal ahead to race. But you may find it amazing that you can back off 4 or 5 seconds, and arrive at the rest stop only 4 or 5 seconds behind the leader, without having to take unnecessary risks.

An obvious spin-off to this tactic is when you discover that the three or four people you've been riding with can't accept your riding style. Maybe you should go back to the motorcyclist store and get some different buddies. And if you're the one who is always looking for a race, that's a hint it's time to consider the advantages of amateur road racing on a closed track rather than risking it all on public roads, as Mark and his buddies were doing.

Wandering Drivers

The other day a minivan driver who had been tailgating me for several miles of double yellow finally zoomed on by, straddling the centerline. Even though my old BMW sidecar rig was maintaining 60 in a 55 zone, I think the close pass was a message, perhaps *you've been holding me up long enough,* or *motorcycles don't belong on the highway,* or maybe just *move it or lose it, biker boy.* While such aggressive actions tend to anger me, they don't scare me quite as much as do drivers who wander over the centerline or the fog line, or those who change speed for no apparent reason. I can only assume that wandering drivers don't have their brain fully engaged in Drive, or their brains are fogged with chemicals. Either way, it's a scary situation for vehicles to be hurtling toward each other at closing speeds in excess of 100 mph, separated only by a pair of 4-inch yellow lines painted on the pavement.

Whether it's an act of aggression or a disengaged brain, drivers who wander over centerlines can pick you off if you don't take action to stay out of the way. There are specific locations where motorists tend to wander out of their lane. You can adjust your line to avoid these areas.

Consider Wandering Willie, who doesn't understand the importance of entering corners from the outside. Halfway around a turn, Willie suddenly realizes the road is turning tighter than the bike, but by then it's too late to prevent an excursion into the opposing lane. Imagine yourself approaching from the opposite direction and noticing that Wandering Willie is drifting into your lane about two-thirds of the way around the corner. Now, let's convert that top view to a perspective more like you'd see approaching the same corner. Place your left index finger on the location

Crossing the centerline is usually a result of apexing too early in a blind turn. Wandering drivers are an important reason to enter turns from the outside of your lane.

where opposing drivers tend to wander over, make a fist with your right hand, and bonk yourself in the forehead while shouting *No! No!* You don't ever want to put your bike in that location.

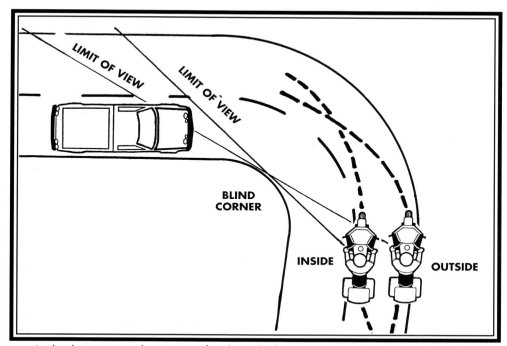

Avoiding that no-no area and entering a turn from the outside also improves your view through the corner.

The View

As it happens, avoiding that no-no area also improves your view through blind turns. The farther you are toward the outside of your lane as you enter a turn, the more you can see of what's coming, whether that's a Wandering Willie, a wild bull elk, or a patch of loose gravel. It's important to maximize your view, whether you intend to putt along and stay out of the way or attempt to increase your velocity. Remember, a longer sight distance enables a higher corner entry speed, if that's what you're looking for.

Out in the country, those right-hand turns present some special problems. The view is more limited than that of a left-hander of the same curvature, and there is a natural tendency to get a target fixation on the inside edge of the pavement, which tends to steer the bike too close to the inside too early. Come to think of it, that's why Willie ended up crossing the centerline two-thirds of the way around, right? Once we allow ourselves to enter a turn pointed toward the inside, it gets awfully difficult to avoid drifting wide a couple seconds later as we pass the road apex.

The smart tactic for staying in your lane is to enter right turns from close to the road centerline. That provides the best view around the corner, which increases sight distance, and puts the bike on a better line to exit the turn without sneaking over the centerline.

Get the Turn Over Sooner

It may sound like a paradox, but entering the turn from the outside allows you to lean the bike later but get the turn over sooner. And this becomes an advantage because you can do the hardest leaning on pavement you can see better. Even if you can see all the way around the corner, surface hazards in the distance will be harder to recognize. And if you can't see the surface all the way around, it's smarter to spend your cornering traction early. If there are surface hazards around a blind corner, you'll encounter them with the bike in a more vertical position and with more traction available for avoidance maneuvers. And what if an oncoming vehicle crosses the centerline? Entering wide gives you the best view of what's coming. If you see a vehicle wandering on the approach, you can reduce speed further, turn tighter, and duck toward the inside to stay out of the way.

One way to think of this is by mentally sliding the apex a little farther around the corner than you think the road apex actually is. To reach the delayed apex, you have to enter the turn on a wider line. A different way of thinking about this is to imagine an entry window out by the centerline through which your tires must pass.

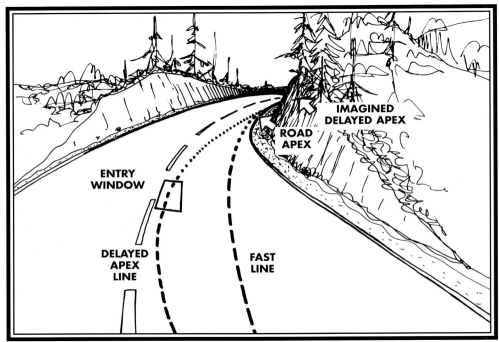

To improve the odds of staying in your lane while cornering, avoid the fast line and concentrate on a delayed apex just around the curve. That gives you the best view of the turn, and puts the bike on a better line.

Avoiding the Bite

Avoiding crashes while riding the twisties is not just a matter of motoring slowly down the center of your lane and waiting nervously to take evasive action. The best bite remedy is to practice smart cornering habits. If you think about all the points I've mentioned, you'll see a pattern emerge. The same wide-entry line that keeps you out of the no-no zone and provides a better view during left-handers is the mirror image of the wide-entry line into right-handers that gives you the best view, helps avoid crossing the centerline, and maximizes traction.

Next time you're out on the back roads, practice that delayed-apex line, and from time to time evaluate your speed habits with a quick sight-distance time hack. Don't be overcautious about using those big brakes to scrub off speed right away when sight distance suddenly closes up. That one little tactic might have saved Norman's and Christine's lives in Boulder Canyon in August 1998.

How Far Are You Hanging It Out?

I don't know how you learned to ride a motorcycle, but I taught myself. Back in the mid-sixties, my old buddy Ricochet Red had started commuting to work on a Honda 90 and quickly graduated to a big Honda 160. I tried Red's 160 and immediately saw the potential for beating automobile traffic on and off the Seattle ferry. Within a week, I found a clean used Suzuki 150 twin for $300.

Of course there weren't many training courses around in the sixties. Red gave me a half-hour lesson behind the grade school one Saturday afternoon. Monday morning I climbed on the Suzuki and zipped off into rush-hour traffic. It rained that very first day, and I remember squish-squishing around the office as I mulled over the implications of traffic and weather. That was the start of my motorcycle education.

Of course there were people around the office who clucked their tongues at my foolishness. Everyone knew motorcycles were dangerous, and riding a motorcycle to work in heavy traffic had to be high-risk foolishness. There were snide remarks and stupid jokes. One coworker even approached me, gripped my shoulder with fatherly sincerity, and offered the opinion, *I sure wouldn't want my son to ride one of **those** things.* When I arrived at the ophthalmologist carrying my helmet, the doctor gave me

When it comes to comprehensive motorcycle statistics in the USA, there has been only one real study completed in all of history—the famous Hurt Report.

Time warp back to 1979. There had been a big motorcycle-buying boom in the seventies, and a lot of those new riders managed to get involved in accidents. That big rise in accidents and fatalities got the attention of the U.S. Department of Transportation, and it decided to get into the act to protect us from ourselves. The National Highway Traffic Safety Administration (NHTSA) let a big contract to study motorcycle accidents, and the University of Southern California Traffic Safety Center got the job. The USC professor responsible for carrying it out was Hugh H. (Harry) Hurt, Jr. The Objectives of the study were to determine the causes of motorcycle accidents, analyze the effectiveness of protective gear such as safety helmets, and then figure out what countermeasures might help prevent accidents or reduce injuries.

Hurt put together a team of investigators who dashed out to every motorcycle accident scene, day or night, over two years. One of the important concepts was that all of the investigators were experienced motorcyclists. The team did an exhaustive study of each accident, determining approximately 1,000 data elements. They took photos, examined the wreckage, measured the skid marks, and interviewed the survivors of more than 900 motorcycle accidents, then interviewed 2,310 passing motorcyclists, and studied 3,600 police reports from the same area. Then they studied the data from every angle for another two years, and published the final report in January 1981.

Now, flash forward twenty years. Traffic is more intense but so is motorcycling. We've got rider training available all across the country, and motorcycles are technically a lot better than the ones we rode in the seventies. Is the Hurt Report still valid for today's motorcycling, and is Harry Hurt Jr. still around? I decided to find out.

I found Harry Hurt still working in safety research, still riding motorcycles, willing to talk with me, and sharp as a tack. Hurt is now President of the Head Protection Research Laboratory (HPRL), a nonprofit corporation formed to conduct research on motorcycle and bicycle accidents. The HPRL also conducts accident investigations and provides training. My first question about the Hurt Report was did Hurt think it was still valid after twenty years?

"We had no idea that study would last so long. We always assumed someone would commission another bigger study. As it worked out, no one ever came up with a contract. Nobody wants to do any new research projects."

Harry confided that he believes the report is still basically valid. It's not just that nothing has come along to replace it, but that he has personally seen evidence that motorcyclists are having the same type of accidents today as they did back in the seventies.

"I still do consulting for police departments and have investigated a num-

REPORT

ber of police motorcycle accidents over the years. Police motor officers get some extensive training. I mean really good training. But even professionals make the same sort of mistakes as novices, and today's riders seem to have the same sort of accidents as those in the NHTSA report."

But what about other evasive maneuvers such as swerving? Did Hurt feel that riders today face the same risks as those in the seventies? And when we did encounter a sudden hazard, didn't we resort to habits? Was there really any reason to practice evasive maneuvers? Hurt sliced through the questions like a hot knife through butter:

"Use the front brake. Use the front brake. Use the front brake."

My next concern was if all the research had been conducted in a big city, that left out a lot of back roads and therefore a lot of country-type accidents such as deer strikes. I wanted to know how Harry felt about that.

"Actually, we didn't limit our research to the city of Los Angeles. Our accident investigation teams went all over the Los Angeles basin, even up into the canyons and up on the Angeles Crest. So we did include "country" accidents in the study. Our data wasn't limited to the city. And the data did include animal strikes."

One of the other questions I had over the years concerns reported versus unreported accidents. If a motorcyclist crashes without involving another vehicle, the accident is likely to go unreported. That would make single-vehicle accidents seem less frequent than collisions. As motorcyclists, it would be important to know whether accidents such as dropping the bike on loose gravel or edge traps were as big a hazard as the infamous left-turning cars. Did the Hurt Report include unreported accidents?

"We studied every accident we knew about, and that did include some that didn't get reported to the police. In some cases, our investigators had to do emergency first aid before they could do the research because they were the first on the scene. And we know that some accidents were never reported to the police. That wasn't our job."

When you think about the technology of motorcycles, it's pretty obvious that bikes are a lot better these days than back in the seventies. For instance, brakes today are powerful, progressive, and fade-free. We've got much better tires, better suspension, and stiffer frames. I asked Hurt whether he felt today's better motorcycles changed the accident scenarios.

"The more time goes by, the less things look different. Riders today have the same sort of accidents as riders in the 1970s, except that today they crash much more expensive bikes."

a 20-minute lecture on the hazards of riding motorcycles and a 5-minute eye exam.

I wouldn't admit it to anyone at the time, but that barrage of antimotorcycle flak caused me to have some serious doubts about motorcycling. I had a wife, two children, and a mortgage. And I sure didn't want to spend the rest of my life in a wheelchair. I recall one day toward the end of the second week when I nearly gave it up. I'd strapped my lunch box to the back of the bike, put on my helmet, and prepared to start the engine, but I was a little reluctant to get rolling. Factory traffic is notoriously aggressive at shift change. I sat on the bike for a long time in the corner of the parking lot, watching cars wedge into the stream and trying to control my rising panic. Eventually, I forced myself to get on the bike and ride home. And I'm still riding. Over the next thirty years, I gradually learned some important lessons about motorcycling. The first lesson was that my coworkers and my ophthalmologist didn't know diddly about motorcycling or motorcycle safety.

Looking back, I have to agree that the basic concern of my colleagues was probably realistic. A lot of people have been messed up in motorcycle crashes, and new riders are particularly vulnerable. But what neither my associates nor I understood at the time is that the risks of motorcycling vary significantly from individual to individual. One rider may have a serious accident soon after taking up motorcycling. Another rider may survive years and years without having a single crash.

Is it just a matter of chance that one rider suffers an accident while another rider avoids crashing? Is swinging a leg over a motorcycle just a two-wheeled form of Russian roulette? I don't think so. During the years I've been riding, writing, and teaching, quite a pile of statistics has been collected, and several important accident studies have been done. We don't have nearly as much data available as we'd like, but we have a much better idea of the risks now than anyone had back in the sixties.

Yes, we understand the discomfort of bringing the risks out in the open and talking about them. After all, part of the thrill of motorcycling is challenging the odds. We ride motorcycles partly because they are more dangerous than other vehicles. Now we can be pretty vociferous about nasty crashes once we have survived them. But we're pretty tight-lipped about our individual potential for crashes that are still out in the future, especially if our relatives, coworkers, or doctors are asking tough questions.

Perhaps not talking about the risks will hold them at bay. Maybe talking about risks is inviting the odds to strike. Or maybe we just don't know enough about managing the risks to know how far we're hanging it out. Road racers understand the need for crash padding because they intend to ride at 99 percent of their limits, and they know how easy it is to punch through the envelope. But the street rider may also be riding at 99 percent of the risk envelope entering a busy intersection. If that's the case, then why doesn't the street rider wear abrasion and impact resistant riding gear?

Let's take a short, fast ride through risk territory. I'll give you a little quiz at the end to help you see how you're doing.

Uh Oh. Statistics

If you ride primarily in city traffic, your specific risks are probably defined fairly well by the "Hurt Report" (Volume I: Technical Report, Motorcycle Accident Cause Factors and Identification of Countermeasures, January, 1981—Final

Report conducted by the Traffic Safety Center of the University of Southern California). The Hurt Report is the only reliable motorcycle accident research ever conducted in the U.S. Unfortunately, more current statistics do not exist. The USC team, lead by Dr. Harry Hurt, investigated 1,100 motorcycle accidents that occurred in the area of the city of Los Angeles over a two-year period and analyzed 900 of those accidents for the report. That study is approaching retirement age, but we suspect that the same sort of accidents occur the same way in any other city even today. So let's take a look at some Hurt Report results.

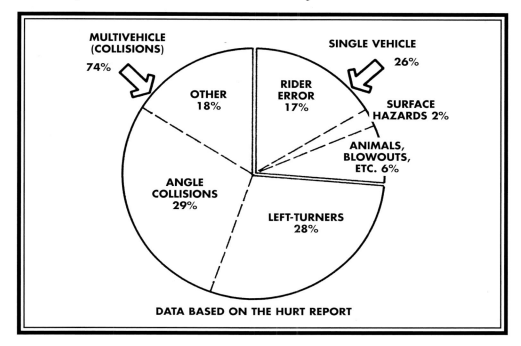

DATA BASED ON THE HURT REPORT

The majority of motorcycle accidents aren't riders exceeding the limits of traction and sliding off into the weeds, but rather they're collisions with other vehicles, mostly automobiles. About 26 percent of urban motorcycle accidents are single vehicle accidents, as when a bike slides out on gravel in a corner. But 74 percent are multiple vehicle accidents, including at least one vehicle colliding with another.

The important point of this big picture is that almost three-fourths of urban motorcycle crashes are collisions. And roughly half of those motorcycle crashes are precipitated by auto drivers. About a fourth of all city motorcycle accidents are collisions with left-turning cars. The two most common errors motorcyclists make are believing the other driver sees them and not taking any evasive action. For example, 32 percent of accident victims rode into a collision without doing anything.

If you ride around in city traffic, it is important to know where collisions occur, what they look like, and the correct evasive action to get out of the way. The Experienced RiderCourse (ERC) offered at motorcycle training sites can help you develop such skills. If you haven't taken the ERC recently, you may have missed some important accident avoidance strategies.

About one-fourth of all motorcycle accidents in the Hurt Report were precipitated by rider error. For example, the motorcyclist goes wide in a turn and sideswipes a car or overcooks the rear brake trying to stop and then slides out. We might suspect that such riders don't really understand how to control their motorcycles. So that's probably a good hint that we ought to study our control skills.

In the meantime, let's consider the experience and licensing status of riders involved in crashes. In the following table, 1.0 indicates the average of those studied. Numbers higher than 1.0 indicate a greater than average accident involvement.

Motorcycle License Status of Accident Victims	Accident Involvement
Motorcycle	0.7
None (or revoked)	2.4
Auto only	2.0
Commercial/chauffeur	0.5
Learners permit	1.2
Hurt Report, January 1981	

Those statistics hint that riders with no license, a revoked license, or only an auto license are about twice as likely to be involved in a motorcycle accident as those with a permit, and three times as risky as a licensed motorcyclist. Now, it should be obvious that just getting a piece of cardboard doesn't change a rider's skill. We might suspect that the different odds are a result of better skills, more experience, or perhaps a different mental attitude.

Let's consider risk in relation to riding experience. Does your risk go down as you gain experience? In the following table, 1.0 would be average.

Experience Riding in Traffic	Risk
0 - 6 mo.	1.40
7 - 12 mo.	0.96
13 - 24 mo.	0.93
25 - 36 mo.	1.52
37 - 48 mo.	0.98
48 mo. +	0.83
Hurt Report, January 1981	

The numbers hint that a rider with less than six month's experience is almost twice as likely to have an accident as the rider with more than four year's. We would expect that. The shocker is that the rider with two to three year's experience is even more likely to crash than the new kid. The lesson here is that riders tend to get cocky as they think they have learned it all—about two years into the learning curve.

What about training? Did Ricochet Red do me a favor giving me that riding lesson in the schoolyard?

Training	Risk
Professional training	0.46
School/club course	0.50
Self taught	0.90
Taught by friends/family	1.56
Hurt Report, January 1981	

I guess Red did me a favor by limiting his advice to a half-hour. Apparently, riders taught by friends or family are about a third more likely to crash than those who teach themselves. But the smart ones who took a rider training class were half as likely to crash as we do-it-yourself types. Since the Hurt Report took place at just about the same time as the Motorcycle Safety Foundation came into existence, it would be interesting to have current statistics. Obviously, a lot more riders are getting professional training these days, and we can see that the motorcycle accident and fatality numbers are gradually decreasing. There's no proof that training is what's bringing down the statistics, but we believe there is a connection.

Booze

It isn't a popular subject to discuss at motorcycle rallies or biker bars, but too many motorcyclists have a serious problem with alcohol. I'm not just talking an innocently sober rider getting squished by a drunk driver, I'm talking about a motorcyclist riding while under the influence and crashing into something.

For comparison, let's consider the alcohol and drug involvement of riders who survive accidents:

Rider Alcohol and Drug Involvement	Survivors
None	86.0 percent
Alcohol or drug use	11.0 percent
Unknown	03.0 percent
Hurt Report, January 1981	

There seems to be a direct link between alcohol or drug consumption and fatal motorcycle accidents. Roughly half of all motorcycle fatalities involve a rider under the influence of alcohol or drugs, mostly alcohol. One big reason for motorcycle accident fatalities is crash speed. The greater the speed, the greater the injuries when the crash happens. And riders who have alcohol in the brain are much more likely to ride faster than their sober speed, even if they are not legally intoxicated. In the Hurt Report, 41 percent of riders who didn't survive crashes had some alcohol or drug involvement.

What's the message here? Well, the bottom line is that around 10 percent of motorcyclists involved in accidents have been drinking, but drinking riders represent over 40 percent of all motorcycle fatalities. If you allow yourself to ride a motorcycle after you've been drinking, even after just a few beers, you're really hanging it out.

Big Bikes vs. Small Bikes

Periodically, we hear suggestions for limiting the power of motorcycles. States with tiered license categories based on displacement assume that big, powerful bikes are potentially more hazardous than small bikes. The insurance industry frequently attempts to show that powerful race-style motorcycles are overrepresented in accidents. Are bikes with big engines more likely to be involved in crashes?

Well, according to the Hurt Report statistics, larger machines are less likely

Engine Displacement vs. Accidents		
Displacement	Percent of Accidents	Est. Machines in Use
000 - 100cc	09 percent	08 percent
101 - 250cc	13 percent	09 percent
251 - 500cc	37 percent	26 percent
501 - 750cc	25 percent	34 percent
751 - + cc	16 percent	23 percent

Hurt Report, January 1981

to be involved in accidents than smaller motorcycles if you factor in the numbers of machines on the road. Part of the reason may be that riders move up to larger motorcycles as they gain experience and perhaps have learned some valuable lessons in traffic survival along the way.

But remember that the Hurt Report statistics are primarily about urban riding. A lot of us live in the country or do much of our serious riding on roads far from the city. Back in the early 1980s, *Road Rider* magazine did a survey to come to grips with the sort of accidents readers had actually experienced, whether reported or not. Of course, the *Road Rider* survey wasn't nearly as sophisticated as the Hurt Report, but the responses were spread over the entire U.S. Among accidents reported to the authorities, *Road Rider* readers indicated approximately twice as many single vehicle accidents most notably due to surface hazards and wild animals. The Hurt Report shows 26 percent of all accidents are single vehicle. The *Road Rider* survey indicated 45 percent were single vehicle accidents. That would make sense, since many of those accidents were out in the country, away from a major city.

The *Road Rider* accident survey brought something else to our attention. A lot of motorcycle accidents don't get reported. Let's say someone slides out on loose gravel and smashes his or her bike into a ditch. If no one calls the police,

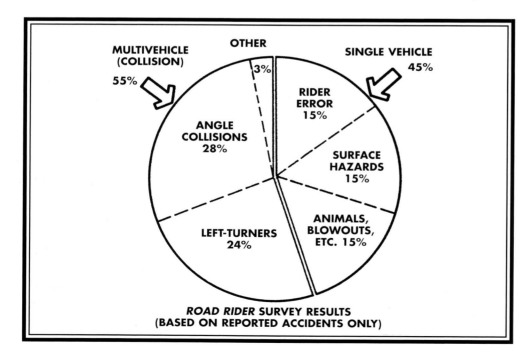

**ROAD RIDER SURVEY RESULTS
(BASED ON REPORTED ACCIDENTS ONLY)**

the rider is still mobile enough to ride, and the damaged bike can either be ridden home or hauled home in a friend's truck, the accident doesn't get reported. When we included both reported and unreported accidents from the *Road Rider* survey, the numbers came out quite differently from the Hurt Report. Single-vehicle accidents accounted for 66 percent of the total accidents, reported and unreported.

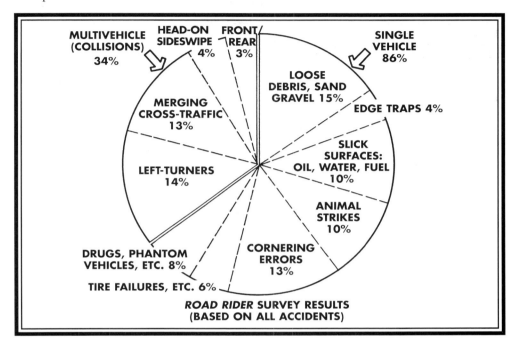

ROAD RIDER SURVEY RESULTS
(BASED ON ALL ACCIDENTS)

Note that the *Road Rider* survey hinted at more single-vehicle accidents, and a much higher percentage of these were caused by surface hazards, animal strikes, and cornering errors than the Hurt Report indicated. That would make sense because outside of cities, we would expect a higher percentage of those types of accidents. The point is you can get hurt just as badly in an unreported, single-vehicle accident as in a collision. And while the *Road Rider* survey isn't one of those huge, government-funded, university projects, we think it hints that motorcyclists face a somewhat different mix of hazards than the Hurt Report showed. That's why I will get a lot deeper into hazards such as edge traps and wild deer than the typical rider training course includes.

Unavoidable Accidents

Even with the best of licensing, training, and skills, some accidents simply are unavoidable. For example, a wild deer suddenly jumps out of the shadows and knocks you off your bike, or an oncoming coal truck swerves over the centerline in a blind corner, forcing you off the road. When you get your chance to crash one of these days, you'll be hitting the landscape in whatever gear you typically wear.

Knee, elbow, and shoulder armor cushions the blows and protects your skin from the pavement. Leg and arm injuries can be painful, but chest and head injuries are more likely to be critical or fatal. That's why some riders wear a spine protector as well as knee and elbow armor. A helmet is designed to pad the brain, but it also can provide facial protection. According to a German study by

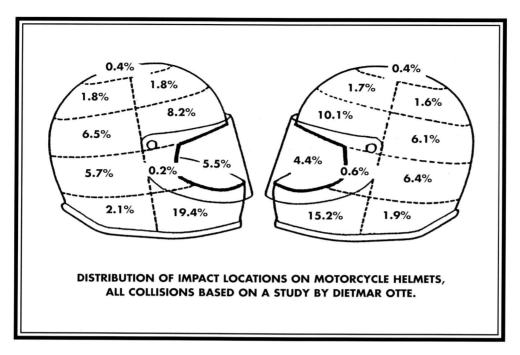

DISTRIBUTION OF IMPACT LOCATIONS ON MOTORCYCLE HELMETS, ALL COLLISIONS BASED ON A STUDY BY DIETMAR OTTE.

Dietmar Otte and Günter Felton that was published in *The Proceedings of the 1991 International Motorcycle Conference,* the majority of helmet strikes in accidents are to the left and right chin areas. You need to remember these points every time you fire up the engine to go for a ride.

Quiz Time

Okay, now that I've rambled through a few of the statistics, put on your thickest skin and tally up your personal score. The numbers are weighted in an approximate relationship to the statistics.

	Add	Subtract
1. Have motorcycle license	10	
2. Commercial driving license	5	
3. Learner's permit, no license	2	
4. License revoked		10
5. No motorcycle license		10
6. Less than six month's experience		2
7. Twenty-five to thirty-six month's experience		5
8. More than forty-eight month's experience	8	
9. Taught by friends or family		2
10. Self-taught		2
11. Passed Motorcycle RiderCourse	10	
12. Passed Experienced RiderCourse	10	
13. No training within last five years		5
14. Sometimes ride after drinking		20
15. Never ride after drinking	20	
16. Often ride in city traffic		5
17. Mostly ride 250 to 500cc		2
18. Mostly ride 750cc or larger	2	
19. Can name twenty common surface hazards	5	

	Add	Subtract
20. Know technique to cross edge traps	5	
21. Practiced quick stops this year	5	
22. Not practiced quick stops this year		5
23. Frequently use countersteering	5	
24. Don't understand countersteering		5
25. Rider age under twenty-seven		5
26. Rider age over forty	5	
27. Always wear armored riding gear	5	
28. Usually wear only denims		5
29. Always wear approved helmet	5	
30. Seldom wear approved helmet		5

Hey, It's Subjective

Sure, sure, we know this is awfully subjective. The point is to be honest with yourself about your motorcycling risk exposure. If you don't like the questions we stacked up, go back through the statistics and write your own quiz. With our quiz, a total score of 80 or higher is a pretty good indication you're doing a lot of the right things. On the other hand, if your score is less than 40, maybe you're hanging it out further than you intended. Wherever you are on the risk scale, I'll be offering some suggestions about managing the risks.

Fixing the Odds

All right, we've looked at an accident, reviewed some motorcycle accident statistics, and offered a little quiz to help you get some perspective on your relative risk. We recognize that such exercises may be way off track. After all, statistics are based on averages, and there are very few Joe Average motorcyclists. What's more, we might also be a little suspect of accident studies that look only at how and why people crashed.

Rider training can benefit almost all riders in one way or another.

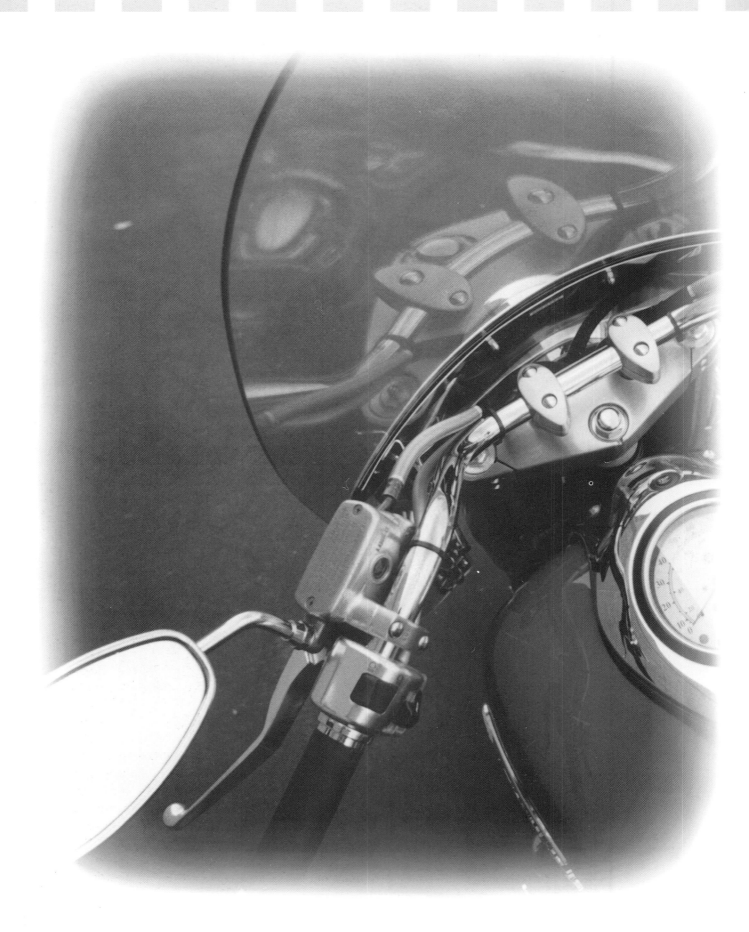

It's sort of like the patient who went to the doctor complaining of a sore tongue:

Patient: *"Doctor, my tongue really hurts."*

Doctor: *"Does your tongue hurt all the time?"*

Patient: *"No, but it really hurts when I bite down hard on it."*

Doctor: *"Well, don't do that!"*

The statistics based on accidents give us hints about what *not* to do, but they don't tell us what successful riders *do* to avoid crashing. The traditional approach to absorbing a helmet full of the right stuff is just to keep riding and riding. *Experience*, the veterans might suggest, *is the best teacher.* In other words, just ride far enough and long enough and life will eventually present you with all the lessons to be learned. That's probably true, but the trouble is some of the motorcycling errors can ambush you before you learn enough to avoid them. It's a lot safer and less risky to learn what you can from other people's mistakes and experiences. That's why I pay attention to the grizzled old motorcycling veterans when they occasionally drop hints about lessons learned.

I happened to be along one day when the *MCN* editors were picking up a test motorcycle for a photo shoot. Mostly, they were engrossed in details of the new machine, the fleeting time, the need to find a photogenic location, and the urgency of beating the evening rush hour. The dealer, obviously a veteran rider, was on a different mental plane. He knew I wrote skill articles, and he offered some advice about one small but important detail: adjusting mirrors. *Most people adjust their mirrors so that the view converges behind the motorcycle. I figured out that it is more important to see more of what's coming up in adjacent lanes. So I adjust my mirrors more toward the sides.* As we rode away with the test machine, I observed that I also adjusted my mirrors far enough outward that I could pick up only a corner of the saddlebags at the inside edges. *Big deal!* you may be thinking. *Who cares how the mirrors are adjusted? Let's get to the really important stuff!*

Well, maybe a helmet full of such small details adds up to the important stuff. Sure, our physical riding skills have a lot to do with keeping the bike under control. But what goes on between the ears is even more important because that's where we decide what to tell our muscles. Novices start out with the physical skills of mastering the clutch, throttle, brakes, and balance. Veterans understand that motorcycling is really more of a mental process of scrutinizing the situation, evaluating the hazards, and deciding what to do with the motorcycle.

Formal rider training courses can give you a big dose of information all at once. But you can also gain a lot of information from motorcycle magazines and books. A year's worth of monthly reading adds up to a big dose of information to help stack the motorcycling risk deck in your favor. A lot of motorcyclists miss out simply because they don't take the time to read what's available.

The trouble with knowledge is that it's a lot like French bread—it doesn't stay fresh very long. A number of veteran motorcyclists have told me they clip and save helpful articles in a notebook to study again on cold winter nights. You'd think the veterans would have learned it all by now, but that's not the way it works. They are still around because they continue to refresh their knowledge.

If you've found time to take the MSF Experienced RiderCourse, you've skewed the odds even more in your favor. The one-day ERC includes both accident avoidance strategies for the brain, and skill exercises for the muscles. I've bumped into a lot of veteran riders who take the ERC every couple of years as a refresher. If you haven't gotten around to taking any rider training, I strongly suggest you make that a high priority. The track schools are useful for learning motorcycle control skills or for getting in some track time, but to hone your accident avoidance skills for public roads, the ERC gets to the basic techniques.

Now and then you'll exit a restaurant to find someone circling your machine. He or she will be a little wide-eyed and irrational, perhaps drooling at the mouth. When you hear the typical questions about fuel mileage and engine size, you know you're talking to someone infected with the motorcycle bug. Do the novice a favor by pointing him or her toward the nearest rider training course, where motorcycling can be tried out under the guidance of a trained instructor. Bikes are provided for those who don't own one. If the novice decides to become a motorcyclist, that initial training provides a good foundation for gaining experience. And if that new rider is a relative or friend, all the more reason to send him or her to the local training site rather than act as a teacher yourself.

Emergency Reactions Follow Habits

One of the important lessons I've learned is that in an emergency, actions follow habits. Riding through the high desert of eastern Oregon one night, two eyes alongside the road suddenly reflected back the headlight beam. I rolled off the throttle and squeezed the brake lever gently. This is deer country, and the reliable tactic for avoiding a deer strike is to stop short of a collision. Those shining eyes were too low to the ground to be a deer, but whether a deer, raccoon, or skunk, I didn't want to hit it.

When the critical moment presents itself, chances are your reaction will follow your habits. If you expect to have the right skills in a crisis, you must practice the right techniques every time you ride.

When the reflecting eyes suddenly darted toward the pavement, my hand squeezed the brake lever, the BMW transferred its weight onto the front tire, and my hand squeezed even harder, braking the front wheel to the maximum just short of a skid. Twenty feet from impact, the headlight beam illuminated a very large porcupine bobbling out toward the centerline, then changing its mind, making a U-turn, and scrambling back toward the verge. As Porky ambled off the pavement, my hand eased off the brake, the suspension stabilized, and I rolled back on the throttle.

What amazes me still, is that I don't recall any decision to brake hard. My right hand just produced a classic quick stop, as if it had been controlled by some animal-sensing device programmed to cover the lever and then make a stop in the shortest distance without falling down. Of course, we all carry such a device. It's located on the bike somewhere between our ears. In an emergency, the brain follows whatever programs have been learned through practice. If you always favor the front brake for normal stops, and you have experienced enough power stops to know what an impending skid feels like, your brain has a quick-stop program available for emergencies.

The moral of that story is that we must constantly practice the right skills if we expect to use them in a pinch. If you expect to be able to handle the loose gravel or the wandering motorist you discover as you round a blind turn, you must practice control skills such as rolling on the throttle in curves, countersteering, and maximum-effort stops, as well as choosing cornering lines that maximize traction.

To put this another way, there aren't really any emergency maneuvers you can pull out of your bag of tricks when something goes wrong. There are only proficient control skills you can practice every day as you ride along. And, if we assume there are physical habits to be practiced, then there must also be proficient mental skills that we must practice so that they become habits.

Booby Traps

The roadways are full of booby traps just waiting to spring shut on the unwary motorcyclist. Road surfaces have potholes, bumps, loose gravel, edge traps, grated bridge decks, shiny steel plates, slick plastic arrows, and spilled diesel oil. Streets may ascend or descend hills right where the railroad tracks cross the pavement. That curve ahead may be the one that tightens up and slants the wrong way halfway around, just beyond your line of sight. That intersection ahead may have offset lanes or a spoke of three or five streets. Freeway lanes may disappear with no warning. Road signs may be placed just far enough from the intersection to mislead a visitor.

The roadways are full of booby traps just waiting to spring out on the unwary motorcyclist.

A critical stop sign may be covered by untrimmed bushes or painted on the road surface where it is obscured by the glare of the morning sun.

Veteran riders allow for such booby traps. They have become veterans by riding a little more conservatively than their personal limits; scrutinizing the situation far ahead; taking a second look at strange happenings; and avoiding sudden, impulsive moves. Swerving across three lanes of traffic to get to your turnoff is a clue that your motorcycle is traveling faster than your awareness of the situation. Sudden darting maneuvers don't leave you the extra observation time, additional space, or reserve traction needed to negotiate whatever booby traps you're likely to encounter. Likewise, experienced riders don't snuggle up to the back bumpers of other vehicles at stop signs because once in a while the driver ahead accidentally selects Reverse instead of Drive when the light turns green, or there may be an open manhole hidden from view just up ahead.

Maintain the Machine

Part of your motorcycle education should include the motorcycle itself. If you believe the Hurt Report, only a small percentage of accidents are caused by defects in the machine. Of course, it may be that on long-distance trips away from the city there are more frequent accidents caused by motorcycle defects. But, whatever the actual statistics, if you happen to have a blowout on your bike while zipping down the superslab, your tire failure statistics will be 100 percent. Tires provide the critical connection between motorcycle and road surface, yet many motorcyclists don't keep their tires pumped up to correct pressure, and many wait too long to replace worn tires. If you find yourself asking any of the following questions, the answer is always the same: Yes.

Should I check the rear tire pressure before the ride?

Should I increase pressure when carrying a heavier load?

Should I replace that worn tire before the trip?

Should I buy the more expensive tire just for a little more traction?

Should I replace that tire just because of a little sidewall cracking?

No one else is going to be as interested in the condition of your machine as you are.

There are a few other mechanical details that you should take care of before a ride. Hydraulic brake systems should be flushed every couple of years or annually in humid climates. Brake pads get hard with age. Worn brake pads should be replaced long before metal screeches on metal. Electrical problems should be traced down and fixed, especially those relating to lights. Critical fasteners such as fork tube clamps, axle bolts, and suspension connectors should be checked for tightness. You don't have to get your hands greasy yourself, but at least take an active interest in the condition of your motorcycle. Don't expect a mechanic back at the shop to keep everything in perfect condition without frequent checks. The bottom line is that no one else is going to be as interested in your machine as you are.

Body Armor

One of these days you will get your turn to crash and try out your body armor. But even if you don't get to crash, your riding gear has a lot to do with your ability to control a bike. I'll leave it up to your imagination how I know this, but a couple of yellow jackets dropping into your boot takes a lot of attention away from the task of keeping your motorcycle pointed between the lines. A sunburned neck can make it too painful to turn your head to find that car hidden in your blind spot. A bouncing stone cracking into your shin can distract you from the left-turning car ahead.

If today is going to be your turn to crash, what do *you* want between your body and the pavement?

Riding gear is more than just uncomfortable body armor worn reluctantly day after day just in case today happens to be your turn to crash. A good riding jacket protects against wind, heat, and cold. A good helmet insulates the head from wind, sun, and cold rain; and a shatterproof face shield also keeps your face from getting chapped. Leather gloves not only protect your palms from road rash during a spill but also keep your knuckles from getting burned by wind and sun, and help your fingers avoid blisters. Tall leather boots provide ankle support as well as protection from a hot exhaust pipe or nasty biting insects.

But if today does happen to be your turn to crash, it's handy if your gear also provides impact and abrasion protection. Competition-weight leather slides for something like 80 to 100 feet on rough concrete before it grinds through to your underwear.

Cotton denim rips to shreds in about 5 feet. Fabric riding suits with armored patches can be almost as abrasion resistant as leather, and a lot easier to clean after a few days under a broiling sun. Of course, we can adjust our gear to the riding conditions. The more hazardous the situation, the greater the need for good stuff. When I'm making a nighttime transit through deer country on my two-wheeled rocket, I'm inclined to wear my leathers. When I'm driving the sidecar rig, I usually wear a two-piece fabric riding suit.

The ultimate purpose of a helmet is to prevent brain injuries during an accident. You can crack your skull and survive, but scrambled brains will bring you to a permanent halt. One really important reason for protecting your brain is that the brain doesn't heal itself like other body tissue. If you bang your head hard enough to black out for a few seconds, you've injured your brain. And a concussion can turn into epilepsy a year or two down the road. So, if you intend to get back in the saddle after the big crash, consider the importance of keeping brain injuries to a minimum. Even a $50 helmet that's DOT approved can provide excellent protection because it's the crushable foam inside that protects the brain, not the outer shell.

Identify Yourself

Consider why a blind man carries a cane painted white. Why not a black cane? The color of the cane isn't for the blind man, it's to warn sighted folks that the man with the cane has a visual handicap. The same principle applies to motorcyclists. Novice riders who haven't yet learned to figure out what's happening around them on the street might be wise to warn others of their handicap. In England, learners must carry a learner plate, a large white rectangular plate with a red L on it.

If you are still going through your novice phase of motorcycling, say your first three years or 20,000 street miles, there is good reason to wear conspicuous riding gear such as a reflective vest. You can't prevent other drivers from running into you, but you can at least make yourself conspicuous enough to give them a chance to see you coming while you're learning how to get out of the way.

If you are just learning to ride, it's smart to wear conspicuous riding gear such as a bright, reflective vest.

ABOUT 18 FEET

EXIT

CENTER OF GRAVITY

ARC OF CP AROUND CG

SHIFT WEIGHT
TO OUTSIDE
FOOTPEG

KEEP ENGINE
PULLING

ABOUT 40 FEET

WEIGHT ON
ON RIGHT

Motorcycle

MOTORCYCLE

Dynamics

DYNAMICS

CENTER
OF MASS

REAR
WHEEL
THRUST

WHEEL

FRONT WHEEL

STEERING HEAD

STEERING AXIS

DECREASED TRAIL

NORMAL TRAIL

INCRE

CHAPTER 2
MOTORCYCLE DYNAMICS

What Keeps It Balanced?

You can get down the road pretty well on your two-wheeler without having to know a lot of details. Once your bike is in motion, it's relatively easy to keep it balanced more-or-less in a straight line. If the bike wanders a bit in the wrong direction, just lean it back toward your intended line. If you want to turn, all you have to do is lean the bike in the direction you want to go. Simple, huh? Well, maybe not so simple. There are a lot of riders around who demonstrate over and over that they are only partly in control of their motorcycles.

Drifting Dan really wants his sportbike to make a nice crisp turn from a stop onto that narrow road, but as he nervously eases out the clutch, the bike seems to take command and swings wide over the centerline. Wandering Wanda wants her cruiser to just motor down the middle of the lane, but it sometimes creeps over toward the edge of the pavement, then back toward the centerline. Wobbling Willie does fine at speed, but when he rolls into the parking lot for the breakfast meeting, his new heavyweight touring machine seems intent on wobbling over toward parked cars, and it's a constant sweaty struggle to keep it between the lines.

One major reason Dan, Wanda, and Willie have difficulty getting their motorcycles to cooperate is that they don't really understand how motorcycles balance and steer. Drifting Dan panics when his sportbike swings wide, and when he attempts to muscle the bars back toward his lane, the bike seems to go even wider. Dan doesn't realize he is actually steering the bars in the wrong direction. Wandering Wanda is paranoid about running wide, and she's absolutely terrified of corners, but she is afraid to try that countersteering she's heard about. Wobbling Willie breaks out in a sweat when his shiny touring machine points itself at car fenders, but he has yet to learn that it is primarily pushing on the grips that controls direction, not simply slamming his knees against the tank.

Dan, Wanda, and Willie have a common problem in their struggle to control their motorcycles. They all understand that you have to lean the bike to change direction. They just aren't sure what really makes it happen. What they need to know is that to lean right, push on the right grip. To lean left, push on the left grip. If your machine tries to snuggle up to a parked car on your right, pushing on the left grip will lean it away from a fender-bender. It's called countersteering because you momentarily turn the front wheel opposite (counter) to the way you want the motorcycle to lean. It also helps to look in the direction you want to go. If you don't want to cross that centerline, look ahead down your lane, don't gawk at the line. Even novice riders who haven't mastered countersteering often gain considerable control just by getting their eyes up and looking where they want the bike to go.

Those are the two big secrets for the average situation: countersteer, and look in the direction you want to go. Now, go out and play. Before you thumb the starter, though, let's note that there are a lot of hazardous situations out there that demand more skill than the average situation. For example, let's say Drifting Dan zooms out of a tunnel in the mountains, smack into a 50-knot crosswind gusting from his right, slamming into the bike and pushing it toward the centerline. What should he do? Dan needs to push hard on the upwind grip to lean the bike over and maintain enough muscle on the grip to hold the bike leaned over but in a straight line. In this situation, he needs to push on the right grip to lean the bike toward the right. With the bike leaned over but not turning, steering isn't going to feel normal, so Dan needs to apply pressure on the grips to make the motorcycle go where he wants it to go, and not just think lean.

Such situations remind us that balancing isn't just a simple matter of nudging on the low grip. To prepare for a wide variety of situations, it might be helpful to look a little deeper into the dynamics of how two-wheelers balance and steer. If you get confused with any of this, I suggest you go out to the garage and try the suggested experiments on your motorcycle.

And, as we get started on balancing dynamics, you should be aware that not everyone agrees about how it works any more than people agree about love or war. From time to time, even experts get into arm-waving arguments about small details, pens hastily scribbling diagrams on lunchroom napkins. What I'm going to offer here is the opinion of one aging moto-journalist/instructor, based on thirty-plus years of arm-waving discussions and napkin scribblings. Also note that for what follows, motorcycle means two-wheelers, not rigid sidecar rigs or trikes.

Two-Wheeler Stability

Occasionally, you'll see a rider let go the grips and lean back in the saddle at freeway speed. You may marvel at the naiveté of a rider willing to ignore hazards such as a groove in the pavement that might instantly yank the front end into a tank-slapper, but hands-off riding is a great demonstration of the unique stability of a motorcycle. The front-end geometry automatically stabilizes a bike in a straight line, self-correcting for minor changes in lean angle.

The simplistic suggestion is that this self-centering action is just a result of the castering effect of the front tire trailing behind the steering pivot axis, similar to the front wheels of a shopping cart at a grocery store. But two-wheelers are quite a bit more complex than shopping carts, partly because they lean into turns. The self-balancing action of a motorcycle's front end is a result of the combined effects of a number of details, including rake, trail, steering head rise/fall, mass shift, contact patch location, and tire cross section.

Rake/Trail

If you stand off to one side of your motorcycle and observe the angle of the front forks, you'll notice that the top of the fork tubes are slanted back. And if you look closer, you'll see that the fork tubes aren't exactly in line with the steering head. When we talk about rake we're talking about the angle of the steering head leaning back from vertical.

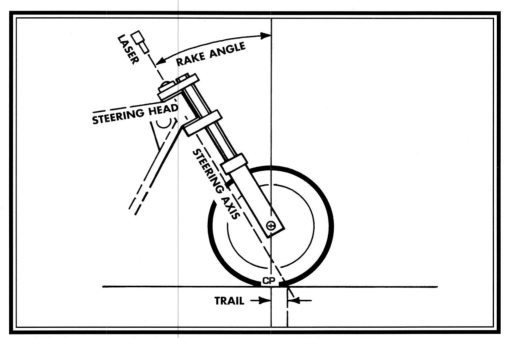

Trail is the measurement along the ground between the steering axis and the contact patch.

You've probably seen choppers with really long, flexing forks. And at the other end of the spectrum you may have observed off-road bikes with almost vertical rake angles. In general, greater rake produces greater straight-ahead stability at speed, and less rake produces low-effort steering. When test riders refer to heavy steering they are talking about a machine that is so stable in a straight-ahead situation that it requires a lot of muscle to get it leaned over and hold it into a turn. What they mean by a flickable machine is one that is relatively unstable, and can be easily leaned over or straightened up with very little muscle. Sportbikes have rake in the 24-degree range, while cruisers are closer to 30 degrees. But rake is only part of the equation.

While you are standing off to one side of the bike, imagine a laser beam passing through the steering head until it strikes the ground. The laser beam represents the pivot center, or steering axis, of the whole front end. For most machines, the steering axis strikes the ground somewhere ahead of where the front tire is sitting on the surface (the contact patch). The distance along the ground from the steering axis to the center of the contact patch is called trail because the contact patch trails behind the steering axis. Typically, street bikes have trail somewhere in the 3- to 6-inch range. In general, longer trail results in a machine that resists leaning into corners, and shorter trail results in quicker, easier steering, or perhaps even a machine that wants to fall into corners. Since rake and trail are interdependent, the figures in bike reviews are usually given as rake/trail.

Steering Head Rise and Fall

One of the interesting results of rake/trail is that the steering head rises and falls as the front end is pivoted from one side to the other. The greater the rake, the more the rise and fall. You can see this for yourself. Straddle your bike, get it balanced vertically, and observe the elevation of the top of the steering head as you turn the handlebars from straight ahead to either side and back. When you turn away from center, the steering head drops. When you turn back to center, the steering head rises.

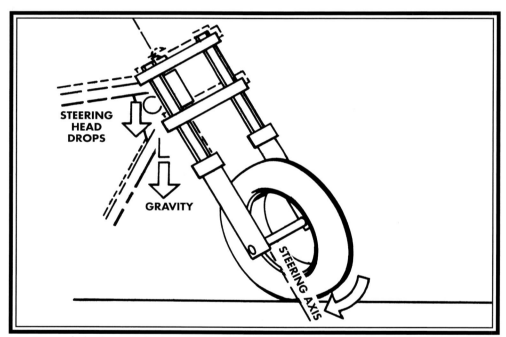

Because of rake, the steering head actually rises and falls when the front end is steered.

Now remember, gravity is pulling down on the bike, which is supporting perhaps half its weight on the steering head. So gravity actually helps turn the front end away from center and resists the front end returning to center. That's not a bad deal, since engineers can balance steering head rise and fall against other steering forces.

Mass Shift

While you are straddling your bike, you might also note that when you turn the handlebars, the steering head also moves sideways (laterally). If you turn the

David L. Hough

bars to the left, the steering head (and the whole front of the bike) shifts laterally to the left of the contact patch. With the front wheel pointed toward the right, you'll feel gravity pulling more on the right because the mass has been shifted to right of center.

In other words, steering can actually shift much of the mass of motorcycle and rider away from center, even if the wheels are not rolling. Of course, as the motorcycle begins to roll ahead, it reacts differently than it does when standing still. With the bike rolling down the street, both the steering head and the contact patch move.

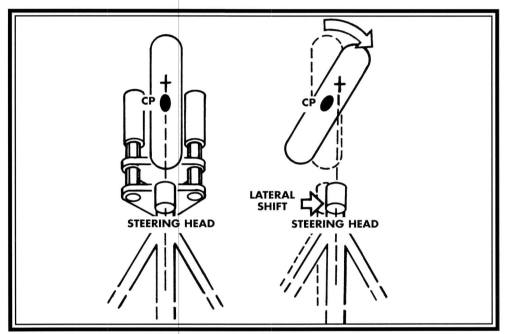

Because of trail, the steering head moves sideways when the front end is steered.

Contact Patch Location

If you were to ride your machine through a puddle of white paint, you'd see a painted stripe all the way around the tread, maybe two inches wide. But even though we could see that this contact stripe is a big ring, it's a lot easier to discuss front-end geometry if we agree to think of it as only a small contact patch (CP) where the tire touches the road at any particular moment. Be aware that the location of the CP can shift forward and back, as well as sideways.

Consider what happens when the wheel rolls over a bump. As the tire hits the bump, the CP instantaneously shifts forward, and then follows the bump backward until the tire rolls onto level ground again. If the bump is steep enough (a curb, for instance) the CP can momentarily jump ahead of the steering axis. That's why a steep bump or dip yanks the handlebars around (and why hands-off riding over bumps and grooves isn't a clever idea).

Now, lean the bike over on the sidestand, with the front wheel pointed straight ahead. Get down on your hands and knees in front of the bike, and look back toward the front tire. Observe that the CP has shifted sideways, away from the wheel's centerline. So, as we lean the bike over into a turn, the CP shifts laterally toward the turn.

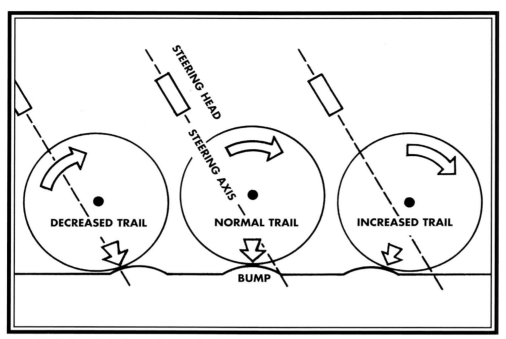

When the front wheel rolls over a bump, trail can decrease or increase.

Tire Cross Section ("Profile")

With a wide, low-profile tire cross section, the CP shifts farther sideways than a narrow, round section tire, for the same lean angle. And the farther out the CP, the greater its off-center drag. The CPs of both front and rear tires shift laterally as the bike leans over, so the sizes and profiles of front and rear tires

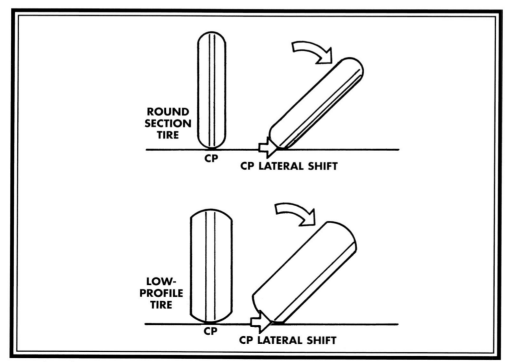

A low-profile tire experiences greater lateral shift of the CP than a round section tire when leaned over.

are interrelated. That's one reason changing tires to different profiles or changing just one tire to a different size or profile can change steering geometry, for better or worse.

Self-Balancing

With carefully selected rake, trail, and tire profiles, a machine can have self-balancing dynamics, whether moving upright and straight ahead or leaned over into a curve, and whether at fast or slow speeds. The point I don't want you to miss is that the front-end geometry is designed to countersteer itself into a straight line. If the bike leans over to the right, the CP shifts farther right, causing the front wheel to steer itself slightly tighter toward the right, countersteering the bike back toward vertical. As the machine returns to vertical, gravity, steering head position, and CPs all balance again. This is a delicate balance, and sometimes the engineers have to walk a tightrope between low effort (flickable) cornering and bad manners such as sudden unexpected tucking, uncontrollable oscillations (speed wobbles), or falling into turns at slower speeds.

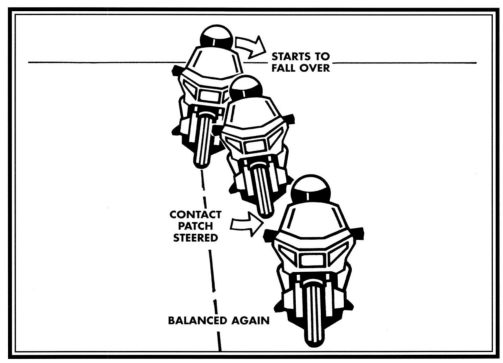

The bike is balanced by steering the contact patch under the center of gravity.

The Snake Track

If you watch a motorcycle cruising down the superslab, you'd swear it follows an absolutely perfect straight line. But if you could measure accurately, you'd discover that it rolls ever so slightly from one side to the other as it balances itself, sort of like a clock pendulum. This self-balancing act is more obvious at slower speeds because the front tire requires more steering input at slower speeds than at higher speeds to get the same effect.

If you were to ride your bike slowly through a puddle of white paint, and then go back and look at the tire tracks, you would see that the front tire sometimes tracks to

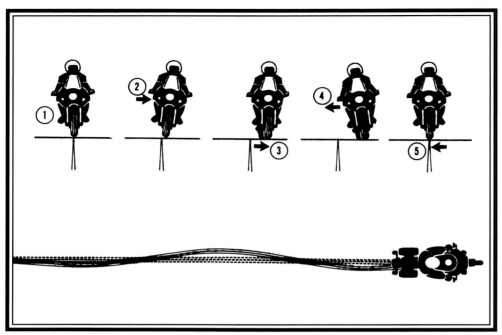

The front wheel makes a snake track as front-end geometry continuously restores balance.

the left and sometimes to the right. In other words, the front tire rolls along in a snakelike track as the bike continuously rebalances itself or as the rider makes small corrections.

Gyroscopic and Inertial Stability

Two big contributors to straight-ahead stability are the inertial effect of the motorcycle/rider mass, and the gyroscopic forces generated by the spinning wheels. Perhaps the best way to think of inertia is that objects "want" to keep on doing whatever they are doing. Kick a brick sitting on the ground, and you'll discover it doesn't want to move. Throw the brick, and it's obvious it wants to keep moving, at the same speed and in the same direction. Putting a name to this "wanting" is tricky. The popular unscientific term is *momentum*. The correct name for this property of matter is *inertia*, but if we start to add vectors and measurements of force, we need to start calling it *kinetic energy*. To avoid a war over definitions, I usually call it *forward energy*.

A motorcycle, once up to speed, wants to keep rolling along straight ahead. Forward energy contributes to straight-ahead stability by pulling the motorcycle's mass back toward center and by providing a resistance against which the tires can react. For example, if the front of the motorcycle is steered away from center, forward energy attempts to pull it back toward a straight line again.

The wheels of a motorcycle also contribute to stability, but in a different way. Spinning wheels generate gyroscopic energy that resists lateral shifts or leaning. A spinning gyroscope wants to stay spinning at the same angle. Basically, forward energy helps keep the motorcycle pointed straight ahead, and the gyroscopic effect of the wheels helps keep the motorcycle from falling over or lurching sideways.

One of the interesting characteristics of gyroscopes is *gyroscopic precession*. What that fancy term means is that if you hold a spinning motorcycle wheel vertically by the axles and turn it toward the left, the wheel wants to lean over toward the right. Since this seems to correspond to what happens when a motorcycle is leaned into a turn, many people are fooled into believing that gyroscopic precession is the

David L. Hough

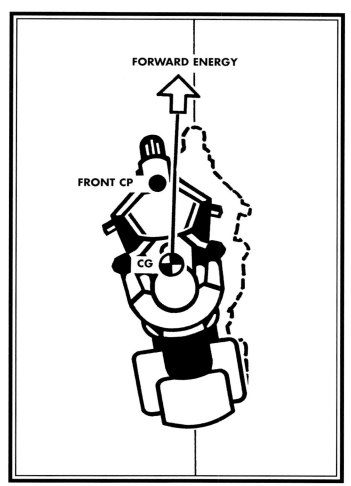

FORWARD ENERGY

FRONT CP

CG

Even if the front wheel tracks off on a tangent, forward energy attempts to pull the bike back into a straight line again.

dominant force that causes a motorcycle to lean into turns. It's a nice, simple theory, but it turns out to be a fable. First, the demonstration suggested is applicable only if you suspend the wheel off the ground, as when a motorcycle is doing a wheelie. Second, when the motorcycle tire is in rolling contact with the road surface, tire traction enters the equation, and traction can produce stronger forces than precession. Third, the front wheel is connected to the rear "gyroscope" via the motorcycle frame. And fourth, there have been experiments that demonstrate that a two-wheeler can be balanced with a very low mass front wheel. Regardless of what makes it happen, you can trust that countersteering will cause the bike to lean.

Feedback

Part of the confusion over motorcycle balancing and steering is that different machines handle differently and give different feedback to the rider. Ideally, if a rider eases pressure on the grips, the motorcycle should settle into a straight-ahead path. If the motorcycle is leaned over into a turn, releasing pressure on the low grip should allow the machine to gradually lift itself up and return to a stable, vertical attitude again. We call this neutral steering.

By comparison, some motorcycles have a tendency to fall into turns at slower speeds. With such machines, you can initiate a right turn by pushing on the right grip, but once the bike starts to lean, it just wants to keep on falling over. The rider may not appreciate what's happening, but once the bike is leaned over, it is necessary to maintain a pull on the low grip to keep the bike from falling. So, the technique to control lean angle is to push on the grip to make it lean, then pull on the low grip to maintain the lean angle. That can be confusing to the rider who doesn't understand what's happening.

Center of Gravity

When you hear someone attributing a motorcycle's good or bad manners to the elevation of its center of gravity (CG), remember that it's mostly steering geometry that makes a machine feel sluggish or top heavy in turns. Certainly, a cruiser that's built low to the ground will have a lower CG. But some cruisers with a low CG have heavy steering. And there are tall dual sportbikes with the engine mass up in the stratosphere but with flickable manners. Next time you hear of a bike that's described as being top heavy or having a high center of gravity, check the rake/trail numbers and consider the sizes and profiles of the tires. And if your favorite machine has some strange cornering habits, be aware that you can do some fine-tuning by changing tire diameters and profiles.

Body English

Remember Wobbling Willie, who can't seem to control the balance of his big road burner by slamming his knees against the tank? It worked fine with Willie's little 250, but it doesn't work with his heavier 1500cc touring bike. Sure, body English can cause a bike to change direction. But the result you get from throwing your weight around depends to a great extent on the relationship of your weight to the weight of the bike. The heavier the bike, the more it's inertial and gyroscopic stability. For instance, slam your knee into the tank on a contemporary 250 lightweight, and it will head off in a new direction. Slam your knee against the tank of a 1500cc tourer, and it may wobble once or twice and then straighten right back up on its original path. With the larger machine, Willie needs to focus more on countersteering and less on body English.

The next time you are out riding, think about what you're doing to control balance and direction. Are you sitting rock-solid in the saddle and just resting your boots on the pegs? Are you pushing or pulling on the grips? Are you shifting your butt? Are you shifting weight from one footpeg to the other? In a turn, do you place more weight on the inside or the outside peg? Are you pushing or pulling on the low grip? I'm not offering any correct answers here, just pointing out that part of becoming a proficient motorcyclist is figuring out what it takes to control your machine, and what your machine is trying to tell you.

What Makes It Turn?

In the previous section, I discussed a number of factors that cause a motorcycle to balance itself and what a rider can do to help. Now, let's consider what we do to make a motorcycle turn. I'll try to keep the concept of turning as understandable as possible, while still giving you the information you need to achieve better control of your motorcycle.

David L. Hough

Turning Equals Unbalancing

As I've already pointed out, a well-engineered motorcycle wants to go straight. The front-end geometry automatically steers straight ahead and vertically, while forward energy and gyroscopic forces help stabilize the bike. To get a two-wheeler to turn, we need to get it leaned over. So turning really is a process of unbalancing the bike to get it leaned over, then rebalancing it in a curving path.

Bikes vs. Cars

One of the big differences between how motorcycles and automobiles turn is that a motorcycle must first be leaned over before it starts to turn. An automobile starts to turn as soon as you yank on the steering wheel. The same is true for a trike or sidecar outfit or any other multitrack vehicle. But two-wheelers are different. Even with a flickable sportbike, it may take a full second to get the bike leaned over before it actually starts to change direction. And with a heavyweight tourer, that initial lean may require more than one second.

A lot of arm waving and heated discussion has taken place around campfires about how we really cause motorcycles to turn. The discussions always get around to countersteering, but there are often disagreements on what we really mean by countersteering, and exactly what the forces are that make it work. Let's see if I can clear up some of the mystery.

The Leaning and Cornering Process

Leaning can be initiated by a number of different factors, including road camber, crosswind, rider's body English, and steering the handlebars. The most powerful factor in leaning is steering the handlebars, so I'll focus on that.

Experienced riders usually refer to a rider's steering input as countersteering because the handlebars are steered opposite, or counter, to the intended lean. Push on the right grip to lean right; push on the left grip to lean left. That's where some of the confusion starts because leaning and cornering is really a process of several steps, while countersteering is just the first step in the process. The process all happens within a couple of seconds, so let's slow down the action and go through it step-by-step. I'll illustrate this leaning and cornering process from the front, and exaggerate the graphic a bit so you can understand what the front end is doing.

Countersteering initiates the lean required for a motorcycle to begin turning. From the saddle, it may appear that the front wheel continues in a straight line while the top of the bike leans over, but what really happens is that the bike and rider lean around the center of mass. The rider steers the front wheel off on a slight tangent, which shifts the contact patch away from the turn. That forces the top of the bike to lean toward the turn.

1. RIDER INITIATES RIGHT TURN BY PUSHING ON RIGHT GRIP; FRONT WHEEL POINTS LEFT

2. FRONT WHEEL TRACKS LEFT; BIKE ROLLS RIGHT

3. BIKE BEGINS TO TURN; RIDER EASES; PUSHES ON GRIP; FRONT WHEEL CENTERS

4. RIDER CONTROLS LEAN ANGLE BY COUNTERSTEERING

Countersteering is just the first step in the leaning/cornering process.

For example, pushing on the right grip steers the front wheel off more toward the left, which forces the bike to lean toward the right.

If you have been practicing countersteering for a while, it may seem as if you just nudge on the grip and hold it. But it should be obvious that if the front wheel continues to track off on a tangent, the bike will continue to lean over until it slams into the ground. So when the bike leans over far enough to achieve the turn you have in mind, you ease pressure on the grips enough to allow the front end to steer itself back toward center.

Now that the bike is leaned over, it starts to turn. Tire traction is actually pushing against the road surface to force the front end into a curving path. The front wheel is pointed slightly toward the direction of turn, and the rider applies just enough steering input to keep the bike leaning and turning. Of course, the bike wants to return to a straight line. We usually refer to that as *centrifugal force*. If you were to tie a connecting rod on the end of a string and swing it around your head, you could think of the outward pull on the orbiting rod as centrifugal force and the string as the front tire. With the bike leaned over, gravity is pulling strongly on the turn side, so you can balance centrifugal force against gravity. You can adjust the lean angle by additional small countersteering inputs, if needed.

Push Steering

If you've never heard of countersteering before, or if you haven't figured it out yet, you should probably start by experimenting with the concept of push steering. The simplest way to describe countersteering is to explain that you push on the right grip to turn the bike right, push on the left grip to turn it left. Take your bike out for a spin, get up to 35 mph or so on a straight, vacant road, and consciously push lightly on the left grip. The bike will lean over slightly left and move toward the left side of the lane. Now push on the right grip. The bike will lean slightly right and move back toward the right side of the lane.

This isn't something new because it's how everyone steers motorcycles, whether they realize it or not. A lot of riders concentrate on body English such as elbow-waving or knee pressure unaware that the important input is through the hands. Accurate cornering is much easier once you realize that the primary input is through the grips. Once you've experimented with push steering, it's time to move on. Different machines and various situations provide different feedback to the grips when leaned over in a corner. So you need to understand countersteering as more than simply pushing on the low grip.

Is It Countersteering?

A fellow rider pointed out an interesting phenomenon about steering input. While leaned over at speed on the racetrack, this rider observed that about half the time he was pushing on the low grip, steering the front wheel slightly away from the turn, and half the time he was pulling on the low grip, steering the front wheel toward the turn, all the while attempting to hold the bike on his desired racing line. He knew whether he was turning the front wheel toward the turn or away from the turn because he was hanging off the bike and could see the front wheel. Does this mean we countersteer only half the time, or is something else going on here?

What this rider's observation points out is that guiding a motorcycle in a curve may require small adjustments of line, not simply constant pressure on the low grip. Remember, front-end geometry steers itself in a slight snakelike weave as the machine attempts to balance itself. Surface camber changes, wind drag, and throttle

David L. Hough

adjustment can all initiate lean angle changes. It's up to the rider to make inputs through body English and steering to hold the cornering line.

Even with the bike stabilized in a turn, we may still be making slight corrections. For example, if the motorcycle is leaned over in a tight left turn and then a crosswind pushes it over a little too far, pulling on the left grip will keep it from leaning over farther. Are we still countersteering, even though the front wheel is pointed to the left of center in a left turn? Sure.

Confusion over the term *countersteering* is often generated by our focus on the grips, when the action is really down at the contact patch. We should understand countersteering to mean shifting the contact patch opposite to where we want to go, whether that takes a push or a pull, whether upright or leaned over, whether fast or slow, and whether the bars are turned left of center or right of center. To put this another way, countersteering is shifting the contact patch in the opposite direction of the way we want the bike to lean at the moment.

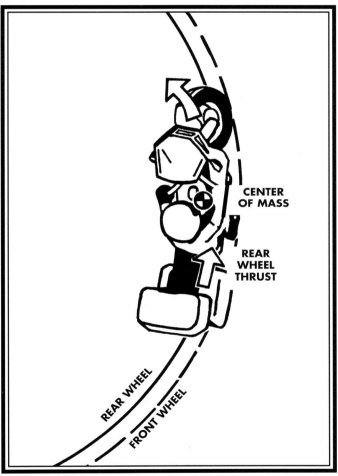

In turns, the front tire tracks outside the rear tire path.

Out-Tracking

When you countersteer, it may seem as if pressure on the grip pushes the bike over without actually pivoting the front wheel. Does the front end actually pivot away from center as the bike leans over into a curve? Yes. The movement is slight, but if the front end isn't free to pivot in the steering head, the motorcycle can't be balanced or turned.

If you could watch a slow-motion video of a motorcycle running through a puddle of paint and then making a figure eight, you would see that the front tire swerves toward the outside during the initial countersteer, then eases back, but it always tracks outside the rear tire in turns. In a left turn, the front tire tracks to the right of center. In a right turn, the front tire tracks outside the rear tire path.

If you'd like another good example of out-tracking, record some motorcycle race footage, and play it back in slow motion. In those shots where the camera is looking back down the straight toward a corner, you can see the lean angle of the bikes head-on. If you mentally plot the path of the motorcycle's CG, you'll see that the bottom of the tires out-tracks, even arcing over onto the rumble strips as the rider uses every last inch of pavement.

Coning

While your bike is leaned over in a curve, you might wonder why it continues to turn even though the front end seems to be pointed straight ahead. Part of the answer is that the front wheel really is pointed slightly toward the curve. The other part of the answer is called coning. To understand coning, let's consider the shape of the front tire where it meets the road surface. Although we can see that the top of an inflated tire forms a rounded shape, we have to imagine that the tire momentarily gets squashed flat where it contacts the ground at the CP. But we also know that the tire CP is really a continuous ring around the tread. It's important to recognize that with the bike leaned over into a turn, this CP ring forms a conical

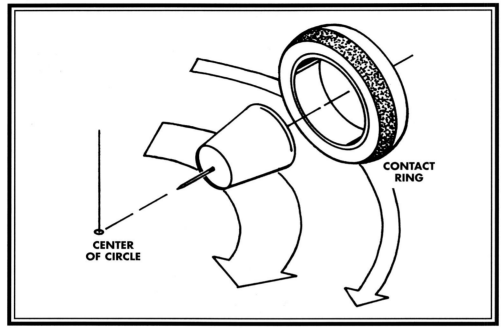

CONTACT RING

CENTER OF CIRCLE

When the tire is leaned over, the contact ring forms a cone, similar to the shape of a foam coffee cup.

shape, similar to a foam coffee cup on its side.

If you nudge the cup forward, it rolls in a circle because the distance around the cup at the closed end is shorter than the distance around the open end. If you stick a toothpick through the center of the cup bottom, the toothpick points approximately at the center of the circle. A motorcycle tire responds similarly when the bike is leaned over. The inside of the tire contact surface covers less distance than the outside. So when leaned, a motorcycle wheel rolls in a circle, with the axle pointed more or less at the center of the turn. In a very tight turn, the axle may actually point at a center that's below the surface of the ground.

Fast Flicks

The more muscle you put into countersteering, the harder the front tire pushes to lean the bike, and the quicker it will lean (up to the limit of traction, of course). And the longer you hold pressure on the grip, the further over the bike will lean during the countersteering input. Those are key points to remember when riding a twisty road where you need to lean the bike left, right, left in a series of turns. Remember, it may take one second to get the bike leaned upright from a tight turn, and another second to get it leaned over the other way before it changes direction.

Is it possible to muscle the handlebars hard enough to snap the tires loose? Yes. You may have seen this in a road race, where a bike suddenly snaps into a heart-stopping wiggle in the middle of an S-curve, or the front tire loses its grip, and the bike crashes off on a tangent.

David L. Hough

Remember, a motorcycle leans (rolls) around its center of mass without a lot of resistance, but resists being pushed up, down, or sideways. That's why a bike speeding over a lumpy bridge on the Isle of Man can go airborne.

Even if you aren't flying over a steep bridge, the bike's inertia will momentarily resist gaining or losing altitude. When a bike is rolled into a turn, the mass needs to lose altitude, and the inertia momentarily resists the pull of gravity, so we must expect less tire traction. But when rolling up out of a turn, the suspension must push the mass upward again, which substantially increases traction. If you consider the arc the contact patches would follow during a quick left-right flick, you can understand why the tires may lose traction as the bike is leaned over, but the bike squats on its suspension as it is rolled back toward vertical. What this means to you as a rider is that the front tire is more likely to lose traction when you are countersteering hard into a lean than when you are pulling it back up again.

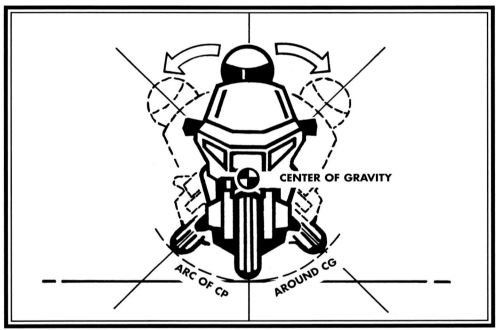

The bike wants to lean around its center of gravity, so the tires may temporarily lose traction as the bike is leaned over, and gain traction as the bike is lifted up out of a curve.

U-Turns

If you're paranoid about slow speed U-turns, you're not alone. Heavyweight machines can be a handful at slow speeds and in tight quarters. The novice technique is to drag the foot-skids, turn the bars to the stop, feather the clutch to creep around, and finally discover that the bike has a larger turning diameter than the width of the road (usually discovered just as the front tire threatens to bounce off the pavement onto a loose gravel shoulder).

The trick for tight U-turns is being aware that as the bike leans over further, the turn becomes tighter. So, rather than drag your boots on the ground with the bike vertical, what's needed is for you to lean the bike into a steep angle. The technique is to lift your butt off the saddle, place most of your weight on the outside footpeg, lean the bike w-a-a-a-y over, and keep the engine pulling. It's okay to slip the clutch if needed to keep the engine from stalling, but squeezing the clutch in a tight turn is usually followed by the sound of a bike hitting the ground. Don't try to coast around

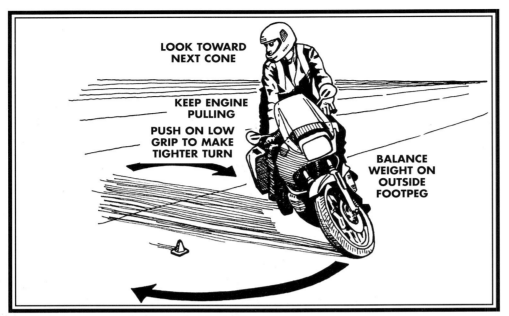

The farther over you can lean the bike, the tighter it will turn.

a tight turn; you need to keep the engine pulling to balance centrifugal force against gravity. In tight turns, it helps to swivel your head around like a barn owl, and look where you want to go. Staring at the ground three feet ahead of the bike may result in finding yourself on the ground right where you were looking.

If the bike seems to go wider than you want it to, you need to lean it over further. Grab those grips and push it over. To avoid any confusion over whether you are pulling or pushing on the low grip, imagine pushing both grips toward the turn to lean the bike over further, and pushing both grips away from the turn to keep it from falling over, or to straighten it up. By now, we know this is really countersteering, but at slow speeds your particular machine may give you some strange feedback.

Ergonomics

If you've been ho hum about the subject of ergonomics (how a rider fits on a motorcycle), consider that how you sit on a bike and reach toward the grips has a lot do with steering control. You'll have better control of the bike if you can reach the grips in a natural position with your arms slightly bent and your feet braced down, not forward. So, if you find your motorcycle difficult to control, take a close look at the ergonomics. It's not just a comfort thing.

Practice

Here's a warm-up exercise for you to practice. It's just a long figure eight in a box. Most motorcycles can actually make a figure eight in an area 18 by 40 feet. It helps to mark the boundaries of the box with cones. Enter at one corner, make a tight turn, another tight turn in the opposite direction at the other end, and continue out the far end. If tight turns make you nervous, this

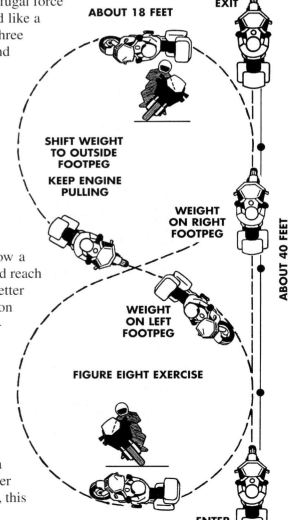

ABOUT 18 FEET   EXIT

SHIFT WEIGHT
TO OUTSIDE
FOOTPEG

KEEP ENGINE
PULLING

WEIGHT
ON RIGHT
FOOTPEG

ABOUT 40 FEET

WEIGHT
ON LEFT
FOOTPEG

FIGURE EIGHT EXERCISE

ENTER

exercise is just what you need to practice. Shift your weight to the outside peg, push both grips in the direction you want to go, and keep the engine pulling. Don't slip the clutch. If you can't stay within the 18-foot width, move the cones out to 20 feet at first, and then pull the box in as you gain skill and confidence.

If you don't have time to lay out the figure eight exercise, try making a figure eight before you park the bike at the end of a ride, or practice a few figure eights as you arrive in the company parking lot each morning. Anyone can ride straight because the bike is doing most of the balancing. It's in the tight turns where we find out who can ride and who is just going along for the ride.

Cornering Habits

We've discussed the basics about how two-wheelers balance and turn. Now, we're ready to take the rubber to the road. First, I'd like you to answer some questions as honestly and realistically as you can about how you control your machine in corners. And if you aren't really sure what you do, take your bike out for a spin and focus on your habits while cruising down your favorite twisty road.

Next time you're out riding, focus on your habits while cruising down a twisty road.

★ **When turning, do you follow more-or-less the center of the lane, or do you follow a different "motorcycle" cornering line?**

★ **Approaching a sharp turn, do you brake or just roll off the gas?**

★ **If you brake, do you brake before leaning the bike, or do you drag the brakes as you continue around the corner?**

★ **If you brake, do you use both brakes, just the front brake, or only the rear brake?**

★ **When rounding a turn, where do you tend to focus your vision? Do you look down at the pavement in front of the bike, at the curb to one side, at the pavement farther around the corner, or where?**

★ **Do you lean your head with the bike, or do you keep your eyes level with the horizon?**

★ **To lean the bike, do you just think lean or do you consciously countersteer?**

★ **As you lean the bike into the turn, do you hold a steady throttle, roll off the throttle, or roll on a little more power?**

David L. Hough

Now, some riders might think such questions are silly. If you've managed to get your motorcycle down the road for thousands of miles without having to think about such boring little details, why do you need to start now? Well, if you're happy with the way you ride and don't feel you could use any improvement, you can stop reading here and get back on the bike. But during your ride, you may start to notice other motorcyclists who wobble through turns, cross the centerline, or suddenly decelerate in corners, forcing you to take evasive action to keep from running up their backsides. You'll probably agree that *those* folks need some cornering help.

Of course, you might want to close the bathroom door, stare at that rider in the mirror, and see if he looks like one of those folks who can't quite put their bikes where they want to. However you perceive your skill level, let's see if we can help you improve your cornering tactics.

You've probably seen a lot of riders who think that cornering is just a matter of stuffing the bike through the bends by grunt and feel and cranking on more throttle until the tires start to squeal. But improving your cornering control (and yes, your cornering speed) is mostly a matter of technique, not fearless throttle twisting. We need to be doing the right things at the right time. That's why I asked those tricky questions. Now, obviously, big sweeping curves such as those on freeways don't need any special tactics. But those twisty back roads really challenge your skills, and there are even a few tricky freeway ramps that tighten up or change direction. The tighter the curve, the more important it is to use the right tactics.

Slow, Look, Lean, and Roll

Different riding schools have different ways to describe the correct cornering techniques. One of the most concise descriptions is the slogan *Slow, Look, Lean, and Roll* used in state rider training courses. Having a slogan helps you remember the details.

Slow

Approaching a curve, you need to decelerate to a speed at which you predict you can make the turn. Most of the time, we roll off the throttle approaching tighter curves. It's smart to decelerate with the bike vertical—while in a straight line—because that allows maximum-effort braking if needed, without the risks of a slide out. Ideally, we apply both brakes in addition to rolling off the gas.

Why brake? Because rolling off the throttle applies braking only to the rear wheel. To conserve traction both brakes

ROLL
AS YOU LEAN, SMOOTHLY ROLL ON THE THROTTLE

LEAN
LEAN THE BIKE

LOOK
KEEP YOUR EYES LEVEL, SELECT CORNERING LINE

SLOW
BRAKE TO CORNER ENTRY SPEED, THEN GET OFF BRAKES

should be used. First, you should be prepared to brake hard for a turn that you discover is tighter than expected. Second, if a hazard comes into view only as you lean over, you should be prepared to use both brakes to the limit of tire traction. If front braking is part of your cornering habits, your survival reaction will be to brake harder on the front, which helps avoid a rear wheel slideout.

Look

Before you dive into a corner at full chat, you really ought to figure out where the road goes, scrutinize the surface for loose gravel and horse poop, and any other debris, and determine whether that's a deer about to leap out of the flickering shadows or just spotted leaves. Note that you'll get the best view of what's happening from the outside of the curve. So, for a right-hander, you'll get the best view if you point the bike way over toward the centerline while you're still decelerating.

When you're ready to dive into the curve, swivel your head around to point your nose toward your intended line. Sure, it looks cool to just shift your eyes behind your blue aviator sunglasses, but turning your head actually helps provide directional control and a smooth entry into the turn.

Lean and Roll

With the bike slowed and positioned for best view, and your chin pointed toward where you want to go, it's time to lean the bike over and roll on a little throttle. Now, there are a number of ways to cause a motorcycle to lean over. You can shift your weight in the saddle, punch your knees against the tank, push down on one footpeg, or apply a little pressure to the handlebar grips. How your machine responds to any of these inputs depends on a variety of factors such as rider-bike weight relationship. But regardless of weight, the most accurate way to lean any two-wheeler is by pressure on the handgrips. Push on the right grip to lean right. Push on the left grip to lean left. Yep, that's correct: Push right to turn right. Hold enough pressure on the low grip to get the bike leaned over and pointed where you're looking, then ease up on the pressure to hold a stable line.

Wait a minute, you may be thinking. I understand that bit about push right to turn right, but back up to that business about rolling on the throttle as I lean over. You're kidding, right? Won't rolling on the gas push the bike wide or cause a rear wheel slideout?

Well, the answer will be obvious as soon as we think through some details. First, as the bike leans over, it's as if your tire diameters shrink. If you don't ease on a little throttle as the bike leans over onto the smaller diameter contact ring of the tires, you won't even be maintaining the same bike speed. And rear wheel compression braking is very much like dragging the rear brake. So rolling on a bit of throttle as you lean over doesn't waste traction, it conserves traction.

What's just as important, rolling on the gas helps balance weight between front and rear, helps stabilize the bike in the middle of its suspension, and maximizes leanover clearance. If you just try to hold a steady throttle through the curve, the bike is more likely to wobble and bobble as it changes lean angle.

What's wrong with just rolling off the gas and letting the bike slow down, you may ask. Well, a trailing throttle not only uses up traction for engine braking but also causes most bikes to squat on their suspension, eating up leanover clearance. If you find your machine making sparks at the apex of a turn, check out your throttle habits. The correct technique is to ease on more throttle progressively to keep the engine pulling smoothly all the way through the curve, which not only smoothes out your line and conserves traction but also maximizes leanover clearance.

Speed 35

I usually get a chuckle from speed signs that say 35, when I know I can make the curve without a lot of drama at 50 or 55. Okay, the signs are posted for everyone, including top-heavy hay trucks. So, is there a rule of thumb for motorcyclists? Yep. But you won't find it posted on a sign. The ideal entry speed into a curve is the speed that will permit a gradual throttle roll-on through the rest of the curve. You'll have to figure out what that speed is, based on what you discover about the road. The key is if you couldn't gradually roll on the gas all the way through the last several turns, it means your entry speeds are generally too high. If you find yourself panicking in mid-corner and snapping off the throttle, it's a message you didn't decelerate enough before leaning the bike over. Sage advice about curves is to go in slow and go out fast.

Cornering Lines

I know a lot of riders who are paranoid about leaning their machines over too far and dropping the bike. If you're concerned about slide outs, it's time to get serious about cornering lines. One of the unique advantages of two-wheelers is their ability to follow a path of travel, or line, that is different from the curve of the pavement. Think about this: side forces on the tires are least when a bike is traveling in a straight line. The straighter the curves, the less risk of a slide out. If you ride around a curve following a car line, your tires are using more traction than if your path of travel followed a straighter motorcycle line. What's just as important is that sudden steering to change direction also demands more traction and eats up ground clearance. A smooth, gradual, stabilized arc is better than a line with constant corrections.

So a big part of cornering is to decide where the pavement goes, and then plan the straightest line that smoothly arcs through the turns. This isn't easy because there aren't special motorcycle markings on the surface to give you any hints about where you should be doing what. We have to imagine our intended lines while also trying to utilize that slow, look, lean, and roll technique I suggested earlier.

One way to put all the elements of cornering together is to imagine windows on the pavement where you'll be accomplishing specific tasks at specific locations. You can figure out where the bike should be leaned over and on the gas, so mentally back up from that window to where you need to be off the brakes, where you need to turn your head to look through the turn, and then way back to where you need to start slowing down.

Following a motorcycle line with a large radius of curve demands less traction than following a car line.

David L. Hough

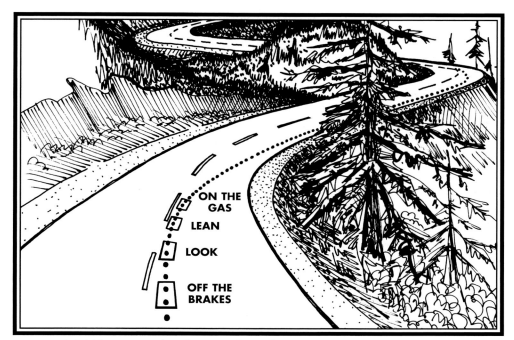

It may be helpful to imagine windows where you need to be off the brakes, look through the corner, lean the bike, and roll on the gas.

Eyes Level

Many riders find it helpful to tilt their heads to keep their eyes level with the horizon while cornering. It's not easy to calculate the curvature of the road at speed, and it's even more difficult if you're trying to triangulate everything at a slanty visual angle. Tilting your eyes level seems to help keep things in perspective. See if it works for you.

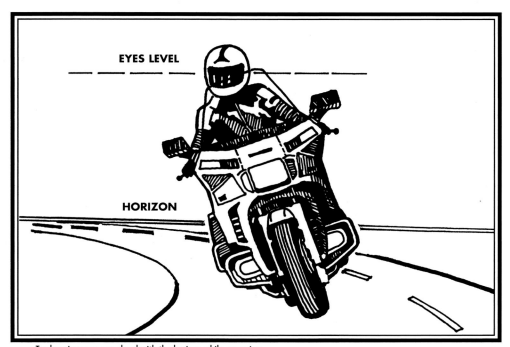

Try keeping your eyes level with the horizon while cornering.

Practice

If you have verified that your habits are good, you're well on the right track to faster, more controlled corners with less risk of slideouts. But if your habits aren't anything like what I've just outlined, it's time to practice some specific skills. One good way to practice is just to take a class at your local motorcycle training site, where an instructor can help you correct any bad habits. But sooner or later you need to take your skills out on the highway.

Why not find some twisty road that's not too busy and focus on the techniques I've described? Slow down to give yourself more time to think about each of the actions. For example, if you know you can stuff the old road rocket down Twisty Hollow Canyon at 50 mph, slow down to 35 and concentrate on doing the right actions at the right locations and the right moments. If you have trouble getting it right, slow down even more until you can do all the steps in sequence, including swiveling your chin around toward the curve and easing on the gas all the way around the turn. Remember, it's the techniques, not just bravado, that lead to better cornering habits. And if you're looking for higher speeds, the correct techniques are essential.

Making Sparks

If your cruiser or tourer has limited leanover clearance, you'll need to be a little more clever about turns. The giveaway is that your machine makes grinding sounds and leaves trails of sparks in every sharp curve.

First off, when you get back from a sparkly ride, check your suspension. Ideally, your suspension should be in the middle of its travel with the bike loaded as you normally ride. The best way to check suspension travel is to sit on the loaded bike and have someone else do some measurements. If you normally carry a passenger, get the passenger on board, too.

If you discover that your machine sits too low when loaded, first jack up the shock springs to maximum preload, and if that doesn't do it, figure on replacing the springs with stronger ones. Sagging front fork springs may be acceptable with spacers to increase the preload. If your suspension has air, carefully add a bit of pressure. Adjusting suspension toward the middle of its travel not only increases leanover clearance but also helps keep the tires in contact with the pavement.

If you've jacked up the shock springs but your low-slung cruiser still makes sparks, you can either lose some weight, or modify your cornering lines. Within limits, you can adjust where you make the tightest part of your corner. For example, you can follow more of a V-shaped line that decelerates on a straighter entry toward a shorter, slower turn, then exits on a straighter line. Sure, you have to slow way down for the tight part of the V, but you can accelerate harder exiting on a straighter line.

If leanover clearance is limited, try modifiying your cornering line to be more like a V.

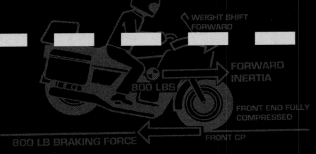

WEIGHT SHIFT FORWARD

800 LBS

FORWARD INERTIA

FRONT END FULLY COMPRESSED

FRONT CP

800 LB BRAKING FORCE

Dynamics
DYNAMICS

Dynamics
DYNAMICS

RETURN AND TRY AGAIN

BRAKE CHUTE AT LEAST 80 FEET LONG, CLEAN PAVEMENT.

LOOK STRAIGHT AHEAD, KEEP BIKE VERTICAL

APPROACH AT STEADY 18 MPH

MAXIMUM BRAKING

COME TO COMPLETE STOP, LEFT FOOT DOWN

CHAPTER 3

DYNAMICS

Getting on the Gas

Interstate Al is motoring cross-country on his big touring machine. Al isn't one of those peg-scraping zoomie bikers who terrorize the canyons. He prefers to ease down the road in the center lane with the motorcycle vertical and the engine idling along in fifth gear. At such a modest pace he can smell the flowers, listen to the tape deck, and allow his mind to wander. Today his thoughts drift toward a question. *Why do some riders get so embroiled in meaningless details of cornering?* he ponders. Al has read about such concepts as delayed apex cornering lines and rolling on the throttle in turns, but frankly he thinks such stuff just isn't related to his riding style. Besides, his big touring bike is better suited to the superslabs where he doesn't have to worry about sharp turns.

It's time for a coffee break, and Al decides to take the next exit. But traffic in the right lane has suddenly closed up bumper-to-bumper, and he must somehow jockey through to get to the exit lane. Al doesn't like to dodge between cars. He breathes a sigh of relief when a space opens up in front of an old pickup truck. He signals, rolls on the throttle to rocket the bike forward, pulls in ahead of the truck with room to spare, and banks off onto the exit ramp, a little fast, but under control for the curve he can see.

Al rolls off the gas as he leans into the off-ramp, but he is surprised when the ramp doesn't curve around in a nice constant circle as he had assumed it would. About halfway around, it suddenly tightens up into a decreasing radius. Al had been pointing the bike toward the inside of the curve, and suddenly he's headed for the outside. Al tries to heave the machine over but can't seem to get the bike to turn as quickly as the pavement, and his scraping footboards limit how far he can lean. With the machine drifting toward the outside curb, his survival reactions take over—he snaps the throttle closed and stomps down on the brake pedal.

In a flash, the rear tire breaks loose, and the bike goes down. The centerstand hangs up on the curb just enough to flip the machine into the concrete divider, and Al is mercifully high-sided into the bushes. Al is only bruised but will later discover that the bent metal and shattered plastic will add up to a total loss of his big road burner.

Consider this: If Al had trusted his tires and just pushed harder on the right grip to lean the machine over to its cornering limits, could he have made the turn without sliding out? If Al had entered the turn more from the outside, and pointed the bike more in the right direction, would he have had a better chance of turning it tighter as the road tightened up? And if Al had not jammed on the brakes while leaned over, would the bike have continued around the curve without sliding out?

Hopefully, Al will realize that his crash has answered his own questions. Serious motorcyclists get "embroiled in the meaningless details of cornering" because the world is full of strange corners, including superslab exit ramps. Good cornering habits are just as important for the touring rider as they are for those who seek out twisty roads for their sportbikes.

Let's consider how throttle control relates to cornering. We usually think of the throttle only as a speed control, but how and when we twist the throttle has a lot to do with traction, stability, ground clearance, and suspension. Conservative riders such as Al may feel that techniques such as rolling on the throttle in corners is something that belongs only on the racetrack, but good throttle control is all about managing traction, and conserving traction is just as important on the road as on the racetrack.

Changing Direction

Inertia makes a moving motorcycle "want" to continue straight ahead. To make the motorcycle change direction, we must force the front end into a curving path, overpowering centrifugal force with tire traction pushing against the road surface. By leaning the motorcycle, we balance gravity and centrifugal force with the position of the front tire.

So, front tire traction is used for both pushing the machine into the curve and for balancing. Rear tire traction resists centrifugal force and also transfers engine thrust to the road. Both tires also can use up traction for braking, but let's keep the situation simple by staying off the brakes for the moment.

Weight Transfer

Think about this: Acceleration and deceleration shift weight. Rolling on the gas shifts weight to the rear. Roll on enough throttle, and you can lift the front wheel off the surface. Rolling off the gas shifts weight forward. And remember that weight on a tire affects available traction.

An unladen motorcycle at rest typically has 50 percent of its weight distributed on each of its tires. And since traction is related to the load on a tire, it might seem that coasting through corners would be ideal, balancing traction equally between the tires. But that isn't ideal for several reasons. First, the rear wheel needs to keep pushing the bike around the corner and overpowering centrifugal force, so we really could use more traction on the rear, say a 60:40 weight balance. Second, just rolling off the throttle isn't coasting—engine compression adds drag on the rear tire, which uses up traction. Keep in mind that it's nearly impossible to match engine speed exactly to bike speed. Even if you squeezed the clutch and coasted, at some point you'd need to get back on the power, with a resulting wobble and possible slideout as traction transferred front to rear. To achieve a wobble-free turn, maintain that ideal 60:40 weight balance and conserve traction. The technique is to be on the throttle when the bike is leaned over.

Roll It On

The ideal throttle technique is to ease on the gas as you lean over and gradually roll on a little more throttle all the way through the turn. *Oh, right*, you may be thinking. *Speed up and run off the road?* Well, let's think about that. Rolling on the throttle does make the engine speed up, but does that always make the bike accelerate? Remember that the contact ring of a tire moves toward the sidewall as the bike is leaned over. When leaned over, the contact ring is smaller in diameter. What this means is that if you aren't rolling on a little throttle as you lean the bike, you're using engine compression to brake the rear wheel, and that uses up rear wheel traction.

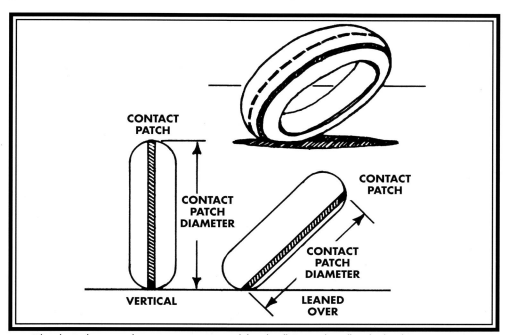

When the tire leans over, the contact ring moves toward the sidewall. You need to roll on the throttle just to maintain the same speed.

And Roll It On Some More

Rolling on a bit more throttle while leaned over happens to do some other helpful things. The added thrust from the rear tire, which helps maintain a desirable balance of traction between the tires, also keeps the front end up on its suspension.

On most shaft-drive machines, and many chain-drive bikes, the torque reaction of power to the rear wheel causes the rear end of the bike to rise. The results are that staying on the throttle while leaned over helps lift the bike up on its suspension at both ends, which increases ground clearance. And more ground clearance means a tighter turn is possible without levering the bike off the tires. Getting around a surprise decreasing-radius turn may require leaning over to the limits.

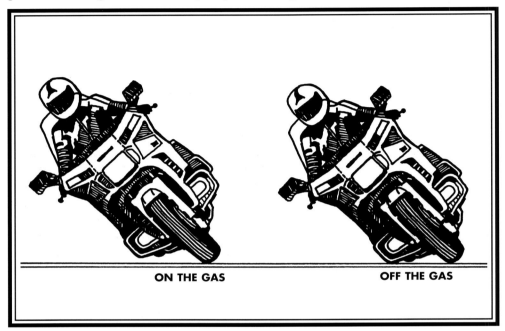

ON THE GAS   **OFF THE GAS**

Rolling on the gas helps keep the bike up on the suspension, and that improves leanover clearance.

Since weight affects available traction on a tire, a weight shift toward the front reduces traction on the rear tire. When carrying a touring load or a passenger, there is plenty of weight and therefore traction on the rear. But when riding solo, any weight shift to the front takes away traction from the rear tire—traction that may be needed to push the bike around a turn. That's why it is important to avoid suddenly rolling off the gas or jamming on the rear brake while leaned over. Al had already rolled off the gas, so his bike had less leanover clearance. He didn't recognize the need to follow a delayed-apex line, so he wasn't prepared for the decreasing radius turn. And braking withdrew more traction than he had in the bank. This combination of bad habits sealed his fate.

Bumps and Dips

Suspension is also affected by throttle control. And how the suspension works is more than just a comfort consideration. Suspension allows the tires to maintain contact with the pavement when rolling over bumps and dips. If the suspension is bottomed out, it can't absorb a bump and will jolt that end of the machine upward. For example, when the front end is down on the stops under heavy braking, it can't absorb a bump. A bump can jolt the whole front end off the ground and cause the tire to skip. If the suspension is already topped out, the wheel can't extend any further down into a dip, and that tire will momentarily lose traction with the surface. Best traction—and smoothest ride—is with the motorcycle floating somewhere near the middle of its suspension travel.

What does throttle control have to do with suspension? Consider what happens to suspension when we twist the throttle. When we roll off the throttle, both ends of the bike drop, putting shock travel closer to being bottomed out. When we roll on the throttle, both ends of the bike rise, and if we roll on hard enough, the suspension can actually top out. In a curve, the suspension is compressed by the pull of gravity and centrifugal force. Get the point? Easing on the gas while leaned over into a turn helps keep the shocks in the middle of their range, assisting the tires in maintaining traction even when bouncing over bumps and dips. So, the ideal throttle technique while cornering is to smoothly and gradually roll on the throttle through the turn.

Roll It On Through the Curve

When approaching a curve, we need to decelerate. Of course that makes the front end heavy and reduces ground clearance, but that's okay in a straight line. The trick is to decelerate in a straight line toward the ideal point where you can simultaneously lean the bike, ease on the throttle, and be able to continue easing on the gas all the way through the rest of the curve.

Now, obviously, we can all think of situations in which rolling on the gas would be stupid. We wouldn't be gassing it during a steep downhill left-hander with a stop sign at the bottom, for example. But easing on the throttle in a curve is one of the keys to better cornering control. It's the best technique for conserving traction, whether you corner leisurely or swiftly. And it's a skill that we can practice while riding.

Next time you're out on your favorite motorcycle, practice rolling on the throttle as you lean into a turn. When approaching an intersection where you intend to turn, lightly apply both brakes while in a straight line, then get off the brakes, look through the turn, and roll on a little throttle as you lean over. If you have to shut off the throttle before you're all the way through the turn, it means you didn't slow enough before leaning. And don't forget to enter turns from the outside. That is, for a right turn, enter from the left side of your lane, unless surface hazards take precedence.

Getting more proficient with the throttle control is more than a way to ride faster. Developing good throttle habits is one of the ways we can expand our safety envelope. And good habits are the key to survival when we are suddenly faced with an unexpected hazard. Ask Interstate Al. He's a lot more interested in those "meaningless" details of cornering these days. He's thinking about better cornering lines and learning to roll on the throttle while leaned over. And he's a little more cautious—on his new bike—about bolting on highway boards that decrease the leanover clearance.

Delayed Apexing

Let's face it. Riding the superslab cross-country is pretty much a no-brainer. Fill the tank, crank up the wick, keep it between the lines, and try to stay out of truck convoys. It's on the twisty roads where we separate proficient riders from those who merely own a motorcycle. If riding the superslab can be compared to line dancing at the local tavern, cornering on a twisty back road is like Gene Kelly dancing in the rain: exactly the right speed for the action, powerful leaps forward at precisely the right time, dramatic lean angles, perfect balance, and an obvious enjoyment of the whole thing.

Road Racing vs. Road Riding

When we talk about cornering, the image that typically comes to mind is of a leather-clad road racer, knee puck scraping the tarmac, race bike leaned over to an unbelievable angle, fat tires drifting at the absolute limit of traction, with the rear end stepping out nervously and the front end twitching. Of course, the goal of racing is to beat the other guys around the circuit.

Risk Acceptance

You'll encounter a lot of other motorcyclists charging ahead aggressively on public roads, seriously captured by a road race mentality, always measuring their worth in terms of who passed and who got passed. Odds are 10 to 1 the road is clear, with no sleepy drivers wandering across the centerline, and no fresh boulders lying on the road halfway around a blind turn. Of course, on every sunny Sunday on twisty roads across America, a few of those daring riders with a higher risk acceptance lose the gamble. Blind corners are one reason aggressive riders don't make it to the biker café. Nine out of ten times you can ride faster than your sight distance and show those other riders your taillight. But when you do round a blind corner at a speed too fast to stop within your sight distance and then discover a hazard in the road, you may not make it to the café at all.

The point is that each of us has a different level of awareness about potentially hazardous situations and a different risk acceptance. There are a growing number of motorcyclists who measure their self worth in terms of their own skill and their personal enjoyment of the ride, not someone else's. As one grows older, it gets easier to understand why riding on public roads must have a very different focus from riding on a racetrack. We're out to have a good time, which includes not only arriving home with body and motorcycle parts unscathed but also enjoying the scenery and taking some satisfaction from having the motorcycle well under control. It isn't necessary to push the limits to have fun. There's tremendous enjoyment in riding a motorcycle at the right speed for the situation, getting the motorcycle in the groove, and knowing you have more performance in the bank should you need it or choose to use it.

Pleasure and Risk

For openers, I think you'll enjoy motorcycling more if you master a few important cornering skills. It can be tremendously satisfying to have your motorcycle completely under your control, knowing how it performs, and being able to make it do what you want it to do. But beyond the enjoyment, there is the matter of risk. Ask yourself this: Even if you ride at the same speed on the same road, will certain cornering tactics increase or reduce risk? Consider some risk concepts that relate to cornering lines:

★ **The largest radius of turn demands the least traction for a given speed and therefore keeps more traction in reserve for dealing with unknown hazards such as loose gravel or wild animals.**

★ **The risk of riding into unseen hazards is reduced by following a line that enters blind curves at positions that provide the best view ahead.**

★ **The risk of collision is reduced by following a line that achieves maximum separation from other traffic at critical locations.**

★ **The risk of falling on surface hazards is reduced by making the sharpest part of the turn on pavement already within the rider's view.**

It should be pretty clear that cornering lines have a lot to do with the relative risks, whether your riding style is to putt along serenely or blitz the countryside at full chat.

Smarter Cornering Lines

One big hazard for aggressive motorcyclists is trying to adapt road racing lines to public roads. On the racetrack, riders don't have to be concerned about opposing traffic or deer leaping out of the trees or farm tractors chuffing onto the road. Racers can concentrate on the track, memorizing each corner and noting reference points for braking. Tire rubber on the pavement scribes an obvious motorcycle line. There may be distance markers to help adjust speed for upcoming corners. And racers know that they will be warned if hazards occur.

If you watch road racing on television, you'll get a lot of views from above, and you'll notice that generally the racing lines curve as smoothly as possible from apex to apex, like a springy board bent around posts at the inside of each turn. Racing lines maximize both traction and speed. But for public roads, we must give priority to the unknown. On a strange road, we have no idea of the curve ahead, or what hazard we might encounter just around the turn. So our cornering lines must be suitable for all manner of strange uphill, downhill, off-camber corners, and also give us the best chance to avoid unannounced hazards as they pop into view.

The View Ahead

Whether or not I can keep my two-wheeler upright often depends upon the condition of the road surface. I would prefer not to discover that the smooth, dry pavement I'm riding on happens to be submerged in fresh diesel oil or cow poop halfway around the blind turn ahead. If the view is limited, it makes a lot of sense to plan the tightest part of the curve where I can see that the pavement is acceptable. Sure, there might be even better traction just around the corner. And if the surface around the corner happens to be smooth, clean, and tractable, I can use it for accelerating. But it's a poor gamble to plan on the condition of unseen surfaces being better than what's already in view.

Wandering Drivers

When a car or truck driver discovers way too late that the corner is a little tighter than it seemed, the other vehicle ends up drifting onto the shoulder or over the centerline with tires squealing. The motorcyclist happening along in the opposite direction is at risk of a collision. A good tactic for avoiding such wandering drivers is to follow a cornering line that moves away from the centerline at the locations where opposing

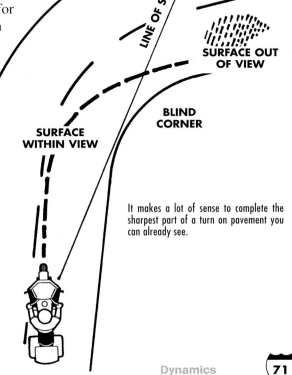

It makes a lot of sense to complete the sharpest part of a turn on pavement you can already see.

traffic is most likely to drift over the line. It isn't necessary to hug the right side of your lane all the time, but it is important to stay away from the centerline at the critical locations—about halfway around the turn.

Wandering Riders

Car drivers aren't the only ones who drift out of their lane. Novice motorcyclists also tend to drift wide in turns. Let's consider how this happens. Visualize a corner coming up. Somewhere along the inside edge is the tightest part of the curve, the apex. It seems to make sense to point toward the apex, following a line similar to road racers. And whether you think about it or not, it's awfully easy to get hypnotized by the inside edge of the pavement rolling into view and point the bike toward the inside way too soon. The problem on public roads is that when a bike is aimed toward an early apex, it is likely to drift wide about halfway around the corner. When you suddenly realize you're running out of road in the middle of a corner, there aren't many options available. You'll either have to risk an excursion into the oncoming lane and gamble that no one is coming around the corner, or squander all available traction swerving back into the right lane and risk a slideout.

A lot of riders who might describe themselves as fast or good assume that frequent excursions across the centerline or onto the shoulder are just a part of aggressive riding, but the embarrassing truth is that drifting wide is a symptom of poor cornering tactics. And drifting wide isn't just a sportbiker

WANDERING DRIVER

You want to stay away from that no-no area, where oncoming drivers tend to go wide across the line.

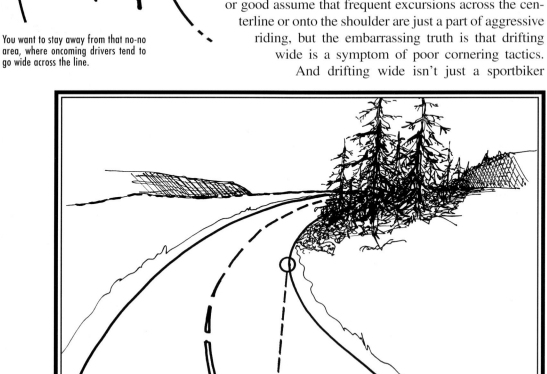

It's easy to get hypnotized by the edge of the road rolling into view and point the bike way too soon toward the inside.

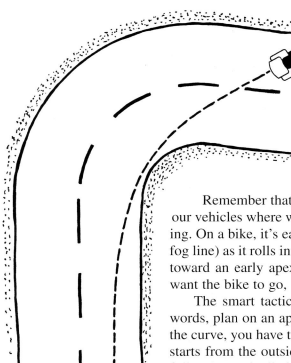

If you apex too early, the bike doesn't get headed around the corner; and once the bike runs wide, you don't have a lot of options to get back to where you belong.

phenomenon. A lot of touring riders drift wide in turns, even at much slower speeds. Drifting wide isn't so much a matter of excessive speed as it is a result of allowing the bike to get pointed in the wrong direction at the wrong time.

If we look at a typical corner from an eagle-eye view, we can see what the problem is. Pointing too soon toward the inside of the curve, the apex points the bike too wide for the rest of the turn.

Remember that people have a target fixation characteristic. We tend to point our vehicles where we are focusing, even if that's not where we think we're steering. On a bike, it's easy to get hypnotized by the inside edge of the pavement (the fog line) as it rolls into view. That's one reason novice riders tend to point the bike toward an early apex without realizing it. It's important to focus on where you want the bike to go, not at that hypnotizing edge.

The smart tactic for driving on public roads is to delay the apex. In other words, plan on an apex farther around the curve. To reach an apex farther around the curve, you have to enter the turn more from the outside. The delayed apex line starts from the outside of the lane, turns tightest as the bike is leaned over, then follows a gradually increasing radius of turn, apexing about two-thirds of the way around the curve.

Delayed Apexing

Okay. Let's assume you want to follow a delayed apex line. How do you decide what the line should look like down at motorcycle level, and how do you get the bike to follow it? One big difficulty with following a delayed apex line is that we can't visualize it from the eagle-eye view. On public roads, we're never quite sure how tight the next turn is, which way it is cambered, if it goes uphill or down, or whether there's loose gravel just beyond. It's especially tricky because we're trying to figure it all out from a vantage point of four feet off the pavement with the world rushing toward us at warp speed.

One way to imagine a delayed apex line is to mentally slide the apex a little farther around the corner than you can see. In other words, as the corner rolls into view, decide about where you think the apex should be and then mentally push that apex farther around the corner. In a blind curve obscured by trees or rocks, you may not actually be able to see where that delayed apex is on the pavement, but that's not important. What is important is that you'll have to enter the turn wider to reach your imagined delayed apex. With your attention focused on a delayed apex rather than the fog line, you're more likely to point the bike in the right direction.

ROAD APEX

SMART LINE

FAST ENTRY LINE

SMART LINE

From the eagle-eye view, you can see the difference between the fast entry line and the smart line.

In a series of turns, you must plan the next turn while you're leaning over into the current one. If you can't get your cranial computer up to bike speed, then slow the bike down to your processing capacity.

Critical Windows

Many riders also find it helpful to imagine locations, or windows, on the pavement through which the bike must pass. For example, when approaching a right-hander, you might imagine an entry window way over toward the center-line. The entry window is the point where you actually start to lean the bike, roll on the gas, and get the machine stabilized in a smooth arc toward that delayed

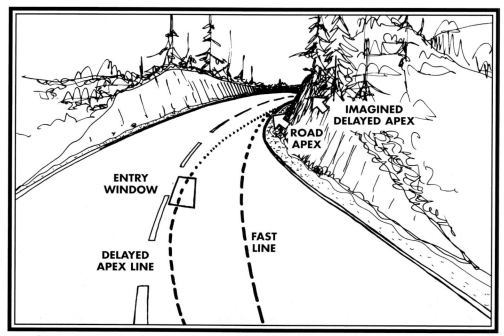

The smart tactic is to plan a delayed apex line. Just mentally slide your apex a little farther around the corner than where you think the road apex is.

David L. Hough

apex. Of course, if the entry window is where you actually lean the bike, you should also imagine the other steps that precede that. Critical windows include *getting off the brakes (Slow), looking as far through the corner as possible (Look), leaning the bike over to make it turn (Lean), and easing on the throttle as you lean over (Roll)*. Try to imagine where these windows are as you approach a corner, and then visualize a continuous ribbon passing through them all.

One important reminder: *Slow* is where you get *off* the brakes, not where you roll off the gas and start squeezing the lever. Remember, the point of being off the brakes before we initiate any serious leaning is so that we're not using traction for braking when we need it for forcing the bike around the corner.

Cranial Computer Speed

On a twisty road where one turn leads into the next, it's important to keep your cranial computer working as fast as your speedometer. Once you've plotted the critical windows in the approaching corner, start scanning ahead toward the next turn and deciding where the next windows should be long before you get there. The sooner you select your line ahead, the smoother your riding can be.

If you don't think far enough ahead, you'll be making quick panic corrections as you suddenly awake to where the line should have gone. And quick corrections gobble traction. If you can't get your cranial computer up to bike speed, the other option is to slow the bike down to your processing capacity.

Homework

All right—it's time for practice. Get those tires pumped up to correct pressures, make sure your brakes are functional, and zip on your most durable crash padding. Find a really twisty road and practice following the delayed apex line. Don't concern yourself with throwing your body weight around just yet. Maintain a modest pace and concentrate on the techniques. Consciously countersteer to follow a smooth, continuous line through the windows. Push on the right grip to lean more right; push on the left grip to lean more left. Focus first on entering turns way out toward the edge of your lane and finding that delayed apex line. Then practice easing on the gas as you lean over. Next, concentrate on braking and getting off the brakes before you need to lean, and turning your head to look where you want the bike to go. In a series of turns, start thinking about the best line for the next corner while still passing through the windows of the current one.

Problems

You find yourself drifting wide in mid-turn:
Either you didn't enter wide enough, didn't achieve correct entry speed, or you aren't pushing hard enough on the low grip to lean the machine over.

You find yourself making sudden steering corrections in mid-corner:
Even as you round a curve, you should be looking toward the next turn, not down at the pavement rolling under your front wheel. Try to achieve one smooth steering input per corner. You'll have to trust us here: the bike will get to that next window where you are focusing your attention.

The bike wobbles when you try to get on the gas while leaned over:
Roll on the gas as you lean over, not halfway around the turn. If you find yourself braking deep into the corner, you didn't initiate braking early enough, or you didn't achieve a slow enough entry speed.

You can't seem to get the bike to follow a consistent line:
Consciously keep your eyes up and point your chin in the direction you want to go. Try keeping your eyes level with the horizon. Don't rush the corners. Concentrate on the critical windows.

Enjoy the Ride

As you master accurate countersteering, smart cornering lines, and proper timing of the critical windows, you'll probably discover that you can corner much more swiftly than before yet still keep your risks within your tolerance level. The big payoff is that smarter cornering tactics give you a greater margin for handling whatever surprises you may encounter, whether you choose to dawdle along or engage warp drive.

The Lowdown on the Slowdown

All right. You've figured out basic cornering tactics, including accurate control of lean angles, positioning for the best view, planning smarter cornering lines, looking where you want to go, and rolling on a little throttle as you lean over. What else is there to know? Well, let's back up to that basic "slow" part of cornering, and take a closer look at hard braking.

Up on that twisty mountain road, hard braking is important. Yes, a lot of experienced riders think it's clever to ride a steady pace that doesn't require any braking, even when zipping along twisty roads. The idea is that smooth is good, and quick

speed changes are the opposite of smooth. But we also know that those back roads contain hazards such as farm tractors, wild deer, loose gravel, and mud-lubricated corners. You don't usually get much advance warning of such hazards, so you may have to do some hard braking at the last moment to avoid a disaster.

And that twisty mountain road eventually comes to a town. As you come off the hill and find yourself slogging through urban traffic, your biggest challenge may be avoiding a left-turning motorist, or a car dodging out of an alley. So, whether you ride conservatively or closer to the edge, hard braking should be a habit. Rather than thinking of smooth riding as never using the brakes, think of smooth riding as being able to brake right up to the limits of traction without upsetting the bike or getting excited.

Laying It Down

Back in the good old days, a lot of people got killed in motorcar and motorcycle accidents exacerbated by weak brakes. Lawrence (of Arabia) didn't die falling off a camel; he died crashing his Brough Superior into a stone wall as an alternative to plowing into some children who popped into view on the narrow English road. In the U.S., the standard quick-stop technique for yesteryear's motor officers was to throw the black and white on its side and hope it would grind to a stop on the axle nuts and crashbars. Many police academies still teach the technique of laying it down, even though officers may be riding machines with sticky rubber and ABS brakes, which can stop a lot quicker on the rubber than on chrome. Frankly, I've always considered laying it down to be a crash.

Smokin' the Tires

Have you ever heard a fellow rider describe a panic stop during which the tires were sliding? For example, here's Zoomie Zed explaining a near collision: *I'm cruising along minding my own business when this chickie babe in a Cherokee zooms out of an alley. I stand on the brake real quick. I'm braking so hard the rear tire is smokin' right to a stop. My engine stalls just as my front wheel ends up about two inches from her front door. You shoulda seen the stupid look on her face!*

Good news, bad news, Zed. The good news is that you didn't score another accident in your file, and you didn't drop the bike. The bad news is that your braking technique needs work. First, the front brake is the one that stops the bike. If you didn't already have your fingers curled around the front brake lever approaching that alley, you wasted maybe a second and 60 feet just reaching for the lever. You should know that cars pulling out of alleys account for almost 20 percent of motorcycle fatalities, so you should have been prepared to make a quick stop when you saw the car nosing out. And jamming on the rear brake too quickly caused the tire to skid, which tossed away another 5 feet of stopping distance, and could have resulted in a high-side flip. One more thing Zed: it helps to squeeze the clutch during a quick stop, so you can concentrate on the brakes and keep the engine from locking up the rear wheel.

Forward Energy

Let's think about how to make quick, painless, maximum-effort stops. A speeding motorcycle "wants" to keep speeding along pointed straight ahead, even if we roll off the gas. It gets a little complex trying to describe the forces in proper physics terms, so let's ask the physics experts to look the other way for a moment. Now imagine the machine's forward energy as a big invisible tow cable pulling on a center of mass, or center of gravity (CG), of the bike, rider, and load. The higher the speed, the greater the forward energy. To slow down a motorcycle or bring it to a stop, we've got to overpower its forward energy.

Of course the bike will slow down if we just roll off the throttle. Wind resistance, rolling friction, and engine compression braking all help overcome its forward energy. But if we need to slow down more quickly, we've got to use the brakes.

Braking Forces

You may have noticed that rear wheel braking can make a lot of smoke and noise but doesn't slow the machine as much as the front brake. That's because the maximum braking force you can apply to a wheel depends upon traction, and traction is limited by the weight on the tire as well as the stickiness of the tire and roughness of the road surface. Braking the wheel to a stop doesn't necessarily stop the bike.

Theoretically, if one half of the total weight of the motorcycle, including rider and load, is carried on the rear tire, the maximum braking force you can get out of the rear tire is one-half the weight of the machine. So, if the total weight is 800 pounds, the maximum rear wheel braking force would be 400 pounds.

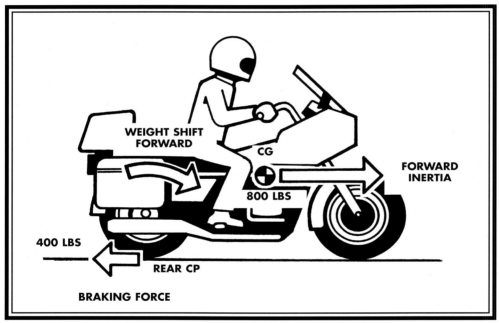

Braking force is proportional to the weight on the tire.

Front Wheel Braking

Now, consider that whether it is engine compression or brake friction trying to overcome forward energy, the braking force is applied way down at the tire contact patches, while the CG is much higher on the machine. The result is that the motorcycle pitches forward. This feels to the rider as if the weight had suddenly been shifted forward onto the front wheel.

Remember, the available braking force is determined by the load on the tire. As the machine pitches forward, there is more weight transfer onto the front wheel, so more traction becomes available on the front, and more front brake force can then be applied. Assuming tractable pavement and sticky rubber, it is relatively easy to brake hard enough on a light bike to do a front wheel stoppie with 100 percent of braking force on the front and the rear wheel in the air.

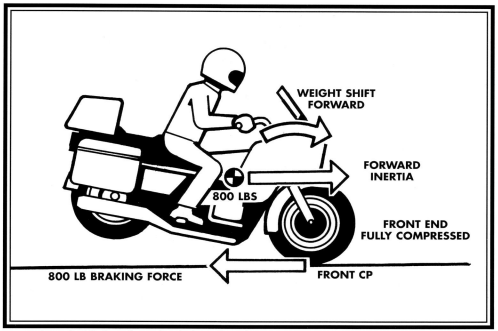

As the weight shifts forward, more front brake can be used.

Theoretically, maximum braking force on a tire is limited to the force of gravity pulling down on the wheel. An 800-pound bike should be able to generate 800 pounds of front wheel braking force, given smooth pavement with a perfect coefficient of friction of 100 percent (1.0). A motorcycle with good brakes should be able to make a maximum effort stop from 60 mph in something like 140 feet.

But if you check the stopping distances in the bike reviews such as those in *Motorcycle Consumer News*, you'll find 60–0 mph braking distances as short as 108 feet. Do motorcycles defy the laws of physics? No, it's just that in real life, the pavement isn't perfectly smooth. Obviously, an extremely smooth surface such as a shiny steel plate will never have traction greater than 1.0. But the little stones in the surface of typical concrete or asphalt pavement act somewhat like the teeth in a cog belt drive, boosting available traction well above that theoretical 1.0.

Endos

Some riders are cautious about braking hard on the front for fear the motorcycle will flip over the front wheel. That wasn't much of a problem in the good old days of harder rubber, but with today's sticky tires on short-wheelbase bikes, it's now the limiting factor. However, most of us could brake a lot harder on the front than we do, even in the rain. Our greatest concern with hard front braking should be smooth, progressive squeezing of the lever to keep the tire from sliding during the time it takes for the bike to pitch forward. It takes about one second for that weight transfer to occur.

High Siding

While many riders are paranoid about sliding the front tire, the greatest danger from overbraking is not on the front, but on the rear. The danger is flipping yourself into a painful high side if the bike slides sideways during a quick stop. If the rider overbrakes on the rear, and the rear end starts sliding out to one side, the unfortunate survival reaction is often to let up on the pedal to reduce the skid, but when the tire spins up, it snaps the rear end back toward center so violently it can flip the bike over the high side.

High-side flips are simple to avoid. Just stay in the habit of using more front brake than rear brake all the time. Lightweight sportbikes are particularly suscepti-ble to rear wheel skids because the weight bias is often more on the front wheel, yet the rear brake is typically a powerful hydraulic disc. When the rear brake is applied on a light sportbike with just a solo rider, it is easy to skid the tire. If you realize that your lightweight sportbike tends to slide the rear tire even with just a light dab on the pedal, ignore the rear brake and use just the front brake.

Directional Control

To keep the bike pointed straight ahead with the rubber side down, we don't want to use all of the available traction for braking. We need to squander a bit of tire trac-tion to keep the rear end straight, and some of that front tire traction to keep the machine balanced. We maintain directional control by modulating, or adjusting, brake lever pressure to keep either tire from sliding at any point in the stop. That's the tech-nique to strive for, whether your machine has integrated brakes, ABS, or linked brake systems. The best antiskid system, though, is still mounted between a rider's ears.

Modulating

During a quick stop, it's important to adjust pressure on the levers to apply max-imum braking just short of a skid. It takes about 1 second for a motorcycle to pitch forward as the brakes are applied. During that 1st second, it is important to squeeze progressively harder until the weight transfer allows maximum front wheel braking.

You can practice that right now. Make a pretend brake lever with the thumb and index finger of your left hand. Now, squeeze the lever while counting out loud *one-thousand-and-one*. If you are full on the brake before you're through counting, that's too fast.

Toward the end of the stop, as forward energy dissipates, it's necessary to ease up on the brake slightly. If the tires cross a slippery spot such as a plastic arrow or an oil slick, it's important to ease off the brakes momentarily as the tires cross the bad surface. In the rain, or if carrying a passenger, more rear brake can be applied because there will be comparatively more weight on the rear wheel.

The Ideal Quick Stop

Let's put all of the details together now and describe an ideal quick stop. You've been enjoying a twisty back road and arrive at a small town. The locals are hurrying around to the various stores and seem to be more focused on getting their shopping done than watching for motorcycles. Entering town, you check to be sure you aren't being tailgated, cover the front brake lever, and watch for pedestrians who might dart across the street and other vehicles that might swerve across your path. Approaching a busy shopping center on your right, you observe a farm truck in the opposite lane that could turn left. You shift down a gear, squeeze lightly on the front brake to reduce speed and prepare for a possible quick stop, and scruti-nize the front end of the farm truck for clues the driver is beginning to turn. The hood of the truck dips slightly as the preoccupied driver decides to turn into the shopping center without looking ahead for other vehicles. Then you see the front tire turn in your direction as the truck begins a left turn across your path. You squeeze the clutch and apply both brakes simultaneously, pressing lightly on the rear brake pedal, but squeezing progressively harder on the front lever as weight transfers onto the front wheel. The left-turner suddenly wakes up to the potential collision and jams on the brakes, stopping the truck halfway across your lane. Concentrating on a quick stop, you maintain maximum braking on the front just short of a skid, and shift to first gear just before you bring the motorcycle to a stop with your right foot still on the rear brake and your left foot on the ground. You glance briefly in the mirror to be sure you're not about to be rear-ended, signal the driver to go ahead, then ease out the clutch and continue on your way. You've taken charge to turn a potential nasty accident into a minor inconvenience.

Quick Stop Practice

Quick stops require skill and experience with the machine you are riding. That's especially important if you are riding a different bike from your usual mount. The only way to build braking skills is to practice the right techniques until they become habits.

I'm not talking just quick slowdowns from 80 to 60 here, I'm talking quick stops from road speed to zero, with no smoking tires, no fall downs, and no high sides. If you intend to ride fast on public roads, you should be as good at hard braking and quick stops as you are at cornering lines and rolling on the gas. Riders of ABS equipped machines are not excused from the drill.

Find a long, smooth, tractable piece of pavement you can borrow for an hour or so. An abandoned section of road will do if it's reasonably clean and dry. Perhaps you have a nearby parking lot that is vacant early in the morning. It helps to set up some cones or markers to define a braking chute, but all you really need is a long strip of clean level pavement. One little caveat: Before you try any skill practice on your bike, do us both a favor and climb into your best crash costume. If you do it all right, we're happy, too. But if you don't get it right, we're not going to be there to point out bad habits or help you pick up the pieces.

Get the machine stabilized at about 18 to 20 mph in second gear. Trust me here, don't try your first run any faster. Maintain speed right up to the braking point. Keep your head up and look forward to where you intend to stop. Avoid glancing down at the instruments or levers. When your front tire passes the braking point, squeeze the clutch, roll off the throttle, and simultaneously apply both brakes, progressively squeezing harder on the front as you count out *one-thousand-and-one*. Stop as quickly as you can without skidding either tire. Toward the end of the stop, shift into first gear. Come to a complete stop with your right foot on the brake pedal and your left foot supporting the machine. The habit of shifting to first prepares you for a quick getaway in case you need to avoid a rear-end collision. Return to the end of the chute and repeat the exercise. See if you can better your previous distance without skidding. As you gain confidence in your front tire traction, bump your approach speed up another 2 mph on each subsequent pass.

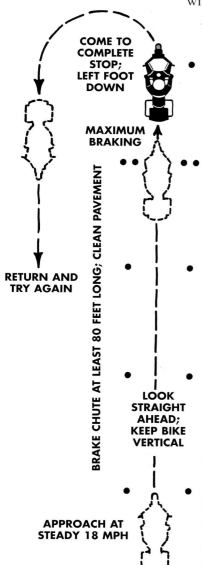

For braking practice, find some clean, level pavement you can borrow for a while. Start your runs at 18 mph and increase approach speed as you gain confidence.

Skids

An impending front tire skid makes the front end feel rubbery. If the front tire does start to skid, immediately release the lever to regain traction (and balance). Be aware that as speed increases the rear tire is more likely to skid due to the increasing inertial forces. If you should accidentally skid the rear tire, my best advice is to stand on it and slide to a complete stop to avoid the possibility of a high-side flip, then make a point of using less rear brake next time. If you can't seem to avoid skidding the rear tire, rest your right foot on the passenger peg and try stopping with the front brake only. A machine with a longer wheelbase has less tendency to lift the rear wheel.

When practicing hard braking, it's helpful to have another rider watching your technique. If you have a buddy to practice with, one rider can signal the other when to stop, to add some spontaneity to the drill.

If you're a little fearful about practicing maximum-effort stops right at the limits of traction, take a rider training course. You'll get practice in straight-line stops, braking in curves, and combinations of swerving and braking, all under the watchful eye of a certified instructor.

Whether you practice on your own or during a training course, the most important part of the drill is to stay in the habit of front wheel braking for all stops, and using the brakes as part of your cornering sequence. Your habits determine what you will do in an emergency.

Taking the Panic out of Panic Stops

Roger Rider is out for a spin in the country. It's a beautiful day, the weather is comfortably warm, and the bike is running sweetly. The road twists and turns

predictably, dipping down into tree-shaded hollows, and climbing back up to snake between the farms and meadows. It's too nice a day to hurry, but Roger isn't loafing, either, because it just feels right to roll on the gas exiting the corners and accelerate through the flickering shadows and sunlight.

But Roger's fun is about to end for the day. Just as he crests a hill, he is startled by a brown object rising up from the roadside ditch and pivoting in his direction. Roger instantly recognizes the two big ears of a mule deer, and hopes it will just freeze there as he rides on by. Without thinking about it, his right hand rolls off the gas, and his left hand nudges the bike over to a course farther away from the deer.

But the deer doesn't just freeze. As Roger gets within 30 feet, the deer suddenly springs to action, bounding onto the road and clattering along in graceful leaps. The deer tries to zigzag away from the motorcycle, and Roger tries to swerve around the deer, but they both guess wrong. Too late, Roger makes a panic grab for the front brake lever. The front wheel slides out, deer and motorcycle careen off each other, and both sprawl onto the pavement. Fortunately, neither rider nor deer is seriously injured, and both manage to stagger back onto their feet after a few seconds. The deer limps off into the trees. Roger limps over to look at his bike, now a mess of broken plastic and bent metal.

Whether it's a deer alongside the road, a stalled hay truck in a blind corner, or a left-turning car at an intersection, a quick stop is often the best tactic for avoiding a collision. Sometimes we call a maximum-effort quick stop a panic stop, because the situation calls for immediate action. Of course, *panic* means sudden, unreasoning terror, and certainly Roger reacted in panic when the deer jumped in front of him. But what Roger really needed was deliberate, reasoned, and correct evasive action. Let's see what we can do to take the *panic* out of panic stops.

Is a Quick Stop the Best Maneuver?

Now, you may not agree that a quick stop is the correct evasive maneuver for a deer suddenly springing into your path. Wouldn't it be better to maintain speed so as not to startle the deer or to speed up to get by the deer quicker? Maintaining speed or increasing speed assumes you can predict what the animal is going to do. Braking reduces forward energy, so a quick stop gives you a good chance to avoid a collision if the deer does get in your way.

When faced with a potential collision on a slick road, would it be smart to toss the bike on its side and let it slide? For example, let's say I have just realized on a rainy morning that the pavement is coated with diesel oil, just as a garbage truck is starting to turn left across my path. Should I try to do a quick stop, or should I toss the bike on its side?

My experience with slick surfaces is that you won't have to make a choice—the situation will decide for you. I intend to stay on the rubber and brake to a stop. My reasoning is that rubber has more traction than metal or plastic, even on oil-slick pavement. In most situations, the bike will stop faster with the rubber side down. You do the best you can, and if you can't keep it upright, you fall. Once the bike is down and sliding, you've lost control.

I'm sure I could think of other scenarios where the best tactic would be to gas it or try swerving around the hazard. But there is only a limited amount of traction, so you shouldn't attempt to swerve and accelerate simultaneously. If you choose to accelerate, it pretty well cancels out the other options. Maintaining speed and attempting to swerve is sometimes the best option, but you need to guess right about which way to swerve. When faced with a deer leaping onto the road, the odds are that

After you've been warned, isn't it smart to be prepared for a quick stop?

When you know farmers are busy, it shouldn't be a surprise when a tractor snorts out onto the road.

you're not going to be successful second guessing which way it is going to leap next.

Hard braking has several advantages over either accelerating or swerving. One big advantage of straight-line hard braking is the potential of stopping short of a collision. The brakes on today's motorcycles are typically more powerful than the engine. More often than not, a quick stop is your best collision avoidance tactic.

If it isn't obvious, the first step in taking the panic out of quick stops is being prepared for them. A big part of that is actively searching the road for clues, and predicting hazards that you can't yet see. When you are riding through a forest at dusk, you shouldn't be surprised when a deer or two leap out of the roadside bushes. In farm country, after you've noticed haying crews mowing, it shouldn't be a big shock when hay trucks snort across the road on the way from the field to the silage pit. If you see a sign warning of moose on that twisty Montana road, wouldn't it be clever to get that logging truck off your tail? Wouldn't it be smart to get out from behind that bus where people can't see you and you can't see what's happening ahead?

Passing through a string of busy intersections in the big city, you shouldn't be amazed to encounter a few car drivers making quick left turns across traffic. Out in the suburbs, wouldn't you expect cars to back out of driveways, kids to ride skateboards out into the street, and dogs to chase motorcycles? If you've got your head in the ride, you'll not only be searching for problems but you'll be thinking well ahead of your front fender.

Once you recognize a hazardous situation, you can get yourself prepared for a quick stop. For example, as you round a blind turn with a barn roof in the background, you should already be covering the front brake lever, and getting yourself psyched up for a quick stop.

The big mistake Roger Rider made was assuming that if he just kept his motorcycle under control, everyone else would stay out of his way. He didn't brake when his sight distance closed up approaching the crest of that hill, because he assumed the road was the same ahead as behind, even though he couldn't see over the hill. And when he did finally spot the deer, he assumed it would stay put while he continued on by. He could just as easily have collided with a wandering cow, or a hay truck entering the road. It isn't sufficient just to keep your own vehicle under control and expect others to get out of your way. You've got to be prepared to get out of the way of other users, whether they are wild animals or other drivers.

A couple of years ago I was having a discussion with a young rider who was limping around in a leg cast. He'd been knocked down in a merging lane by a driver who didn't yield the right of way.

Young Rider: "I can't believe he hit me! He was supposed to yield!"
Me: "Did the driver get injured?"
Young Rider: "Heck no. But I got a broken leg!"
Me: "So, why did you let him get you?"
Young Rider: "He should have stopped. I had the right of way!"
Me: "Does your leg hurt?"
Young Rider: "Sure it hurts."
Me: "So, why did you let him get you?"

It doesn't make any difference whether a motorcyclist has the right-of-way or not, the rider is the one most likely to get hurt. The way to avoid the pain and expense is to get out of the way. My father used to repeat a little ditty on the subject:

He was right, dead right, as he sped along.
But he's just as dead as if he'd been wrong.

If you wait until the last second before making the decision to brake hard, whatever you do is going to be in panic. It's important to get on the brakes early, when you first see or predict a potential collision. When sight distance closes up or another vehicle gets into a position where it could turn across your path, you should already be on the brakes, scrubbing off a bit of forward energy and heating up the discs.

If the other driver doesn't yield or makes a sudden swerve across your path, you can just squeeze a little harder and make a quick stop to avoid a smash. If the other guy stops after all, you can ease off the brakes and get back up to speed without a lot of fuss. You don't have to make quick stops every time you see a problem, but you should be prepared.

Okay, let's say you're riding a busy urban arterial with many confusing intersections and a lot of cross-traffic. You are predicting the possibility of other drivers making sudden moves. You've passed that creeper car with the out-of-state plates, you've moved out from behind the view-blocking bus, and you've changed lanes to let that aggressive cabby get on by. You are scrutinizing the road surface for slick spots and edge traps, observing the hoods of oncoming cars for potential left-turners, and glancing at the tops of front tires to get the first indication of cars beginning to pull out from side streets. What more can you do?

Veteran Tactics

Let's review six veteran techniques for making successful quick stops with a minimum of panic.

★ **Get in the front brake habit. Stay in the habit of using the front brake every time you brake, even if your machine has integrated front/rear brakes or antilock brakes. There is a reason the front wheel has the big stoppers: in a quick stop, it is the front tire that gets pushed into the pavement. It is tempting to fall into the habit of just rolling off the throttle, or using just the rear brake and believing that you can reach for the front brake on those rare occasions when a quicker stop is needed. The trouble is very few of us can out-think our habits. In an emergency, we will do whatever we have been in the habit of doing, then think about it after the fact. If you get in the front brake habit, you'll use the front brake in a crisis without even thinking about it.**

★ **Approaching turns, use your brakes. Braking should be part of your cornering sequence. Sure, rolling off the throttle slows the bike but, remember,**

Stay in the front brake habit.

David L. Hough

Approaching turns, use your brakes.

engine compression functions as a rear wheel brake only. Adding a touch of front brake to help decelerate prior to leaning over into corners makes two-wheel braking part of your habit pattern. If you're in the habit of braking when approaching turns, you will automatically brake harder when you realize the curve ahead is a little tighter than you thought or when you spot a gravel spill at the apex or the view suddenly gets blocked by roadside trees and bushes or a pedestrian steps off the sidewalk as you make your turn.

★ **Brake early.** When you approach a hazardous situation such as a busy inter-

Brake early when approaching a hazardous situation.

section, get on the front brake to reduce both reaction time and stopping distance before you are faced with an impending collision. All of us require a half-second or more to make the decision to brake and another half-second if we have to reach for the lever. Reaction time can eat up a lot more distance than you might think. At 40 mph, you are covering almost 30 feet every half-second. And even if you are quick enough to reach for the brakes in only a half-second, it takes at least another half-second of progressive squeezing to get the front end loaded before you can get full on the brake. One wasted second at 40 mph eats up about 60 feet of critical road space—just about the same distance it takes to brake to a stop from that speed.

If you are already on the front brake lightly to get the discs heated up and transfer a little weight onto the front tire, it shouldn't take more than a half-second to squeeze harder and initiate a maximum effort stop. Getting on the brakes early can make the difference between stopping 5 feet short of the car fender or bashing into it at 30 mph.

Slow down 10 mph for problems.

⭐ **Slow down 10 mph for problems.** As you approach a hazardous area such as a busy intersection with a car waiting to turn left or a driveway with a bumper sticking out, ease on the brakes and decelerate just 10 mph, shifting down as needed to keep engine revs up. Typical urban intersection speeds are 30 to 40 mph. Slowing just 10 mph, from 40 mph to 30 mph, reduces forward energy by almost half. That means the same brakes and tires can stop the same load in half the distance.

⭐ **Reduce speed to sight distance.** There is a tendency to settle into a steady cruise speed, rather than speeding up or slowing down for changing conditions. One accomplice to that is an engine with a narrow power band, which encourages the rider to maintain speed comparable to the torque band rather than shift up and down constantly. But your view of the road ahead changes dramatically as you ride along. And when the view closes

Reduce speed to sight distance.

up, it is important to immediately shed speed, so that you can always bring the bike to a complete stop within the roadway you can see.

What that really means is that when your view ahead is suddenly blocked, you should immediately get on the brakes and scrub off speed. That's especially important on any twisty road where you can't see around corners or over hills. And the faster your speed in the straights, the more important it is to brake hard approaching blind situations. The more you are assuming where the road goes even though you can't see all of it, the

At least once each year practice your quick stops.

more you are hanging yourself out. If you are interested in being quick on public roads, remember that crashing really ruins your average speed.

★ **Practice.** Reading is okay to improve your mind, but you've got to practice on the bike to hone your skills. If Roger had practiced a few quick stops, maybe he would have been able to stop short of that deer collision without dropping the bike. At least once each year, practice maximum-effort stops to sharpen your skills.

The goal of quick stops is decelerating from traffic speed to zero in the shortest distance, without losing control. Even if your favorite road burner has integrated brakes or if you spent the big bucks for ABS, don't excuse yourself from practicing the skills. You must be able to separate braking from swerving quickly, and be able to do a quick stop on dry pavement or in the rain, pointing uphill or down, in a straight or in a corner. All of the veteran techniques we've suggested work equally well for riders of ABS machines.

Less Panic

Once you make those veteran tactics part of your own riding habits, you may discover that you are encountering fewer and fewer sudden hazards, and it may seem that you have more time to deal with the problems that do occur. That's because we almost always have more than 3 or 4 seconds prior to impact to take evasive action. Most of those victims in motorcycle accidents offer the excuse that they didn't have time to react, but that's really an admission they weren't monitoring the road far enough ahead.

By predicting hidden situations, looking farther ahead, being prepared, and practicing the tactics we've mentioned, the skilled rider will do a perfect quick stop without wasting any time, then marvel about it afterwards.

Right Pace, Right Place

A few months ago I was getting a quick tour of the back roads north and south of San Francisco. A couple of local motorcyclists were showing me some really fun secondary roads that snaked over the hills and down into canyons shaded by giant redwoods. We even stopped for lunch at Alice's Restaurant, the famous biker hangout on Skyline Boulevard, and checked out the fancy sportbikes in the parking lot.

Every sunny weekend, the Skyline is a steady toccata of high-strung motorcycles. And tow trucks. We passed by one shiny yellow Ducati being winched uphill out of the trees. All we could see of the bike was the rear end being hoisted back over the edge, but we could recognize the exhaust pipes sticking out under the tail cone.

There was no obvious reason the rider should have crashed here. The location wasn't a blind intersection or a decreasing-radius sucker corner. The pavement wasn't littered with tree needles or wet leaves. It wasn't raining. We didn't see any deer. There were no cars nearby with dented passenger doors. As near as I could figure, the Ducati rider had been flirting with the laws of physics and gotten slapped. He'd probably been a little hot, started to drift wide, panicked, did something dumb, and sailed over the edge into some heavy-duty tree trunks. We didn't stop—this sort of thing happens all the time up on the Skyline.

If you believe the covers of today's motorcycling magazines, the purpose of motorcycling is to ride as fast as you can and lean over in the curves until your knee sliders get hot. Road racers are held up as our heroes, and race-replica sportbikes are what you really want. Of course, today's sports machines really are good. If you could roll most any box-stock contemporary sportbike off the showroom floor and into a time machine, transporting it back just ten years, you'd have a faster, better handling motorcycle than the big buck factory race bikes of the day. And that's really a dilemma for today's motorcyclists.

I have this image of me on a high-zoot sportbike, passing every other motorcyclist on the road, half Mike Hailwood and half Joey Dunlop. But I don't ride the track. The dreamy perfect racer image gets pushed aside by the nightmare of a gravel truck chugging out of a hidden driveway, a horse escaping from a pasture, the sudden odor of

Attempting to keep a race replica bike under control on public roads is a challenge many of us aren't up to.

spilled diesel oil, or a rusty pickup truck weaving across the line as the driver flings an empty Jack Daniel's bottle into my path. Sure, I'd like to think of myself as a good rider, but I'd like to stick around for a while longer. And I can't escape the knowledge that public roads are full of hazards that can quickly and permanently end my motorcycling. There are a lot of riders like the guy on that yellow Ducati who are willing to push the envelope on public roads, but they seem to have very short riding careers. For most of us, jacking up the risks of a ticket or a crash is unacceptable. I've also discovered over the years that what's important is to enjoy the ride, and only a modest part of that enjoyment relates to speed.

If you find that your bike often seems to have a mind of its own or you often get a panicky feeling that you aren't really in control of the situation, those are clues that the bike is too much in control of the ride, and you're just going along as baggage. There are a couple of messages here, if you choose to listen. First, think about your machinery. Those shiny 100-horse sportbikes are sinfully seductive parked in front of Alice's, but attempting to keep a 170 mph race replica bike under control on public roads is a challenge many of us aren't up to.

We can imagine the scenario for that Ducati rider. He's pushing his limits heading up Skyline Boulevard, his head swimming in adrenaline but scarce on high-speed skills. He goes into the curve a little too hot, and somewhere in the middle of that sweeper, his brain registers that those trees are approaching awfully fast, and the bike isn't turning as tight as the road. He panics. His right hand slams the throttle closed, and his right foot nails the rear brake lever. Adios, baby.

The Right Machine for the Ride

My first motorcycle was a 150cc. A year later, I moved up to a 305, then a 450, followed by various 500, 750, 800, 850, 900, and 1000cc bikes. A couple of years ago I added a 350cc dual-sport to my stable and have rediscovered how much fun a smaller motorcycle can be, both offroad and on pavement. On that San Francisco trip, I took the 350. It turned out to be the right machine for those twisty back roads around San Francisco, and for slipping through downtown traffic. *A little 350*, you might be wondering, *running with the big dogs in the canyons of California? Didn't you get blown into the weeds?*

Yes, I did get some funny looks from the other riders. Before one ride, the leader asked about maximum speed and fuel range. I'm not sure he believed me when I said it would cruise at 70 mph, with a fuel range of 200 miles. What was more surprising to the other riders was that once we hit the back roads, the 350 could maintain the same pace as the group, and even leave some bigger bikes behind. A lighter bike can corner as quickly as a heavier bike, and with less risk of making a mistake. The 350 was a lot of fun to ride on the twisty little roads and highways. I'm not sorry I didn't take my 1000cc fire-breather on that trip.

If you're thinking about buying a different machine, or adding another bike to your fleet, don't overlook the dual sportbikes in the 350cc to 650cc range, or 600cc sportbikes. Sure, if you normally carry a passenger, cruise the superslabs from coast to coast, or carry big loads of camping gear, a big 1200 or 1500 tourer is the right tool. Just don't forget that mid-sized bikes can be a lot of fun. Whatever your choice of machine, the same general riding skills apply. Let's consider some cornering tactics that will help you stay out of trouble and enjoy the ride more.

The Right Pace

Most of us enjoy the performance of a high-powered bike. We like the feel of leaning a massive machine over into curves and the kick in our pants as we accelerate down the straights. But, somewhere between road racer and plonker, there's room for spirited riding, and if we do it right we don't have to jack up the risks to unacceptable levels. That's really what *Proficient Motorcycling* is all about.

Most of the time, we're talking about techniques. Steering. Braking. Throttle control. Cornering lines. But motorcycling also involves rhythm. A large part of the enjoyment of motorcycling comes from setting the right pace for the right place.

Consider a musician who plays every piece the same way: loud and fast. A galloping allegro tempo might be fun for something like the *Flight of the Bumblebee,* but it would be silly to rush through the blues, or country/western, or an anthem. The mood of the piece determines an appropriate tempo. That's the way it should be with motorcycling. The road, the situation, the bike, your companions, the weather, and your attitude all help determine an appropriate riding pace. It's up to you to find the pace—the right tempo—for today's ride. That's not simply a matter of road speed, but of the rhythm at which you approach a corner, apply the brakes, lean the bike, or roll the throttle.

For example, the force you apply at the grips determines how quickly your motorcycle leans into a turn. Shove hard on the inside grip, and the motorcycle snaps over. Push gently, and it eases over. Push hard enough, and you can slide the front tire out from under you. Push too lazily, and you can run into the weeds before you get the bike turned. Different corners demand a different pace. As you experiment with different cornering lines, you also need to adjust the tempo.

Braking Tempo

If the number one survival skill in traffic is maximum-effort braking, the number two survival skill is being able to set an appropriate corner entry speed without having to brake hard or late. Road racers may talk about late braking, or trailing the rear brake deep into corners. But late braking on the road has a way of eating up too much cornering traction and pushing the bike wide, either of which can bring your riding career to a sudden end. Timing is an essential part of braking.

When braking, how quickly do you squeeze the lever? How firmly do you squeeze? How quickly do you release the lever? Isn't the tempo for getting off the brakes just as important as how you apply them? If you are full on the front brake with the suspension compressed, and you suddenly let go of the lever, the front end will jump back up, upsetting the bike and changing the traction equation. Smooth *on* the brakes; smooth *off* the brakes. Remember, you should be squeezing progressively harder over one full second as weight transfers onto the front wheel. Now release the brake over one full second and ask yourself when you should be off the brakes. The bottom line is that you really don't want to be squandering traction on braking when the bike is leaned over. The wise rider sets cornering speed early, and gets off the brakes before leaning the bike into the curve. Adding a little rear brake while leaned over (trailing brake) is basically a technique for keeping the engine pulling smoother without increasing speed. Late braking is a hint you didn't achieve the correct corner entry speed.

At this point, you might be wondering what's wrong with just riding along at a modest pace and controlling speed with the throttle. A lot of riders do that, but then a lot of riders end up bashing into hazards because their survival habits didn't include braking. If you expect to be able to brake hard someday to avoid a hazard that suddenly pops into view, you should stay in the front brake habit, and use both brakes as part of your cornering sequence, even if you just lightly touch the levers.

Cornering Tempo

We've suggested the importance of finding the right entry speed for corners. The only good guideline for entry speed is what happened in the last corner. If you had to roll the throttle closed or brake after you leaned over, you didn't go in slow enough. Your target entry speed should be whatever speed will allow you to roll on the throttle smoothly through the rest of the curve. You'll also get some clues from a series of bends. If you discover that you're a little late and a little wide in turn two then drifting even wider in turn three, and headed toward the gravel in turn four, that means bike speed is faster than your thinking speed. Slow down a bit more entering corners, get the bike under control, and enjoy the ride at a more relaxed tempo that matches your thinking pace.

Throttle Tempo

We've asked this before, and we'll ask it again: When do you roll on the throttle during a curve? Do you roll off the gas and let engine compression slow the bike halfway through the turn? Do you wait until you lift the bike up again before rolling on the gas? Or do you ease on the throttle as you lean the bike over? Unless it's a really strange downhill turn, the correct time to ease on the throttle is when you lean the bike over, long before you pass the apex.

If you get the bike slowed to the right entry speed, then lean the bike over into a nice stable arc and simultaneously roll on a little throttle, everything will feel a lot smoother and more enjoyable. We're not talking a sudden burst of power here, just a smooth roll-on all the way through the turn. If you find yourself panicking in the middle of curves because the bike is drifting wide, think about your cornering lines and what you're doing with the throttle.

Leaning Tempo

You don't want to lean the bike too early because that points the bike toward the inside of the lane, and then it's pointed too wide at the apex. Delay the turn-in slightly, keeping the bike closer to the outside of your lane, then smoothly and forcefully lean the bike over, pointing toward a delayed apex. It's better to push firmly on the low grip and hold it a little longer than to slam the bike down with a quick, hard push because a smoother, longer push results in less chassis wobble as the machine

Start the left-hander from the far right side of the lane, braking lightly to a speed at which you can roll on the throttle as you lean left.

David L. Hough

Starting wide while approaching that right-hander ahead points the bike toward the center of the road.

Approaching the right-hander, brake lightly, decelerating to a speed at which . . .

. . . you can roll on the throttle as you lean right, pointing the bike toward a delayed apex just around the corner behind those rocks.

Now you can see the left-hand turn coming up, followed by another right-hander. Point toward the outside again . . .

settles into its cornering line. The smoother you are at leaning the bike, the more traction you'll have for cornering, with the least risk of a slideout.

At the tail end of the corner, it's time to straighten up the bike. There is no advantage in pushing hard on the "up" grip to suddenly straighten the bike, unless you have to swerve around a hazard. Just roll on a little more throttle and let the bike lift itself up as it follows a smooth arc toward the outside of the curve. Unless there's another vehicle in the way or a surface problem, you can use all of your lane. Okay, let's put it all together, riding through a series of corners.

. . . and decelerate to a speed at which you can roll on the throttle as you lean the bike left. As soon as you can see the next turn ahead, you should already be planning your critical turn windows and lines.

Enjoying the Ride

The point of all this is that you might enjoy the ride more when the emphasis is on perfect control of the motorcycle rather than on what the speedometer says. And finding the right timing is the key to better control. What many riders discover, to their amazement, is that the right pace results in higher cornering speeds as well as better control. For many of us, a brisk but controlled ride down a favorite twisty road on a good handling bike is a most enjoyable way to spend an afternoon.

David L. Hough

Urban Traffic

Survival

CHAPTER 4
URBAN TRAFFIC SURVIVAL

City Traffic

O ccasionally, I get the opportunity to go motorcycling through some faraway places. The travels have always been great, but I'm constantly surprised at what the folks back home think about the relative dangers of riding around a foreign country on a motorcycle. A few years ago, I had the opportunity to join a tour across South Africa on a BMW GS Dual Sport. The most frequent question my coworkers asked about the trip was, *Aren't you concerned about your personal safety?* Well, sure, I was concerned about my safety, but I wasn't as concerned about getting caught up in a race riot as I was concerned about surviving South African traffic. Let's face it: riding around in traffic on a motorcycle involves some big risks, no matter what country you're in.

Sure, you could get assassinated in Afghanistan or firebombed in Bloemfontein, but you're more likely to get crunched by a cabbie in Cincinnati or totaled by a truck in Toledo. In other words, getting mugged, shot, torched, or blown to bits by some fanatical terrorist isn't a traveler's worst nightmare. The traveling motorcyclist's greatest hazard—most anywhere in the world—is motor vehicle traffic.

Best Advice for Travelers

So, if you are concerned about personal safety, my absolutely, positively best advice about travel is: (drum roll please) STAY OUT OF CITIES. Go anywhere you want, but just don't ride into big cities. Cities are a combat zone of cars, trucks, busses, trains, trolleys, donkey carts, bicycles, skateboards, and other assorted wheeled vehicles; all seemingly trying to smash into each other at high velocities. It's not the sort of environment a clever person would choose to ride into on a motorcycle.

But You're Going to Do It Anyway, Right?

Well, okay, I know you're going to ignore my advice and ride into cities anyway. Maybe you live in the city. Or maybe you live in the suburbs but you ride into the big city because a motorcycle is the only vehicle you can find a parking place for. Or maybe you have a burning desire to snap a photo of your motorcycle with the statue of Liberty in the background, or you're headed for Disneyland and you've got to get through San Bernardino, or you are headed for Sturgis, and somehow end up on a one-way street into downtown Chicago. Maybe, like myself, you get really nutzo and choose a motorcycle for the daily commute to work. Whatever the reasons for zooming into the city on motorcycles, we'd be wise to work on our traffic survival skills. So, park your "scooter" outside the garage door there, pour yourself a cup of your favorite beverage, pull up that creaky chair, and let's get started.

Sudden Collisions

The first thing to realize about "sudden" collisions is that they seldom occur as suddenly as most accident victims think. Now, if you suddenly realize you are on a collision course with a Chicago cab, just a second or two away from impact, the rest of the crash may seem awfully quick. But the suddenness is often a matter of not observing what is happening until too late in the process, typically within the last second or two. If you know where to look, how to look, and what to look for, you can almost always spot a potential collision several seconds before the point of impact. And once you understand what is happening, you can usually make a little correction to avoid riding into the problem.

One of the reasons cities are so hazardous is just the amount of stuff going on all at once. We've got multiple lanes of traffic, vehicles weaving around in all directions, cross-traffic squirting out at intersections, double-parked cars, jaywalking pedestrians, aggressive bicyclists, roaring trucks, oil-dripping busses, slick plastic arrows, sunken railroad tracks, grated bridge decks, man-eating potholes, and millions of traffic signs and signals—some of which are confusing—and that's just the good stuff. Whatever is out there demands our attention at once, and any one problem is capable of causing us grief. The paradox is that we've somehow got to be aware of all the hazards at once, but there are usually too many hazards to keep track of at any one moment. Let's share a few ideas on how to deal with this paradox.

The first idea is to separate the hazards. Although it often seems as if everything is demanding our attention at once, it is possible to separate our awareness of the hazards, if only by a few feet or a few milliseconds. Of course we can't make the other guys move farther apart or go more slowly, but we can observe them over more distance or more time by looking farther ahead.

One trick is to get in the habit of scrutinizing stuff w-a-a-a-y down the road. The farther ahead you spot trouble, the more time you have to observe it, make a decision about it, and deal with it. You won't have to do any sudden panic maneuvers because you will make a few simple adjustments early on, and just stay out of harm's way. The safety experts often recommend looking 12 seconds ahead. That's the distance you will be covering during the next 12 seconds, which translates into about as far ahead as you can see any details. To put this another way, you want to spot any problems 12 seconds before they get close enough to become a hazard to you.

Look 12 Seconds Ahead

Looking 12 seconds ahead is a good habit to get into, but we're talking about more than just staring down the road with glazed eyeballs. We need to be good observers. By *observe* I mean really keeping our eyes moving to take in as much as possible, and making judgment calls about what's happening.

Try this exercise right now: Go back and read the previous paragraph again, but this time read one line at a time, and spend 2 seconds scrutinizing the world around you before reading the next line. See if you can remember what you're reading while also observing details of what's happening around you—the current time, what TV channel is on, who else is in the room, the color of the car driving by, what pictures are on the wall behind you, and so forth. It's not easy, is it? The temptation is either to look around and stop reading, or continue reading and ignore the observing. But don't we do something similar as we simultaneously ride the bike and observe traffic around us? And consider this: Once you record in your memory what time it is or who else is in the room, you have a pretty good idea of what's going on. The only items you need to study on subsequent glances are things that have changed.

It's the same way in traffic. We need to be aware of everything, but we can focus momentarily on those things that are in the process of becoming potential hazards. For example, the big rattling car transporter rolling along in the next lane may scream for attention, but one or two glances may confirm that it's not really a problem. That oncoming car approaching the intersection ahead isn't demanding attention, but I know that left-turners are a frequent hazard for motorcyclists, so I need to focus on that car, not on the noisy truck.

Danger Zones

Intersections are danger zones where we especially need to focus our attention. Folks with poor judgment are very likely to make mistakes at intersections, pulling out in front of other drivers, making quick turns, jamming on the brakes, or motoring through red lights. Recognize that intersections are anywhere vehicles can cross paths, whether they be divided eight-lane arterials or two lanes that cross in the shopping mall parking lot.

Intersections are danger zones where we especially need to focus our attention.

For the record, about three-fourths of all motorcycle crashes are collisions with cars, and about one-fourth of all motorcycle crashes are the result of car drivers making quick left turns across the paths of motorcyclists.

It's also worthwhile to note that collisions with cars zooming out of alleys account for a good percentage of intersection smashos, and a disproportionate share of motorcyclist fatalities. Never mind who is at fault, the motorcyclist is the one who gets hurt.

Separate the Hazards

Just as we can mentally separate our observations of what is happening around us, we can physically separate ourselves from hazards. We can move the motorcycle farther away from hazards and we can separate one hazard from another by changing lane position or speed. For example, if that rattling car transporter is too much of a distraction being so close, I can speed up, slow down, or change lanes to get farther away. Likewise, I can move away from a slow-moving car that's in the process of collecting a gaggle of trouble around it, or I can change lanes to move further away from a car that's poking its nose out of an alley.

Since intersections are trouble enough, I try to separate myself from other hazards before I get to an intersection. If I am being tailgated by an aggressive driver or paced by someone in an adjacent lane, I take steps to move farther away. If at all possible, I move away from trucks or busses, primarily because they block my view. I'd rather not allow myself to be a victim of whatever happens, and I prefer not to let the hazards multiply. Take control of the situation to continuously improve the odds in your favor. Don't be squeezed into a corner or boxed into a trap if you can help it.

Move away from view-blocking trucks or buses.

I Didn't See You

If you allow another motorist to knock you down, you'll hear the same excuse: *I didn't see you.* Sometimes an errant driver has looked down at the poor motorcyclist lying miserably crunched under a bent motorcycle and let slip: *Gosh, I didn't see you. You were coming so fast, and you were wearing black leather, and, besides, you didn't have your headlight turned on.* Certainly there are occasions when the other driver really couldn't see the motorcyclist, but many veteran motorcyclists have a sneaking suspicion that the excuse is mostly a cop-out. When a driver attempts a sudden left turn in front of a motorcyclist and doesn't make it in time, we shouldn't expect to hear, *I saw you but I was in a hurry and I figured you'd get out of my way.*

This repeated *I didn't see you* excuse of the knocker-downers has led some safety experts to believe that the problem simply is that motorcycles are inconspicuous in traffic. The solution, theoretically, is to be more conspicuous. The suggestions are to wear bright colored riding gear, blind everyone else with the headlight on high beam, and screw on a Yosemite Sam *Back Off* mud flap.

Most of the high-mileage riding friends I know roll their eyes at the conspicuity stuff. *Friends don't let friends wear pink leathers,* they sneer. Perhaps the veterans have a more realistic understanding of the *I didn't see you myth* and suspect that conspicuity stuff is more of a magic talisman than a dependable safety device. (Magic talismans are supposed to ward off evil with no effort on the part of the wearer.) Conspicuity devices are based on the assumption that the other guy will get out of the way of the motorcyclist if only he can see you. The veterans know that avoiding collisions depends on being prepared to get out of the way of the other guy, whether he sees you or not.

We can't control every situation, though, and like it or not we often depend upon other motorists not to run us over. Motorcycles are narrower and more difficult to see in traffic. Other motorists don't always comprehend how rapidly a motorcycle is approaching because a single 7-inch diameter headlight doesn't really give them a clue about its approach speed. So a case can be made for motorcyclists to be a little more visible for the benefit of those drivers on the road who are really trying to avoid collisions. Most importantly, if you are still in the process of learning the tactics of traffic survival, you really are more dependent upon other drivers to stay out of your way, and you should help them out by being as conspicuous as you can. Whatever your experience level, you'll have to arrive at a level of conspicuousness that meets your needs and fits your limits of sensibility.

If you think it might help to increase your conspicuity, here are some suggestions:

★ **Consider light colored riding gear such as tan, silver, yellow, or bright blue. Add brightly colored vanity stripes to your darker colored leathers, or wear a bright reflective vest over your jacket.**

★ **Choose a helmet in a lighter, brighter color, or a helmet design with bright stripes.**

★ **When shopping for a new machine or repainting your faded bike, give priority to a bright paint scheme.**

★ **Use amber running lights on the front of your bike, as widely spaced as practical and legal.**

★ **For nighttime rides, add reflective tape to the back end of your saddlebags, tour trunk, and helmet. Add multiple red taillights, preferably spaced wide apart.**

Move It or Lose It

I've already suggested that the wise rider can learn to make simple adjustments to avoid hazards, reducing the need to make rapid evasive maneuvers.

Okay, I wasn't quite honest about that. We can learn to avoid almost all accidents, but once in a while we really do encounter a sudden hazard we had no way of seeing or predicting. For example, a large rock suddenly tumbles down onto the road just as you come along, or a black horse escapes his corral on a rainy night and stands in the middle of the road. When you suddenly realize you're 2 seconds from impact, you'll do whatever you're in the habit of doing. If you're in the habit of using the front brake to the limits of traction, you'll squeeze the brake lever without thinking about it. If you're in the habit of pushing on the grips to quickly lean the bike, you'll do a quick swerve without wasting any time. That's why I keep repeating the same advice: Practice emergency avoidance maneuvers such as quick stops and emergency swerves at least once each season, and practice all the right cornering techniques even when you don't have to. But surviving city traffic requires more than just perfect evasive maneuvers. You've got to figure out what's going on in traffic and learn to predict what's going to happen before it happens.

Booby Trap Intersections

Cities are full of booby traps for the unwary motorcyclist. Collisions with other vehicles are high on the motorcyclist's danger list. Novice street riders may assume that keeping the rubber side down is simply a matter of learning skills such as balancing, shifting, and throttle control. Experience soon teaches us that avoiding motorcycle accidents involves outsmarting as well as outmaneuvering other motorists.

The classic left-turner

Intersection booby traps are often disguised as a car waiting for us to ride through. Suddenly, the car zooms across our path and **Snap!** the trap closes. Statistically, about two-thirds of all motorcycle accidents and half of all motorcycle fatalities occur at intersections. The unwary get about 2 seconds to avoid a collision, and a lot of novice riders slam into the side of the car without even reaching for the front brake.

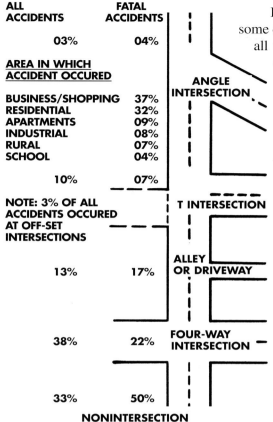

ALL ACCIDENTS	FATAL ACCIDENTS	
03%	04%	ANGLE INTERSECTION

AREA IN WHICH ACCIDENT OCCURED

BUSINESS/SHOPPING	37%	
RESIDENTIAL	32%	
APARTMENTS	09%	
INDUSTRIAL	08%	
RURAL	07%	
SCHOOL	04%	

10%	07%	

NOTE: 3% OF ALL ACCIDENTS OCCURED AT OFF-SET INTERSECTIONS

		T INTERSECTION
13%	17%	ALLEY OR DRIVEWAY
38%	22%	FOUR-WAY INTERSECTION
33%	50%	NONINTERSECTION

If we are to survive booby trap intersections, we need to develop some collision avoidance strategies. Let's define *intersection,* so we're all thinking about the same situations, and describe the types of crashes that occur at intersections. Then let's consider some practical tactics for spotting and avoiding collisions.

An intersection is anywhere two traffic lanes connect, including entrances to gas stations, alleys, driveways, traffic lanes in shopping malls, and anywhere else two vehicles are likely to cross paths. The diagram shows the breakdown of the type of intersection and the relative percentages of accidents and fatalities.

According to the Hurt Report, roughly half of all motorcycle accidents are caused by other motorists (usually car drivers) violating the motorcyclist's right of way. If you compare the percentages of all accidents to fatal accidents, it is interesting to note that only 13 percent of accidents happen at alleys, but alley collisions generate 17 percent of all motorcycle fatalities. Obviously, we need to pay more attention to vehicles coming out of alleys and driveways. Four-way intersections generate the majority of accidents, accounting for 22 percent of fatalities, so let's first consider how accidents occur at such locations.

A whopping 28 percent of collisions occur between cars and motorcycles with the motorist making a left turn. Typically, the driver turns left in front of the motorcyclist, and the bike slams into the side of the car.

While the left-turner often approaches from the opposite direction, there are several variations we need to watch for. A driver can turn left from side streets from either our left or our right. When such vehicles are hidden behind busses, trucks, or parked cars, they can appear in our path suddenly.

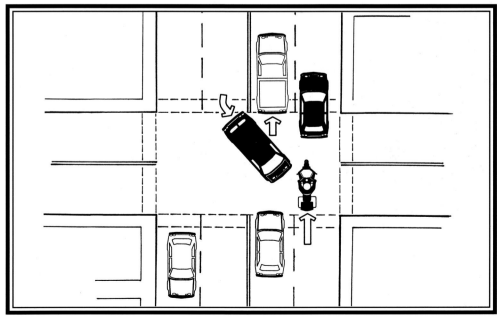

The classic left-turner, top view

Left-turner from street on your left

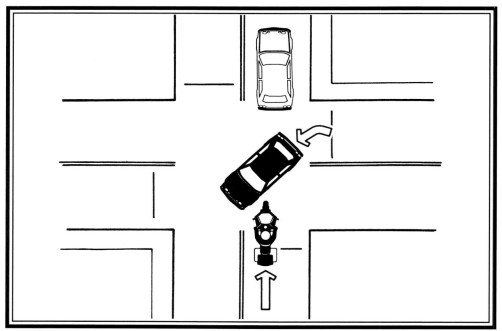

Left-turner from street on your right

One booby trap that catches a few riders by surprise is the driver in the right lane of a one-way street who suddenly turns left across the path of the motorcyclist.

As we try to figure out some collision-avoidance strategies, let's note that accidents are only "sudden" when neither motorist has looked far enough ahead to spot the problem. Riders who report a mere 2 seconds between the time they saw the offending driver and the time they hit the door are simply admitting they weren't looking far enough ahead, didn't know what to look for, or didn't believe there was potential for a crash.

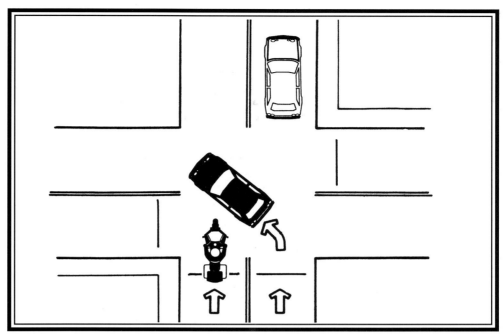

Left-turner from a one-way street

Eyes Up

Previously, I discussed looking ahead at the road over which you will be traveling in the next 12 seconds. At a street speed of 40 mph, 12 seconds covers more than 700 feet! If you can't see that far ahead because of other traffic or obstructions, slowing down gives you more time to react to whatever suddenly pops into view. Large vehicles can really limit your view ahead and also prevent other drivers from seeing you.

Be wary of passing trucks or busses waiting to make a turn. The problem isn't just that you can't see what's happening ahead, it's that other drivers can't see you

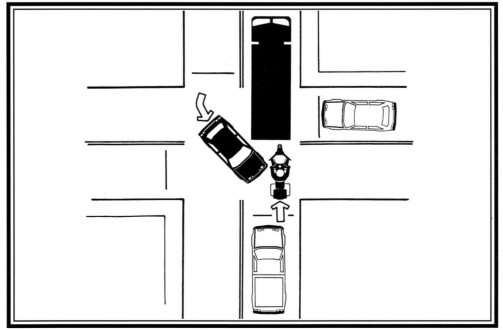

Why it's not smart to follow trucks or busses through an intersection.

hidden behind the truck or bus. The driver in the opposite lane who is waiting for a chance to turn left may think that space behind the bus will provide just enough room to zip across traffic. Wise riders don't follow immediately behind big obstructions such as busses.

To identify potential left-turners approaching from the opposite direction, watch for some important clues:

★ **The vehicle begins to slow as it enters the intersection.**
★ **The hood dips slightly as the driver begins to brake.**
★ **The car enters a left-turn lane or eases over close to the centerline.**
★ **The front wheel begins to turn in your direction.**

Of course, the driver could be signaling a turn, but that doesn't tell you when the car might actually pull into your path. Some safety experts suggest establishing eye contact with the driver, but eye contact is no guarantee he or she won't make the turn anyway. Once you identify a car that could turn in front of you, you need to know if it is actually starting to move into your path. We'll get into the nitty gritty of evasive action shortly.

Alleys produce a disproportionate share of fatalities partly because we get complacent about alleys and driveways. Alleys are narrow and often hidden between buildings, so you need to search aggressively for evidence of a vehicle about to pull out. Clues may be as subtle as a flicker of light reflected from a chrome bumper or the momentary pause of a pedestrian on the sidewalk. Streets, alleys, and driveways on your right are more of a danger because vehicles emerging from them are closer to your path of travel. Moving farther away from alleys definitely improves your odds of avoiding a collision with a car that suddenly pulls out onto the street.

When observing vehicles on side streets, watch the top of the front wheel. The top of the wheel moves twice as fast as the bumper, so the top of the tire starting to roll is your first clue that the vehicle is starting to move.

Sure, you may have the legal right of way at intersections, but having the legal right of way is little consolation when you're looking up at a trauma doctor. When you can't see what's going to happen in the next 12 seconds, what are the smart tactics? Right—slow down to give yourself time to react to the unknown, move to a lane position that maximizes your view, and be prepared to take evasive action to get out of the way.

Intersection Approach Tactics

When you are approaching an intersection where you predict the possibility of a collision, try to prepare yourself for avoidance maneuvers. Keep in mind that stopping distance depends upon your speed, your reaction time, and your skill, as well as your equipment. Position yourself for best view and maximum separation from other vehicles. For example, where buildings or large vehicles block your view of traffic on streets to your right, you can get a better view by moving to the left side of the lane, or moving to the left lane. That same tactic works for narrow alleys.

The higher your speed, the greater the distance required to stop, even with instantaneous reaction and perfect braking technique. Stopping distance just about doubles for every 10 mph increase. For example, it takes you 40 feet to stop from a speed of 30 mph, it will take you at least 80 feet to stop from a speed of 40 mph. The moral is, slowing down just 10 mph can cut 40 feet, or just about the width of two lanes, off your stopping distance at typical urban street speeds. You don't have to putter along urban arterials at 30, but if you're approaching a busy intersection with multiple left-turners, slowing down 10 mph can make the difference between a quick stop and a collision. And remember, you have to squeeze the lever before the brakes can do anything. Your reaction time to get on the brakes might consume half a second or more if you don't already have your fingers squeezing the brake lever. Half a second doesn't sound like much, but it represents about 30 feet at 40 mph. And regardless of when you manage to get on the brakes, your actual stopping distance depends greatly upon your braking skill as well as your equipment.

Riders who haven't actually practiced quick stops from 40 to 0 typically can't pull off a good stop. In rider training courses for experienced motorcyclists, even veteran riders often can't stop quickly without sliding the rear tire, or they don't know how to do a quick stop in a curve without losing control. If the thought of practicing quick stops makes you nervous, that's probably something you should take care of before you're confronted with the big test out in traffic.

Once more, I'll remind you that in a panic situation our muscles follow our habits. Too many riders don't use enough front brake or don't use the front brake at all. That's why some machines have integrated brake systems that automatically meter rear pedal brake pressure to one of the front discs as well as the rear. But the quickest stop still requires proficient use of the front brake lever in addition to the pedal.

Riders who have spent the big bucks for an antilock brake system (ABS) are sometimes under the delusion that they don't need to be proficient at braking, since the ABS will save them from a spill. Yes, ABS can help avoid a spill if you over-brake on a slick surface, but ABS won't prevent the tires from sliding out if you overbrake while leaned over in a curve. And even with ABS, quickest stops can usually be made if the rider brakes to a maximum just short of where the ABS activates. ABS doesn't stand for "automatic brake system." So, whether your bike has inter-locked brakes, ABS, or independent brakes, you need to be proficient at making quick stops, whether in a straight line or in a curve.

The Possibilities

Let's add up the tactics, and see what they mean in terms of stopping distance from a typical street speed of 35-45 mph:

TACTIC	EFFECT
Slow from 40 to 30 mph	-40 feet
Already on front brake lever	-30 feet
Marginal braking technique	+57 feet
Proficient braking technique	+37 feet
Potential difference in braking distance:	127 ft. vs. 37 feet

Looking Good

Remember, your motorcycle tends to go wherever you are looking. If you stare at the side of a left-turning car, that's where the bike will go. If you'd rather miss the car, focus on the open street where you want the motorcycle to go. If you're making a quick stop to avoid punching into the right front door of a left-turning car, wouldn't it make sense to focus on the pavement in front of the car where you intend to stop short of a collision, not on the side of the car?

Rider Training

To help develop good habits, smart riders practice swerves and quick stops in a training environment at least once each year. Braking and swerving practice is smart, but don't overlook some study time to hone your accident avoidance strategies. Some riders take the ERC every year or every other year as a refresher. To locate your nearest training site, call the Motorcycle Safety Foundation hotline (800) 446-9227 and give them your zip code. They will put you in touch with the closest training facility.

Whether you've taken a training course or practiced by yourself, it's important to stay in the habit of using the front brake during every stop and to include braking as part of your cornering sequence prior to leaning the bike into a curve. When the chips are down, you'll do whatever you've been in the habit of doing. As I mentioned at the beginning, avoiding booby traps in the city involves both out-maneuvering and outwitting a wide variety of urban hazards.

Suburb Survival

Bigdawg Dan has been fidgety ever since he watched the European road racing on *Speedvision* last Tuesday. His right hand has been twitching, and his soul is itching for a twisty road fix. As the week unfolds, Dan checks his tires, tops off the oil, runs a rag over the chrome, oils up his leathers, and polishes his face shield one more time.

The weather report Thursday night promises a sunny day on Friday, but rain on Saturday. While he's been futzing with the bike, Dan has been formulating a believable medical excuse for the boss. The weather report clinches the decision: Friday morning, instead of heading for work, Dan points the bike through commuter traffic to get out of town and onto his favorite back road. Even as he carves through frustratingly slow traffic, he's slicing through those turns in his mind. To make better time, Dan cuts over to the side streets he knows so well.

But before Bigdawg can get out of Dodge City, a posse of sleepy commuters pulls a hold-up. With no warning, a van zips out of an alley, directly into Dan's path. Like the sleepy driver, it takes Dan a moment to switch from dreaming to reality, and that extra reaction time seals his fate. Too late getting on the brake, Dan slams into the driver's

When you escape from the freeways, busy arterials, and heavy traffic, and cruise down a quiet side street, it's easy to let your guard down.

door and catapults over the roof. Luckily, he isn't seriously injured, thanks to the riding gear he had decided to wear. But the bike's front end is wrapped back under the engine, and this machine isn't going to go anywhere soon. The ride is over. Now Dan can honestly fulfill his sick leave prophesy with a sprained shoulder.

I bump into a lot of veteran riders in my travels. And I get a pretty good idea of what's on their minds. One top-level priority seems to be riding the twisty back roads as quickly as possible. Yes, drifting through the twisties is exciting. We're basically trying to emulate the road racers without having to buy track time. In my opinion, there's nothing wrong with enjoying quick riding, but there's a lot more to motorcycling than emulating the racers. Remember, a lot of your riding time is in the suburbs. Even if you're headed out to the country, you've got to get through the suburbs first. And what many motorcyclists seem to overlook is that suburbs generate a lot of motorcycle accidents.

Freeways might appear to be a hazardous riding environment, what with the big volume of traffic and the higher speeds, but the statistics hint that freeways are safer than undivided highways. Most motorcyclists have figured out that urban (city) intersections are our biggest nightmare, complete with cross-traffic, multiple lanes, strange intersections, confusing signals, pedestrians, taxi cabs, delivery trucks, busses, and a lot of aggressive driving as frustrated motorists attempt to get somewhere faster than everyone else. Sometimes just getting through a busy parking lot can be a major skirmish. When you can escape from the freeways, busy arterials and heavy traffic, and cruise down a quiet side street, it's easy to let your guard down.

Familiarity Breeds Complacency

You probably already know that the majority of motorcycle accidents occur in business or shopping areas; on sunny days; on straight, level, dry roads; at speeds below 40 mph; and that about three-fourths of all motorcycle accidents are collisions with cars and pickup trucks. What you may not realize is that most accidents occur within the first 12 minutes of the intended trip or on trips of less than 5 miles.

Think about that. When you're close to home, you are familiar with your surroundings. *I've traveled this street a thousand times and have never had a car pull out of that alley before. I've ridden past these same parked cars on this residential side street for five years, and have never had anyone back out of a driveway into my path until today. I never figured that other driver would swerve into my lane to get around the bicyclist.* Familiarity tends to breed complacency. Obviously, it's a lot quieter on the side streets. But if you happen along at the same instant and same place as someone else who suddenly gets in your way, you need to be just as prepared to avoid the crash as you would be on the busier arterials.

Get Your Head in the Ride

Consider Bigdawg Dan's mental state at the time of his accident. He was dreaming about the future, not thinking in the present. He was squandering his thoughts on the ride, which in his mind would commence when he got to his favorite road. He wasn't focusing on the ride already in progress or the situation immediately in front of his machine. For Dan, getting through city traffic was just an inconvenience prior to the real ride of the day. It is important to get your head in the ride before you ease out the clutch, whether you're shifting down for that first of a hundred fun curves on the coast highway, heading out on the next leg of a cross-country trip, or just zipping down to the local coffee shop for breakfast.

And while we're talking about thinking, let's note the importance of keeping your self fed and free of toxins. You can't expect your brain to function correctly if it isn't well nourished and free of dizzying drugs. Have a good breakfast before a morning ride, or at least stop early for some healthy food. Leave the bike in the garage if you're on any pills that make you drowsy or light-headed. Most importantly, avoid alcohol while you're riding a motorcycle.

Yeah, alcohol has a bad reputation for being involved in fatal accidents, and it deserves it. Alcohol degrades most of the physical and mental functions you need to operate a motor vehicle. Automobile drivers seem to be getting smarter about not driving under the influence, but motorcyclists don't seem to be paying attention, and riding a bike requires greater skill and judgment than driving a car. According to the National Center for Statistics and Analysis, approximately 20 percent of automobile drivers in fatal accidents had a BAC of 0.10 or greater. Of motorcyclists involved in fatal accidents, 40 percent had a BAC of 0.10 or greater. There are some folks who dispute the exact numbers, but it should be

Way too many riders are willing to risk a cocktail of booze and bikes.

obvious that there are still way too many riders who are willing to risk a cocktail of booze and bikes.

Timing, Timing, Timing

You might be amazed that there are significant differences in the accident and fatality numbers depending upon time of day. The hours when frustrated workers head home from the job and drunks head home from the bars on weekends are especially hazardous. Be aware that afternoons between 3 P.M. and 6 P.M. generate about one-fourth of all motorcycle accidents and fatalities. There is also a surge in accidents around midnight on Friday and Saturday. By comparison, early mornings between 3 A.M. and 6 A.M. have a low accident frequency, even on weekends. So, Bigdawg Dan actually faced a much lower collision risk heading out on a Friday morning than if he'd waited until Saturday afternoon. That ought to be useful information when you're scrambling for an excuse to slip away from the job for a day in the canyons. But whatever the time of day or week, the risk of an accident never drops to zero. Those suburban side streets have some peculiar hazards we need to understand.

Parked Cars

With all those parked cars lining the side streets, it's easy to start thinking of them as permanently fixed objects. Just remember, most of them are auto*mobiles.* They move occasionally. The clever rider looks for clues that a parked car is about to go mobile. For cars parked parallel along the curb, watch for a driver behind the wheel or eyes reflected in a side mirror. Look for exhaust emanating from the tailpipe, for an illuminated brake light, or flickering backup lights as the driver shifts into drive. Beware of a front wheel turned toward the street, and remember that the top of a wheel moves twice as fast as the bumper.

Don't ignore cars parked in narrow driveways just off the street. A driver

Do you see there's a driver in that station wagon?

It shouldn't be a surprise when that station wagon pulls out in front of you.

backing into the street isn't likely to have a good view of a motorcycle zipping along. This is especially important where cars are parked on steep inclines or partially hidden behind retaining walls, hedges, or fences. When you do spot any clues that a vehicle might move, get prepared for evasive action, preferably a quick stop.

Kids, Dogs, and Skateboards

You're more likely to encounter people and animals dodging into the street near residences. Kids playing along side streets may also become complacent about traffic and may chase a bouncing ball into your path without thinking about the consequences.

Bicyclists, in-line skaters, and skateboarders are also common on suburban streets these days. For whatever reason, many of these folks believe that the traffic laws don't apply to them. It's fairly common to encounter an adult bicyclist or skater zipping through an intersection against a red light or sailing off the sidewalk and into the street against the flow of traffic. And keep in mind that a vehicle in the opposing lane may swerve across the line to avoid a skater or bicyclist. Young children can be excused for not really understanding the risks, but adults who should know better are just as likely to be the victims. Sixty percent of bicyclist fatalities are in the over-fifteen age bracket.

Darting into the road is the single largest contributor to pedestrian accidents. Of the 5,412 pedestrians killed in the U.S. in 1996, 84 percent of the fatalities happened at locations other than intersections. It may also be helpful to know that 27 percent of pedestrian fatalities occurred between 4 P.M. and 8 P.M., during that evening rush hour when frustrated workers are trying to get home, and 37 percent occurred between 8 P.M. and 12 P.M. on weekends (from the Bureau of Transportation Statistics (BTS), U.S. Department of Transportation in cooperation with NHTSA).

In a collision between a motorcycle and a pedestrian or a motorcycle and a skateboarder, the motorcyclist is more likely to come out on top. But even if you aren't hurt and your bike is undamaged, don't assume you'll survive the accident unscathed. Even if you had the green light, the sympathy of the court is more likely to lean toward the pedestrian than toward the motorcyclist. And your insurance company won't like the deal either. So, even if you have the right-of-way, consider all pedestrians and human-powered vehicles moving targets to avoid.

Evasive Action

The first step in avoiding any of these suburban hazards is planning ahead. The basic evasive maneuver (for everything except loose dogs) is a quick stop. The key to quick stops is to use the front brake every time you brake, and to get familiar with maximum-effort braking without skidding the tires. If you haven't actually gone off to a vacant parking lot and practiced quick stops, you're probably not prepared for riding around in traffic.

Whether you are riding a freeway or a side street, you should always be able to stop within your sight distance. The big problem with narrow residential streets is that your sight distance may be only to the end of the car you are riding by, or to that overgrown hedge at the next corner. A child could be ready to dart out from between the cars, for example, or a skateboarder could come zipping out from behind the hedge. So, your speed through residential neighborhoods must be slow enough that you can make quick stops with little warning. That's why it is unwise to hurry along side streets, as Bigdawg Dan was doing.

When approaching a blind intersection, where you can't see traffic on the side street, plan on a stop to look, just as if there were a stop sign. Assuming you have the right-of-way is an invitation to an embarrassing get-together. And when you do encounter a stop sign, get in the habit of making a complete, left-foot-down stop. A lot of riders who only intended a slowdown when rolling by a stop sign or blind intersection have been surprised by cross-traffic, and have ended up stopping their machines horizontally.

When approaching a blind intersection, where you can't see traffic on the side street, plan on a stop to look, just as if there were a Stop sign.

Surface Hazards

Side streets often have more surface hazards than busier arterials. Street crews tend to ignore problems such as pavement ripples or sunken drains on little-used side streets. So, while you're scrutinizing the situation for the usual vehicle, child, and animal hazards, don't ignore the road surface.

This wooden bridge deck is treacherous in the rain.

Older cities still have streets with brick paving and bridges with wooden decking. Brick and wood may seem to have good traction when dry but can be amazingly slippery when wet. What happens is that the brick dust or wood fibers

Don't ignore that bump over the tree roots while you're bringing your bike to a stop.

David L. Hough

mix with water to form a slimy lubricant that is the same color as the surrounding surface. You can't see the slippery stuff, so just remember that wood and brick surfaces can be treacherous when wet, even from a little dew.

You're also more likely to encounter pavement ripples and grooves on side streets. Where mature trees line a street, expect ripples from tree roots growing under the paving. On many side streets, the paving may suddenly change to gravel or the road may narrow or the sidewalks may disappear.

In newer neighborhoods, you can expect edge traps, dips, and bumps created by the installation of underground pipes and wires as new houses are constructed. Expect manhole covers or drain grates that didn't work out to be the right elevation for the paving but never got fixed. Remember, manholes and grates are usually located at intersections, right where your attention is focused on moving targets.

Slip in Spring and Fall

In climates where winter temperatures dip below freezing, expect loose sand at the edges of the wheel tracks each spring. Wintertime street-sanding operations often leave sandy berms that are most obvious for a month or two after the thaw. Watch carefully at intersections where the sand berms collect near the curb and close to the centerline. Try to keep your tires out of the loose sand.

In autumn, treat fallen leaves with respect. You may get this creative idea to go blasting through a big pile of leaves in the gutter, but think twice about that. Even if the leaves are dry on top, there is often a soggy, slippery layer of rotten vegetation on the bottom, down where your tires are looking for a grip. Or perhaps there are some hidden "ball bearings" in the form of acorns or chestnuts. Maybe there is a loose brick or a sunken drain grate hiding under the leaves, waiting to bend your wheel rim. You can chance the leaf blast if you want, but let's not hear any sniveling if it doesn't work out as creatively as in your imagination.

You may want to think twice about blasting through a big pile of leaves in the gutter.

Wear Your Gear

One final admonition: Wear your riding gear especially when you don't think the situation demands the precaution. Like Bigdawg Dan, you know there are hazards of taking a soil sample when you're blitzing a twisty road at warp speeds, so it's a no-brainer to suit up in the good stuff. But hey, for a 1-mile trip to the convenience store, it's a lot of bother to zip on the armored pants and jacket, right? Just remember that those quiet, innocent-looking side streets can spring sudden hazards on you just as quickly as your favorite twisty road, and that a collision with a left-turner can be just as violent as sliding off a curve.

Superslab Tactics

I happen to live in the country, where I can ease out of my driveway onto a quiet farm road miles from city traffic. I realize I'm in the privileged minority. Most motorcyclists are finding themselves riding busy urban arterials and multilane superhighways more often than not. Even if you're just headed out into the country to get to your favorite twisty road, it's usually a lot easier and quicker to get on the nearest freeway and make an end run around urban traffic. And if you're making a cross-country transit on a limited time schedule, you'll be spending most of your time on the interstates. Let's consider some tactics for surviving those high-speed multilane highways we call freeways, parkways, tollways, motorways, autostradas. For our purposes, we'll call them all superslabs.

Statistically, superslabs are much safer than city streets or two-lane back roads. The old standby Hurt report from 1981 indicated that only 10 percent of motorcycle accidents occurred on freeways. Later data on fatal crashes based on type of roadway hints that superslabs are getting even safer.

NUMBER OF LANES	NOT DIVIDED	DIVIDED
One	42	163
Two	21,276	6,218
Three	315	1,745
Four	2,261	1,753
More than four	253	655

U.S. Fatal Accidents, All Vehicles, 1994, data from DOT Bureau of Transportation Statistics

Take a look at the difference between a two-lane undivided road (a typical secondary highway with a painted centerline) and a divided three-lane or four-lane highway (a typical superslab with a grassy median or a concrete "Jersey" barrier separating opposing traffic). Run the numbers through your calculator, and you can see that there are about twelve fatal accidents on a secondary highway for every one fatal accident on a freeway.

Now, while the superslab does look like a pretty safe environment compared to those dangerous two-laners, people do get killed and seriously injured in superslab accidents. To help you avoid becoming a statistic on the BTS hard drive (not to mention an odd stain on I-80), let's ramble through a bit of philosophy about superslab riding, and then get down to some nitty-gritty tactics.

The Times They Are A-Changing

Back in the good old days, when American traffic and drivers' thinking were much more sedate, it was fairly obvious that traffic in Europe was faster and European drivers more skillful. An English friend of mine who flew across the "pond" to Seattle in 1982 to tour the West Coast by motorcycle described American traffic as moving in slow motion. Things have changed a lot over the last couple of decades. Today, traffic in America is zipping along just as fast as in parts of Europe, and in some big cities, drivers are just as aggressive as their European counterparts. And we also have more of a problem with road rage.

Twenty years ago, motorcycles had the performance advantage. Even on the bikes of yesteryear, we could out-accelerate, out-corner, and out-brake the average passenger sedan. Thanks to competition from the Japanese and German auto industries, just about every mid-sized passenger car today has performance that whittles away most of the advantages of motorcycles. Sure, there are a lot of superbikes that can still out-accelerate cars, but today's higher traffic speeds are getting faster than many riders can process information. On top of that, we've still got our thinking, vision, and hearing being buffeted by the wind stream.

Thinking Skills

Where we might have held our own with performance back in the good old days, staying out of trouble in today's traffic environment requires that we get smarter rather than just quicker. Obviously, we need to be really proficient at skills such as cornering on slick or grooved surfaces, emergency swerves, and hard braking. But we also need to be mentally sharp enough to plan our moves well ahead and predict what's going to happen *before* it happens. Sudden, unplanned moves encourage accidents. Indications that your planning skills need a tune-up are if you find yourself making lane changes on a whim, or frequently accelerating and decelerating, or diving across four lanes at the last second to peel off onto your exit.

Let's also remember that little of my advice will help if you're preoccupied with social problems, woozy from prescriptions, or "bulletproofed" by alcohol. It is essential to focus on today's ride, even if you've done the same trip every day for the last twenty-four months. When you snap up the sidestand, snick your brain in gear before you ease out the clutch.

If you're traveling cross-country, you need a better plan than if you're close to home. You can't afford to glance down at a map while you're also attempting to negotiate a decreasing-radius cloverleaf that slam dunks you directly into a warp 7 through-lane. One veteran long-distance tactic is to pull out the map before hitting the road, and write down the names of the next big towns and the highway numbers on a slip of paper clipped to the windshield or in the map pocket of a tankbag. Just before getting to a confusing interchange, glance down at the names and numbers to refresh your memory.

When traveling, you should expect a lot of very strange intersections that don't look anything like the road map, and fraudulent signs pointing to lane five when the local commuters all know you should be in lane one just around that curve ahead. What's important is not to panic and jam on the brakes or make quick lane changes when you realize you've taken the wrong road or can't get to the exit lane in time. Take the next exit, get out the map, plot a course back in the right direction, and make another short list.

There are also some electronic devices to help you navigate, including GPS receivers, which can show you exactly where you are. If you're serious enough about navigation to install a GPS receiver, you're probably way ahead of us here.

Lane Positioning

You'll hear all sorts of advice about superslab riding that begins with "always" or "never." *Never ride in the center lane. Always ride in the left wheel track. Always ride in the left lane.* The trouble with this type of advice is that the superslab environment is constantly changing, which means you should continuously reevaluate what you're doing. Which lane you ride in, or which wheel track, depends on conditions at the moment, including surface hazards. One "never" rule that does make sense is never ride in the blind spots of other vehicles. If you can't see a face in their mirrors, they probably can't see you either.

Traffic Gaggles

You might be amazed at how much open space there is on a busy highway. One of these days, park your scooter and walk out onto an overpass (One with a

Drivers tend to flock together into gaggles, leaving open spaces in-between.

sidewalk, eh?) where you can study traffic for a few minutes. One phenomenon you can observe is that drivers tend to flock together into gaggles. Often you'll see a gaggle of ten or fifteen cars all elbowing for position, then a clear space with no vehicles, then another gaggle.

The smart motorcyclist stays away from the flock, either intentionally dropping back into a clear space, or aggressively moving on by a congested gaggle of creeper cars and motoring into the next clear space.

Lane Splitting

So, here you are on the superslab at 4 P.M., just trying to get across town. Traffic is jugged up, and now slows to a crawl as four lanes shrink to two in a construction zone. Why not take advantage of that "motorcycle" lane between the creeping cars? Yes, narrow motorcycles fit between the cars most of the time. But is it smart to ride the white lines in traffic?

When traffic is jugged up, is it smart to ride between the cars?

There are several key questions involved. First, is white lining (lane splitting) legal or tolerated in the area in which you are riding? In congested areas of California, white lining is common, expected by most drivers, and more-or-less tolerated. The attitude is, *Well, here comes another stupid biker splitting lanes. If he dings the mirror on my new BMW, he better watch out!* By comparison, in Seattle white lining is not only illegal but not tolerated. The attitude is, *Who does that scofflaw jerko biker think he is? I'm going to swerve over and teach him a lesson.* In almost all states except California, lane splitting—sharing the same lane with another vehicle—is either not legal or not tolerated by other drivers. In many foreign countries, lane splitting by motorcyclists is common.

If you find yourself in California, or in countries such as England or Italy, where lane splitting is standard practice, you may decide to join in. Lane splitting may appear to be dangerous, but the risks don't appear to be any greater than the risks of being rear-ended while creeping along in a line of cars. A little later, I'll offer some suggestions for successful lane splitting.

Sudden Problems

One essential mental requirement for superslab riding is looking far enough ahead to predict what's going to happen in time to do something about it. You've probably seen this situation many times: You spot a few brake lights coming on ten or twenty cars ahead, ease off the throttle, and squeeze on some brake. But the driver in front of you doesn't seem to be aware of anything except the back of the next car. You feel like shouting, *Hey, Particleboard-Brain! Wake up and get off the gas! Don't you see the brake lights ahead?* As you see the brake lights coming on in a wave traveling backwards, you head for the shoulder, clamp on the binders, and consider climbing over the guardrail for a little extra protection. Sure enough, old P-Brain is so dense that he doesn't do anything until the brake lights of the car ahead suddenly light up in a blaze of red. You don't have to multiply this scenario by more than a few vehicles to have a whammo-bammo chain reaction with several dozen vehicles involved.

So, what was the obvious difference between you and old P-Brain? First off, you were looking 12 seconds ahead. You were looking over the tops of cars and around trucks to scrutinize the situation w-a-a-a-y down the road. Second, when you saw the flicker of brake lights ahead, your mental hazard buzzer went off. You predicted that it wouldn't be long before whatever was happening up ahead would affect you up close and personal. By looking ahead and predicting what was likely to occur, you could take evasive action to get out of the way before you got caught up in the mayhem.

Scrutinizing the Road Ahead

If it isn't obvious, one key to avoiding crashos on the 'slab is looking far enough ahead. We've discussed looking 12 seconds ahead, which amounts to the distance you'll be covering in the next 12 seconds. As the speedometer climbs up the dial on the 'slab, that 12 seconds stretches way out toward the horizon, and that's a lot more territory than most of us have the mental capacity to monitor. The trick is to summarize what's happening. We don't need to study every vehicle in detail; we look for certain patterns or ripples in the flow of traffic ahead, similar to predicting treacherous rocks under the surface of a river by observing the swirl of the water over them. We're looking for the big picture, not small details, so you can use your peripheral vision more. It's sort of a Zen thing.

You can practice this right now. Focus on the middle of the wall on the other side of the room. Now, without changing your focus, become aware of the line where the wall meets the ceiling. Now become aware of the lower left-hand corner of the room, the number of windows, what's on the TV, who is in the room, and so on. You can keep track of what's happening, without having to focus on specific objects.

Here are some common traffic "swirls" that often lead to accidents:

★ **A vehicle traveling either much faster or much slower than others;**
★ **A vehicle making sudden, erratic speed or lane changes;**
★ **A car in a Turn Only lane suddenly slowing;**
★ **Traffic in one lane suddenly starting to slow for no apparent reason;**
★ **The second car on an on-ramp charging faster than the first;**
★ **A driver ahead using a cell phone, reading the newspaper, putting on makeup, or lighting a smoke;**
★ **A poorly maintained car, or a truck with a loose load.**

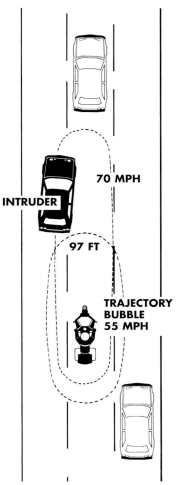

The trajectory bubble concept

When you observe such traffic "swirls," take some action to move away from the problem. Change lanes, accelerate, decelerate, or head for an off-ramp. Don't just hang in there hoping the problem will go away by itself.

The 2-Second Bubble

To help maintain awareness of all those other cars, trucks, busses, and bikes around me in traffic, I find it helpful to visualize a two-second "trajectory bubble" circling me. Sure, I'm looking for ripples in the traffic stream within 12 seconds ahead, but I'm especially interested in intruders who are closing on my 2-second bubble. Anyone who intrudes on the bubble (anyone closer than 2 seconds away) gets my immediate attention. At slower speeds, the bubble is shorter but wider. As speed increases, it stretches farther and farther out in front.

Same Dumb Stunts

While cars may be better these days, people still pull many of the same dumb stunts as their ancestors, even at higher speeds. And some locations generate a lion's share of the accidents. Curves, on-ramps, off-ramps, and merging lanes are locations where we can expect people to make last-second decisions and sudden changes of speed or direction. Next time you're out riding, take a close look at dividers and walls on curving off-ramps, and you'll often see tire tracks partway up the sides.

And while we're on the subject of ramps, make a point of positioning yourself in traffic so you aren't between another vehicle and a merging lane. That driver coming up fast on your left may just be in a hurry to pass. Or he could be an off-ramp dodger, desperate to make this exit even if it's over your dead body. If you're in the right lane and aren't planning to exit, you really should make a fist and smack yourself in the forehead while shouting *Dumb! Dumb!* And if you see an on-ramp dodger coming up fast on an on-ramp, you'd be wise to get out of the way.

Watch out for the On-Ramp Dodger!

Lane Crunching

When you are changing lanes, consider not only the space in the next lane but also the other drivers who might be deciding to jump into the same space you are ogling. If you have decided to change lanes, why not turn on your blinkers first, then check for other vehicles parallel to your position. If you spot nervous head turns in your peripheral vision, that's a clue a lane cruncher is about to make a move. If there is any question about who might get to the space first, either move ahead or move back so it's harder to have a get-together.

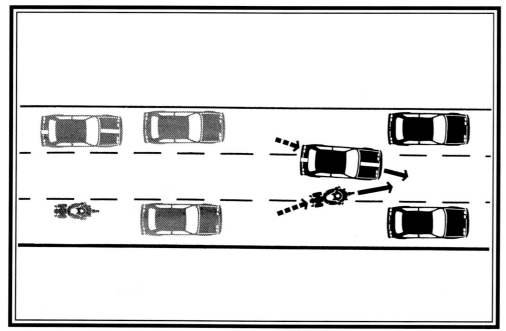

When changing lanes, watch out for that guy who has the same idea two lanes over.

Road Sharks

If you haven't encountered road sharks, let's introduce them. You know, those folks in fast cars with dark windows, racing through traffic about 30 knots faster than everyone else, zipping from lane one to lane four and back in one big swoop like you see in some computer games. You'll know 'em when you see 'em. Road sharks are one good reason to maintain your awareness of what's coming up in adjacent lanes behind you.

I know a few riders with big dog attitudes, who feel they can hold their own with the road sharks. *Think they could push me around, did they? They didn't know who the @#$% they were dealing with. I passed these jerks at a hunnert and ten going through the S-curves. I guess I showed 'em a thing or two.* Look, the reality is that in skirmishes between aggressive drivers and aggressive bikers, the biker almost always lands at the bottom of the heap.

Road sharks can really slicker you into stupid behavior. I've been suckered into more dumb stunts than I'd care to remember over the years. We all need to file this important message away in the back of our brains for future use: If someone makes you mad, it is important to take a break and cool off. Don't get mad. Don't get even. Don't get stupid. Most importantly, don't keep riding. Take a break until you get over the anger and can think clearly again.

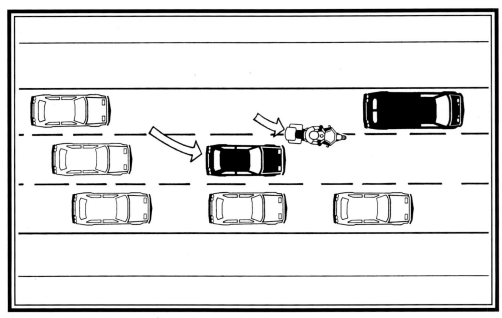

Before you make a quick lane change, watch for that road shark behind you.

Statistics, Statistics

If you're interested in some statistics, about 55 percent of all U.S. motorcycle fatalities involved a collision between a motorcycle and another vehicle. The fatalities stack up like this:

Collision Between:	Other Vehicle	Motorcyclist
car/motorcycle	17	596
light truck/motorcycle	0	386
large truck/motorcycle	0	114
motorcycle/motorcycle	na	28
bus/motorcycle	0	7
other/unknown/motorcycle	0	29
from Bureau of Transportation Statistics, U.S. Fatalities, Two-vehicle Collisions, 1994		

If you're a gambler, the odds are just about 115 to 1 that the biker wins the ride in the coroner's wagon. If you want to avoid getting scrunched in a superslab accident, it doesn't seem smart to challenge other drivers for road space.

Rear-Enders

You may also be getting a bit paranoid about being rear-ended. The BTS numbers hint that rear-enders aren't a big problem. The majority of all motorcyclist fatalities involved the motorcycle crashing head-on into something. The score: 1,540 front-of-bike fatalities vs. 76 rear of bike. But do pay attention to other vehicles in adjacent lanes. In 1994, 168 riders were killed by colliding with something on the right side, compared to 113 on the left side. Additionally, there were 214 noncollision fatalities, and 193 others/unknown. That adds up to 2,304 motorcyclist fatalities in 1994.

Serious Maintenance

One final note: Today's traffic on the superslab puts serious demands on your

David L. Hough

motorcycle. You can't afford to have a failure while you're zipping along in heavy traffic. At today's higher speeds and increased traffic aggressiveness, there isn't much extra slack for coddling underinflated tires, sacked shocks, spongy brakes, or loose steering head bearings. If you're going to go play with the big boys on the superslab, it's important that your motorcycle be up to the task.

Aggressive Drivers

We've suggested that motorcyclists face a variety of booby traps. The pavement may have a groove that snags your front tire and upsets the bike, or the road may tighten up or change camber partway through a blind corner, or someone may have dribbled a puddle of diesel oil onto an off-ramp, or a railroad crossing may have an X-trap waiting to snag your front tire. Sure, the road itself can have hidden hazards, but other motorists also can create some booby traps. Let's consider overly aggressive drivers, who often slicker others into road rage.

As traffic gets more congested, drivers get more impatient and resort to self-centered tactics. Remember, drivers are people, and most people take out their frustrations and aggression in their driving. Around big cities, we must expect more drivers to be zooming along at super-legal speeds, darting from lane to lane without signaling, and sneaking through a signal light just after it has changed. But a growing number of frustrated drivers go over the edge, carving through traffic with total disregard for laws, intentionally running red lights, and even threatening other drivers with collisions if they don't get out of the way.

A common estimate among professionals is that one out of every ten people has some sort of mental health problem, from depression all the way to schizophrenia. That's something to think about as you motor down the road minding your own business. Of course, there are also a lot of people out there who are more-or-less "normal" but are in a big hurry today, or angry at their significant other, or happen to hate motorcycles. There are druggies and drunks weaving along, and others with 400 CI engines and the social skills IQ of 40. It's no wonder that collisions between cars and motorcycles account for the majority of motorcyclist accidents and fatalities.

"Though this be madness, yet there is method in't." (*Shakespeare,* **Hamlet**)

Here's Rider Ralph, who has been following a "creeper car" for too long on a narrow highway. The driver is apparently unwilling to exceed the speed limit, and slows down below the limit for intersections and tighter corners. With a steady stream of oncoming traffic, Ralph can't get around, so he closes up behind the slower driver and switches to high beam to encourage the driver to speed up or move over. Finally, Ralph has had it. He rolls on the gas and zips by the slow driver so close the bike is only halfway over the double-yellow lines. Ralph's right handlebar barely ticks the driver's mirror on the way by, before Ralph swerves the bike back into the right lane inches ahead of the creeper. But the other driver suddenly goes bonkers, zooming up behind Ralph, beeping the horn, shaking a fist, shouting, and weaving from side to side. Ralph accelerates, but the crazy driver jams the accelerator to the floor and roars around Ralph, forcing an oncoming school bus onto the shoulder, then cuts right in front of the motorcycle and slams on the brakes.

Now Ralph is enraged. First this creeper held him up, and now he can't tolerate being passed. Ralph's first urge is to zoom alongside the car and kick a dent in the driver's door. Fortunately, Ralph has just enough survival instinct left to realize that he could get seriously hurt in a confrontation with a car. His fight or flight response flickers over to flight, and he backs off to separate himself from the angry driver.

Now, did Ralph just happen to stumble upon one of those 10 percent who have mental problems, or did he do something to trigger the road rage? Without realizing it, motorcyclists can stimulate aggressive situations or create a brewing anger that affects others later. For example, Ralph had no way of knowing that the "crazy" driver's next-door neighbor had stayed up late last night tuning the carbs on his unmuffled chopper and that a few miles back two thoughtless riders had been motoring along side-by-side carrying on a rolling conversation and holding up traffic. Then Ralph came along and tailgated the driver, blinding him with the high beam, and passing in a no-passing zone.

It didn't help that Ralph is one of those "loud pipes save lives" guys. He actually believes that more noise will reduce his risks. The noise had been annoying the driver for miles, and when Ralph roared on by inches away with his off-road-only drag pipes barking, the driver finally snapped. In this scenario, the driver wasn't someone with a serious psychological problem—he was just a guy who had been angered by one too many motorcyclists, and Ralph was the final straw.

"Whom the gods wish to destroy, they first make mad." (*Euripides*)

Remember, we can encounter aggression for a wide variety of reasons, and those drivers around us can come in all grades of mental health. Someone who is already angry or frustrated could be triggered into rage by a single thoughtless act. Worse yet, someone with a serious mental problem such as schizophrenia might initiate aggression for no apparent reason. Maybe that extraterrestrial voice in her brain said *Get that motorcyclist.*

David L. Hough

To help you avoid getting snared by an aggressive driver, let's think through the scenario. First of all, did Ralph do the right thing by backing off when the other driver showed aggression, or should he have attempted to fight back? I know of a rider who got a pushy driver to back off by pulling a handgun out of his fairing pocket. I've talked with macho riders who think it is appropriate to toss heavy steel ball bearings or lug nuts over their shoulder to help educate aggressive tailgaters. I once knew a rider who was very proud that he had punched an overly aggressive driver in the face, right through the glass side window.

When someone cuts me off, I get mad too. I used to think it was my job to educate drivers about their transgressions against motorcyclists. Once I put my bike on the sidestand in the middle of the street and marched back to explain sarcastically to an errant driver: *Apparently, you haven't discovered this little shiny thing on the outside of your door. It's called a mirror. Why, some drivers even glance in it before they change lanes.*

But trying to educate other drivers on the road is a little nutso. In the first place, an unstable driver could easily be triggered into doing something really dangerous by a simple act such as a rude gesture. You can create a bigger problem than you expected or get an innocent bystander injured.

Remember that an unstable driver could easily be triggered into doing something really dangerous by a simple act such as a rude gesture.

Once I almost caused an accident. A car had been tailgating me on the freeway. Traffic was light, but the other driver, a silver-haired woman, didn't want to pass me. I was thinking about pulling over onto the shoulder, when she suddenly swerved halfway over into the passing lane, and tromped on the gas. I swerved over to avoid getting sideswiped, and then had to slow down as she pulled back into the right lane inches away. Her apparent arrogance really ticked me off.

I thought it would be clever to give her a demonstration, so I accelerated up behind her, passed close to the dotted line, and swerved back into the right lane a few feet ahead of her, just as she had done to me. My pass startled her, and she instinctively swerved and braked, almost losing control. I realized she was just a preoccupied old lady with poor vision and low driving skill, who probably had no idea she had triggered road rage. I suddenly felt very embarrassed.

One big reason for not trying to retaliate for transgressions, or attempt any driver education on the road, is the proliferation of handguns. Before you ease up alongside a car door shaking your fist, or walk back for a cheesy chat, imagine the driver reaching under the seat for a loaded gun. Getting your pride injured is nothing compared to bullet holes.

Get Over It

The most important reason for swallowing your pride and just getting out of the way is that cars and trucks are bigger than bikes. Given the difference in weight between a bike and a car, or a bike and a truck, we pretty well understand who's going to come out second best in a bump-a-thon. There isn't much you can do on a motorcycle to protect yourself against a driver who goes into a rage, other than to get out of the way.

Sure, sure, you're thinking. *Stay calm when some idiot is trying to kill me.* Well, it isn't easy to just get over it, but that's what's needed. One calming tactic psychologists suggest is to imagine the other person as something really silly, say a purple Easter bunny, or a human-sized Daffy Duck, or a cigar-smoking alligator. It's harder to take a comic figure seriously. If you can just see a flicker of humor in the situation, you're on the right track. If you can't get over it, that's a message you may have some psychological problems to work out.

If you can stay calm, you can use your wits plus the performance and maneuverability of your motorcycle to get out of the way. In the serious situation where a raging driver seems intent on running you over, take immediate action to get lost. You might be able to position yourself on the opposite side of a truck or a highway patrol car, for example. I have even made a quick exit from the freeway and paused at the on-ramp for a few seconds to separate myself from an aggressive driver. On one occasion I evaded an aggressive tailgater by accelerating to warp speed until he was out of view, then braking hard and dodging off onto a side road. The point is, don't just ride along hoping an aggressive driver will go away.

You're Only Paranoid If They Aren't Out to Get You

When I'm riding along in traffic, I have no way of knowing the attitude or intent of other drivers, but I can watch for actions I feel are suspicious. For instance, I am suspicious of another vehicle pacing me, especially if its a carload of macho-looking young men with no signs of friendliness or a vehicle with tinted windows. It could be that these folks are just curious about my bike, or just a coincidence that a vehicle speeds up or slows down when I do, but I'd rather err on the side of being paranoid. I don't even acknowledge their existence. I simply change speed or lanes to put space or other vehicles between us, and get on with the ride.

Other drivers are more likely to give you respect when you give them respect. You don't have to be a wimp to be polite. When you enter a busy highway, dial on some speed quickly to avoid holding up traffic behind you. Signal your lane changes and turns at least 3 seconds in advance. In city traffic, avoid the obnoxious habits of sudden or frequent lane changes, tailgating, or blipping the throttle. Keep your headlight on low beam in the daytime, and adjust it properly for nighttime use. When other drivers are trying to change lanes in busy traffic, back off and give them some room.

When following or passing another vehicle, maintain at least 2 second's separation. When passing, don't crowd the other vehicle. Move entirely over into the other lane. Once you have passed, keep rolling fast enough to avoid holding up the vehicles you have just passed, even if they respond by speeding up.

Would a Sharper Image Help?

Think about this for a moment: the motorcycle you ride and the gear you wear have an effect on others. Moviemakers and advertising agencies continue to portray motorcyclists as criminals or dangerous scum, such as those bad guys in *Road Warriors*. And some riders seem to enjoy fulfilling that image. If your image evokes distaste or loathing in other drivers, you are sending the message that you are not worthy of their respect—and therefore not worthy of your road space. To put this another way, if you look like one of the bad-guy bikers in a movie, you shouldn't be surprised that other drivers treat you as the enemy rather than as a fellow motorist.

You can help defuse aggressive situations just by maintaining the appearance of a skilled motorcyclist who is in charge of the situation but polite to others. Part of that is what you do and part of that is what you wear. Consider the implications of quality riding gear in a color other than black, and a clean, quiet machine with no-nonsense luggage.

Some riders believe that a noisy bike decreases their risk of a collision. Others apparently think loud pipes are related to their rights, or that noise isn't anybody's business but the rider's, or that it's justifiable to make noise if that's the only way to make more horsepower. Contrary to those pseudo-serious Loud Pipes Save Lives stickers, noise basically annoys people. Road closures targeted at motorcycles are almost always a response to excessive motorcycle noise.

But does noise affect your risks of riding? I suggest that it does. It is obviously true that the drivers and bystanders within earshot at the moment may be more aware of your presence, but what's more important is the attitude they form about motorcyclists. We should expect that a noisy bike will generate aggressiveness toward the rider. But does the driver who is annoyed by one rider's loud pipes take out his frustration on the next motorcyclists to happen along? My suspicion is that loud pipes cause more accidents than they help avoid.

If you know your machine is loud, pay attention to what other people are doing and where the pipes are pointed before you fire it up. For example, don't fire your drag pipes directly at the restaurant window. Don't be accelerating through a quiet residential neighborhood at 5 A.M. And see if you can stop blipping the throttle while you're waiting for a red light in front of the church on Sunday.

Being polite, neat, proficient, and quiet won't guarantee that you will avoid all the aggressive crazies out there, but it will go a long way toward reducing the tensions that can trigger aggressive confrontations with other motorists.

And when you are confronted by an aggressive driver, remember that your job is to get out of the way and get over it.

Evasive Action

On more than one occasion, I have suggested that if you understand what's likely to occur in traffic, continuously scan ahead 12 seconds, and know what to look for, you can usually make a few small corrections early enough to avoid riding into a problem. If you wait to react until the problem gets closer, you have less time to take any evasive actions. Frankly, if you wait until the last couple of seconds prior to impact to do something, it's probably too late to make any difference.

Sooner or later you'll encounter a problem you couldn't have predicted.

But once in a while we just don't get much advance warning of a problem. When teaching rider training courses, I used to pull ridiculous situations out of the hat as examples of emergencies that might occur with little warning. For example, you're riding down the freeway when a portable toilet tips out of the truck ahead of you. Should you brake or should you swerve? You're cruising across town when suddenly an escaped zoo elephant charges out into the street. What evasive action would you take? What surprised me is that I would often have a student come up to me after class saying something like, *You're not going to believe this, but I did have an escaped zoo elephant come charging out at me once in Minneapolis.* I discovered that whatever strange hazard I could think of had occurred to some rider somewhere. Sooner or later, most of us will encounter a problem we couldn't have predicted, and we'll either take evasive action or "bite the elephant," so to speak.

Battle Stations!

When you are faced with an impending collision, there are only three evasive actions you can take while riding a motorcycle: speed up, swerve, or slow down. The trouble is, evasive maneuvers all depend on traction, and traction is a limited commodity. If you attempt to swerve while also braking hard, the bike tends to swap ends, fall down, or flip into a high-side barrel roll. To pull off a successful evasive maneuver requires us to make a split-second decision and then pull off the maneuver we've selected. To help prepare for that split-second decision, let's think through the advantages and disadvantages of those three evasive maneuvers.

Accelerating

Let's say you observe a car approaching an intersection from the other direction and suddenly the driver swerves left across your path without slowing or signaling. There's a remote chance you could gas it and squirt around the front of the car. Then again, maybe the driver will beat you to it, and you'll just end up planting your chin into the car hood at a faster speed.

Maybe you could gas it and squirt around in front of this car. Then again, maybe you'll just end up planting your chin into the car hood at a faster speed.

The big advantage of accelerating is that motorcycles typically have a lot of power. It's easy to accelerate—all you have to do is roll the throttle open, and hang on. The big disadvantage of accelerating is that speed increases forward energy. Kinetic energy increases much faster than speed. That means if you're moving at a faster speed and you do end up in a collision, the impact forces will be much greater. For instance, the impact force at 40 mph is just about twice what it would be at 30 mph.

Speeding up also makes it harder to change direction. You might be able to swerve around a car at 30 mph but not at 60 mph. And even if you do manage to accelerate around the left-turner, and then realize you've got to brake hard to avoid slamming into the back of that garbage truck, your chances go into the garbage, so to speak. Once you've accelerated, you've pretty well canceled out the other options.

Swerving

Of course, there are times when swerving is the best maneuver. Maybe you could swerve around behind the offending driver. Swerving doesn't increase forward energy, so it is possible to swerve and then straighten up and brake hard, without increasing braking distance. Of course, swerving successfully depends on both being able to predict which way the obstructing vehicle is going to move and being able to swerve the bike without dropping it. If you choose to swerve, it would be helpful to know whether the driver is going to continue or panic and screech to a halt halfway across your lane, but the behavior of other drivers is difficult to predict.

Swerving isn't too clever when encountering animals in the road, either. A loose dog may be homing in on your front wheel, no matter which way you swerve. And a wild animal such as a deer or raccoon is likely to try to evade you with sudden, unpredictable changes of direction. If you manage to swerve around an animal scampering on the pavement, it's probably more luck than skill.

Be aware that swerving can eat up all available traction, even at modest street speeds. If you're trying to do a maximum effort swerve, you really can't afford to squander any traction on accelerating or braking. You could brake first to scrub off some energy, then get off the brakes and swerve. Or, you could swerve first to clear the car, and then brake. You could swerve and then accelerate. But swerving while either accelerating or braking is likely to result in a slideout.

The big problem with swerving is that our natural survival reaction to an emergency is to snap off the throttle, and that eats rear wheel traction as the engine tries to brake the rear wheel. A successful swerve requires that you maintain a steady throttle until the bike is straightened out again. Frankly, when faced with an obstruction in our path, most of us will panic and roll off the throttle before we can resist the urge. That's why few riders manage to pull off a maximum effort swerve without dropping the bike.

Several different swerving exercises are included in the Experienced RiderCourse, but you might question whether there's such a thing as an emergency swerve. If you aren't prepared, do you think you'll be able to pull an emergency swerve out of the hat in the final 2 seconds prior to impact?

There's a lot of evidence that in emergencies we revert to our habits. If that's true, the best practice for swerving is probably just riding a really twisty road that requires a lot of aggressive leaning, so that pushing forcefully on the grips becomes habit. If you are paranoid about leaning the bike over into sharp turns, it is unlikely you'll do more than a gentle swerve. If you're used to leaning the bike over to steep lean angles in tight curves, you'll probably swerve when it's called for, without having to think about it.

Braking

Hard braking is a reliable evasive maneuver, and probably the best tactic for avoiding intersection collisions and wild animals. On today's motorcycles, the front brakes are typically more powerful than the engine, and today's tire compounds have excellent traction. With the correct technique, you can probably bring the bike to a stop in less distance than it took the engine to accelerate up to that speed.

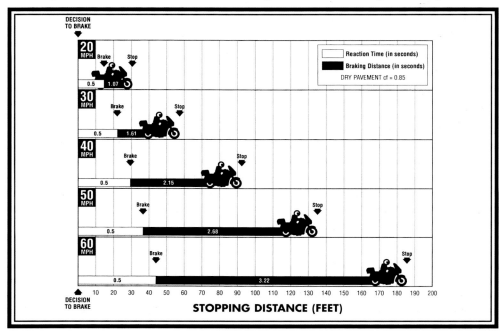

Including a half-second reaction time, a proficient rider can stop the typical bike going 40 mph in less than 100 feet.

One reason quick stops (sometimes called panic stops) are so useful is because of the amount of power the brakes can muster. Antilock brake systems (ABS) provide the advantage of avoiding a spill if you brake too hard. ABS works by releasing the brakes in pulses when the wheel sensor detects that wheel rotation has suddenly slowed. The ABS momentarily releases brake pressure to allow the wheel to spin up and regain traction, then reapplies the brake. ABS can save you from a spill if you overbrake on a slick surface, but the shortest stop requires that you brake to a maximum just short of a skid. In other words, you should consider ABS a safety net, not an automatic brake system, and even ABS riders should learn to apply the brakes to the limits just short of a skid. That's doubly important for braking in curves, since ABS doesn't sense slideouts, only wheel rotation.

With integrated brakes, such as the systems on Honda Gold Wings, there is a proportioning valve on the rear brake that automatically applies one of the front brake calipers. The proportioning valve supplies about 30 percent of the pedal pressure to the rear wheel and 70 percent to one of the front calipers. The front brake lever on the handlebar provides 100 percent of its lever pressure to the other front caliper. The concept is that unskilled riders are more likely to use only the rear brake pedal, and the system will make up for the rider's lack of skill by applying one of the two front brake calipers. But it requires all three brakes to make the shortest possible stop, so it is essential that riders of machines with integrated brakes stay in the habit of using the brake lever as well as the brake pedal.

Neither ABS nor integrated brake systems will save you from the mistake of attempting to swerve while braking hard or attempting to brake hard while leaned over in a curve. And lightweight sportbikes with double-disk systems, multiple-piston calipers, and sticky tire compounds add up to awesome braking power that can literally flip a motorcycle on its nose with a modest squeeze on the brake lever. So regardless of your machinery, hard braking requires some practice.

What if You Can't Stop in Time?

In spite of your best efforts, you might not be able to stop short of a collision. Some riders have suggested crash jumping, a technique of standing up on the pegs at the last second and vaulting upward off the bike to clear the other vehicle. Police academies still teach laying it down to motor officers, even though many motor pools these days are full of ABS-equipped BMW patrol bikes. Other riders think it might be better to just leap off the bike to avoid getting caught between the bike and the offending vehicle.

It might sound a little macabre to think about crashing into things, but if you realize that you are going to crash, wouldn't it be best to reduce the impact forces? None of the above tactics do much to reduce forward energy, and all of them assume you've got the time and the focus to do something other than hang on with wide eyes.

Yes, crash jumping might allow you to fly over the left-turner as your bike slams into the side of the car, but you're still going to make a touchdown on the other side. Sure, you could lay it down, but a bike doesn't stop just because it's grinding along on the footpegs and axle nuts.

From my perspective, if you've got time to do anything, you've got time to brake, and braking reduces the impact force. Rubber has a lot more traction than plastic or steel. If you can't avoid a smasho, wouldn't it be a lot better to smash at 5 mph than 25 mph? I'll keep it on the rubber, thank you, and brake hard right up to impact.

Booby

BOOBY

Traps

TRAPS

CHAPTER 5
BOOBY TRAPS

Surface Hazards

Here's Biker Bob tooling along his favorite curvy back road, braking smoothly before each turn, scrutinizing the shape of the curve ahead to plot the right line, leaning the bike by pushing on the low grip, and rolling on the gas to maintain speed and ground clearance. You can't see his expression inside his Shoei, but he's had a grin on his face for the last 50 miles. This, thinks Bob, is what motorcycling is all about.

But as Bob rolls on around the next apex, the front tire momentarily steps sideways. Bob's heart leaps into his throat, and his survival reactions take over; he snaps off the throttle. The rear tire instantly releases its grip on the pavement. Before he can comprehend what's happening, the machine slams down on its side and squirts off into the ditch in a trail of sparks and shattered plastic. Bob won't even remember coming off the low side. His next memory is of sliding, sliding, sliding, and how unforgiving the pavement feels hammering through his leathers.

As he painfully gets up, Bob reaches for his throbbing left elbow and recoils as he feels something slippery. In spite of the pain, he twists his elbow around to look for the source of the blood. There's a liquid, but it isn't blood. Rubbing his glove finger in the liquid, he smells it. Diesel oil! Biker Bob has just had a lesson about surface hazards. He had been so engrossed in the curves and the speed that he had failed to notice a trail of spilled diesel oil.

The very thing that makes motorcycles so much fun to corner is also their Achilles' heel: Two-wheelers demand traction just to balance upright. If a car or sidecar rig loses traction on one or two tires, the driver can be pretty ho-hum about it. But if a two-wheeler loses traction on even one tire, the rider will be lucky to avoid a fall-down.

Instinctively, we all know this. But we may not understand how to detect surface hazards, or what to do about them. Even when we see changes in the road surface, we don't always consider how different surfaces change the traction equation. And when a tire suddenly loses its grip on the road, our survival reactions tend to work against us. Let's think about some common surface hazards and then consider some techniques for keeping the rubber side down even when we encounter slippery spots.

Remember that two-wheelers are balanced by constantly steering the front wheel from side to side. Front-end geometry helps balance the machine automatically by constantly steering itself into a balanced condition. To turn, we unbalance the machine until it falls over into a lean, and we control the angle of lean by adjusting pressure on the grips. Balance is so automatic that we may not think about how traction is related to balance. But it is important to understand that balance depends on front tire traction, whether it's the front-end geometry balancing itself or the rider making steering inputs. You can slide the rear tire in a straight line without necessarily falling down, but a front wheel skid usually results in a fall-down.

Traction

That rolling grip between the rubber tire and road surface is really a matter of the rubber changing shape slightly to conform to the little dimples and bumps in the road's surface. So we need to consider both the tire and the surface. Slide your hand over some carpet and you'll feel resistance as your skin tries to conform to the lumps and bumps of fiber. Slide your hand over a plastic countertop, and there is much less resistance, or traction, because there are fewer lumps or bumps into which your skin can squeeze. Dribble a little water on the smooth countertop, and you'll see that traction decreases even more. A rough concrete road provides more traction than a shiny steel plate.

Hard rubber has less traction than soft rubber because compliant rubber can quickly squish into the surface irregularities. That's also why too much pressure in a tire reduces traction. If a tire is overinflated, it can't as easily squish into conformity with the pavement. Lower pressure improves traction, which is an advantage for unpaved roads but would overheat the tire carcass at highway speeds. So tire pressure is a compromise between traction and reliability.

With correct pressure in your tires for highway speeds, how much surface area would you guess your tire contact patches have? Would you say that both tires together have about as much area as this page you're reading? Would it surprise you to know that the total contact patch area of both your tires is about the same size as the palm of one hand? Considering that tire traction is the connection between the bike and the road, we should never scrimp on tires, and we should check frequently to ensure that tire pressures are correct for the load we intend to carry.

David L. Hough

Study the Surface Texture and Color

Biker Bob crashed because he was allowing his mind to wander just enough to be distracted from the road surface. Creative thoughts, scenery, and even cornering lines must always be secondary to surface traction. What should Bob have been looking for?

One key to spotting surface hazards is recognizing that you have a pretty good idea of the available traction of the surface under your tires at the moment. A change in the texture or color of the surface ahead indicates a possible change in traction. For example, if your tires are on slippery mud, you know by the feel that the road is slick. The color and texture of the mud are visual cues that the road is slippery. A change in the color and texture of the mud is an indication that the road surface is changing, and you can predict the traction changes. If the road ahead looks more like dry asphalt, traction may improve. If the light-colored concrete you're riding on has streaks of something dark and shiny, you can predict that traction might be worse if your tires cross over the streaks.

The change in color and texture of these side-by-side lanes is a clue that there are also changes in traction.

So, the technique for spotting potential traction changes is looking for changes in surface texture and color. Had Bob been observing the surface, he might have noticed the shinier look of the spilled oil dribbled down the road, the slightly darker appearance, or the rainbow colored sheen, and realized that traction was getting scarce.

Slick Surfaces

Most of us understand that frost is slippery, and we know what frost looks like. We can see the white color or perhaps observe the twinkling crystals of frozen water. White plastic lane markings are almost as slippery as frost, and they are just as obvious. But some riders haven't yet figured out how slippery white plastic can be. Shiny steel construction plates are obviously smooth textured, hinting at very little traction. Railroad tracks get polished smooth by passing traffic. Less obvious are the grease traps left in the center of left turn lanes by idling vehicles, spilled fuel

White plastic arrows and other markings can be slippery when wet. Just keep your tires off the plastic.

That steel construction plate ahead is not only slick but the rough texture at its edges could be loose gravel.

that blends with the color of the asphalt, and various contaminants that collect on the road surface during dry weather.

As with that countertop experiment, slick surfaces get even slicker when wet. Rainwater mixes with the contaminants to form a slippery lubricant. It takes about a half hour of downpour to wash off the accumulated drippings and droppings, especially if it hasn't rained for a while. That's why smart riders take a break during the first half hour of a fresh rain.

Any soft paving material that wears away quickly can be slippery when wet. Bricks have reasonably good traction when dry, but the brick dust mixes with rain-

It takes about a half-hour of steady rain to wash away road contaminants.

water to make slippery clay. Wooden bridge decks and railroad crossings can be slick when wet, as the wood particles mix with water to form a slimy paste. You won't get reliable texture or color clues about such hazards because the particles look the same as the rest of the surface. Just file away in your brain that when wet, bricks and wooden surfaces get just as slippery as wet clay.

Loose Stuff

We must also be aware of flat debris such as a flattened soda can, a pizza box, or a crushed plastic oil bottle on the road's surface. If you put your tires over any such loose objects, your tires could lose traction with the road. For instance, if you happen to be braking when your front tire rolls up on top of that crushed plastic oil bottle, the tire can grip the plastic, causing the plastic to slide down the road like a ski under your front wheel. If it isn't obvious, you'll lose steering, and if you don't quickly release the front brake, you'll lose balance.

Gravel acts like little ball bearings, rolling around under the tire and lifting the rubber off the pavement surface. In many parts of the country, highway crews seal coat the road's surface by spreading loose gravel over tacky oil and then letting traffic grind the gravel into a new layer. They don't always put up warning signs, or the signs may not follow the crew down the road. Loose gravel on the road has a rough texture and often a lighter or different shade of color. A companion clue for loose gravel on the pavement is the painted lines disappearing under the stones.

Sand, dirt, and mud are more insidious with gravel, because such loose stuff may be the same color and texture as the hard surface underneath. Best clues for such hazards are how the pavement relates to the surrounding roadside. When you see construction taking place ahead, whether a shopping center or a bungalow is going up, be prepared for dirt and mud to be tracked out onto the surface by the tires of construction vehicles. In farm country, be aware of field work adjacent to the road. Farm equipment can track a lot of fresh mud or dirt onto the road. Be wary of pavement downhill from a field being irrigated.

The seal coating operation is obvious here, but if there are no signs or cones, your only warning may be the different surface textures.

In the spring, in climates where temperatures drop below freezing in the winter, leftover sand from wintertime maintenance tends to gather near intersections, usually collecting as a berm toward the outside edges of the wheel tracks. Out in the country, roadside dirt and sand can drift onto the surface at any time of year, yet look just like the hard paving. Here, the relation of the road to the roadside is the best clue. Wherever there is a dirt bank uphill from the road, be wary of loose dirt or sand that may have drifted out onto the surface.

Narrow canyon roads in the southeastern U.S. typically don't have ditches. Such roads in dry climates are infamous for loose sand being blown out by strong winds

That may look like only a little water on the road, but actually it's 6 inches of slippery mud, which has washed out of the fields.

David L. Hough

or washed onto the surface during thundershowers. A rain shower can flush several inches of slippery mud over the surface wherever the road dips to a lower elevation than the surrounding landscape, especially where there is no ditch to catch the spillage. You may catch a glimpse of dirty color, but your best clue is simply being aware of where mud could wash out, and conserving traction when you see any evidence of a traction problem.

Conserving Traction

If the whole lane has a traction problem, such as loose gravel, it is important to reduce lean angles in turns, and to avoid any sudden throttle, steering, or braking inputs. On slippery or loose surfaces, it is just as important to avoid suddenly rolling off the throttle. In Biker Bob's situation, his panic survival reaction to roll off the gas transferred weight off the rear tire and applied engine braking that demanded more traction. The front tire wiggled on the diesel oil, but the rear tire slid out. Maybe Bob couldn't have saved the day by smarter control, but perhaps staying on the gas would have conserved just enough traction to slither through the oil without falling.

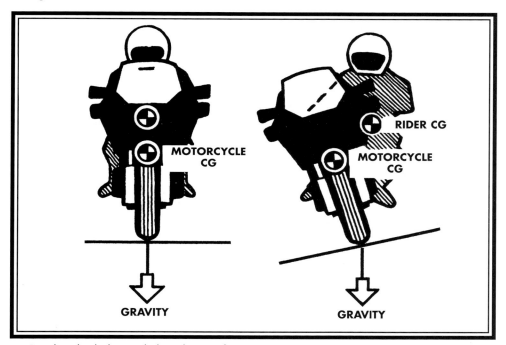

Try to keep the wheels perpendicular to slippery surfaces.

Okay, let's assume Bob knew what to look for, and he spotted the oil. What could he have done about shrinking traction? The trick is to conserve whatever traction you've got. On Bob's road, the oil was in only one lane. Bob could simply have slowed down and kept his tires out of the oil. And even if the oil spill covered the whole road, Bob could have modified his line to get the bike vertical as he crossed the slippery section.

What about road camber? What if the road slants off to one side? The veteran tactic is to counterbalance the motorcycle to keep the tires perpendicular to the road surface. If the tires do slide, the bike can slide sideways with less risk of falling down. It's the same tactic that's used for riding across a patch of wet grass, glare ice, or loose gravel on a surface that isn't level.

Reducing speed for corners also reduces traction demands. The slower the speed, the less the side loads on the tires to push it around the corner. Let's imagine Bob approaching what appears to be a seal-coated section of road with deep, loose gravel. Bob could straighten the bike up and brake hard to scrub off speed before reaching the gravel, then release the brakes and roll back on just enough throttle to stabilize the bike.

For loose gravel, follow the slick surface tactics, except for using the throttle. The dirt bikers use the throttle to steer through loose gravel. Of course if you don't have those big doggie knobby tires, you won't be able to throw a rooster tail, but follow the dirt biker's advice: When in doubt—gas it! Unless you've got knobby tires that provide better sliding control, it's best to keep your feet on the pegs and your speed down.

Ah, but you never ride off pavement, right? Except for detours. Faced with a detour on some highway construction project, you can either turn around and go home, or ride the dirt. If you are faced with a muddy detour, remember that a narrow motorcycle doesn't have to follow the truck tracks. Look for the best traction. Find a strip of road that hasn't been churned to a mess, put your tires over the best surface, and follow the slippery surface techniques, including leaning the bike to keep the wheels perpendicular to the surface.

If your motorcycle does get stuck in a muddy rut, it becomes difficult to balance, and the bike may fall over. Don't be a hero. Let the bike fall but get out of the way so you don't fry your calf or break your leg in the process. Plastic is cheaper than surgery.

Faced with a detour on a highway construction project, you can either turn around and go home, or ride the dirt.

Riding Practice

If the thought of riding on wet grass or slippery mud makes you nervous, you aren't alone. But sooner or later you're going to have to ride on a slick or loose surface. The solution is to gain skill rather than worry about trying to avoid surface hazards. Borrow someone's dirt bike and practice with those knobby tires at first.

Find a nice gravel farm road or explore those dirt roads up in a national or state park. Wait for the snow to melt, put on all your crash padding and go find some slippery and loose surfaces to ride on your street machine. Ride slowly around the back lawn. Try that fire road or power line road.

Watch for texture or color changes ahead. Remember the techniques:

- ★ **Reduce speed;**
- ★ **Weight on footpegs;**
- ★ **Pick best surface, follow smooth lines;**
- ★ **Steady throttle hand;**
- ★ **Bike perpendicular to the road surface.**

Once you've put in a few hours on some unpaved back roads, you'll lose a lot of paranoia about a few little patches of gravel or a slippery wooden bridge on that coast-to-coast trip.

Despite the rough road surface, the real hazard is that raised edge of pavement on the right.

Curbs Ahead

Rider Ralph is cruising down a four-lane divided arterial on a warm summer evening, minding his own business and thinking about what he will do when he gets home. As he rounds a curve, he notices some construction cones and then his headlight illuminates a sign that says Bump. Ralph observes that the pavement ahead has a different texture, and when his front tire bounces down onto the road's surface, he realizes the old asphalt has been ground away in preparation for repaving. A novice rider might have been unnerved by the tires wiggling around in the grooves, but Ralph is a veteran rider, and he knows the bike will find it's way through a little uneven pavement.

Ahead on his left, a pile of construction debris is cordoned off, and cones direct traffic back toward the right lane, where there is a section of smooth concrete. Ralph eases the wiggling bike over toward what appears to be smoother pavement. But suddenly, just as his front wheel reaches the concrete section, the handlebars are yanked from his grasp. The bike seems intent on falling over on its right side.

Pushing as hard as he can on the grips to countersteer the machine upright, Ralph can't maintain balance. The bike crashes over hard on its right side with Ralph's leg trapped between the frame and the road. His motorcycle ride is over for the evening and for the months it will take for the torn flesh and broken bones to heal.

What Happened?

What caused Rider Ralph's crash was the exposed edge of a slab of concrete pavement that had been left in place with the surrounding asphalt ground away. The raised edge of the concrete formed what you can think of as a curb right out in the middle of the street. For an automobile driver, merging into a curb in the middle of the street might have resulted in a front end bent out of alignment, or a dented wheel rim. For a motorcyclist, attempting to cross a concrete edge can quickly result in a spill and serious injuries to both bike and rider.

Rider Ralph isn't the only motorcyclist who has been surprised by a hard pavement edge, and that includes veterans who you would think have learned everything. What appears to be just a bump or a crack in the pavement suddenly upsets the bike, and the hapless rider can't maintain balance. Let's call such raised pavement edges *edge traps* because of the way a motorcycle wheel gets trapped against the edge of the raised "curb."

The basic problem is that two-wheelers are particularly vulnerable to raised pavement edges and grooves. Too many riders don't understand how hazardous an edge trap or even a small groove can be. And road maintenance departments don't seem to understand enough about two-wheelers to understand why so many motorcycle accidents occur in construction zones, or what to do about it.

Countersteering

Remember, a two-wheeler is balanced mostly by steering the front wheel, whether that's a result of front-end geometry or rider input at the grips. For example, if a motorcycle starts to fall over to the left, we can steer the front wheel more to the left to rebalance. The term for this balancing act is *countersteering* because we initially steer opposite, counter to, the direction we want the motorcycle to lean. It's also how we control direction. To turn right, push on the right grip. To straighten up from a right turn, push on the left grip.

Countersteering explains why edge traps are so hazardous to two-wheelers, while only a jarring, wheel-bending inconvenience to other vehicles. A car or a sidecar rig can slide sideways without losing balance, but if a two-wheeler loses traction on the front wheel for more than a couple of seconds, it becomes difficult to maintain balance. Easing up to a curb, you can maintain balance right up to the point where the front wheel contacts the edge. After that, with the tire scrubbing along the edge of the curb, you can't countersteer to maintain balance.

When you find yourself in a lane where the pavement has been gouged away, the feeling of the rough surface prompts you to start looking for a smoother place to ride. There's that smooth shoulder beckoning you to ease on over, or that nice new pavement on the other lane. But if you try to ease over the edge, your front tire is likely to get trapped, and you'll lose balance. It's important to recognize that even a modest pavement edge can cause a spill if you attempt to ease over it at a narrow angle.

In tests conducted years ago by the Motorcycle Safety Foundation, professional riders attempting to swerve around an obstruction from pavement to a gravel shoulder and back onto the pavement again were amazed when several crashes occurred.

David L. Hough

These steep edges are a big hazard to motorcyclists.

Looking a little more closely, the experts discovered that a spill was more likely if the rider swerved back toward the pavement edge at less than a 45° angle.

Edge traps come in a variety of disguises. You'll have to spot them for yourself because you're probably never going to get a warning sign that says edge traps. Newer asphalt often sinks under the pounding of traffic, exposing the sharp edge of adjacent concrete pavement—a common situation where an older road has been widened or lanes repositioned. Old paving several layers down may shift or sink, allowing a groove to form at the surface. When a road is repaved, there will be a steep raised edge above the shoulder until it is filled and graded. And even when the

Heads up! That pavement edge ahead wanders across your lane.

shoulder is graded level with the pavement, your front tire can sink in the soft gravel and be trapped on the edge. Any location where you must cross a raised pavement edge is a serious hazard.

Changes in Texture or Color

Whenever you approach a work zone or observe a change in the pavement ahead, think of Rider Ralph and start looking for edge traps. As with all surface hazards, the trick is to look for changes in surface color or texture. You already have some idea of the surface you're riding on. When you see a different surface ahead, you should be prepared for the transition from this surface to the next. Even at night, you should be able to distinguish between asphalt and the smoother, lighter appearance of concrete, or the shinier appearance of a polished steel construction plate or streetcar rail.

If you don't have to change lanes, just stay away from those edge traps, especially those "curbs" at the sides of a lane where pavement has been ground away. Even if there is a pavement edge sauntering into your lane, you can usually sneak by a few inches away. The key is to avoid letting your front tire get close to a raised edge or groove.

If you have to cross a raised pavement edge in the street, treat it like you would this curb. Point your front wheel straight at the curb, and roll on a little throttle to drive the tire up and over.

But what do you do when cones force you to cross over a hard edge, as in Ralph's situation? How do you get across an edge trap without falling? The trick is to cross aggressively at a maximum angle, rather than attempting to ease over, and use a little horsepower to bounce the front wheel up. Imagine trying to ride your motorcycle over a curb, up onto the sidewalk. First, you'd want to slow down to avoid bending a rim. Then you would want to get the bike pointed straight at the curb, or at least at a 45° angle, and roll on some throttle to bounce the tire up over the edge. To change lanes over a hard pavement edge, first swing away, then steer back at a wider angle, get a good grip on the bars, and roll on some throttle to drive the front tire up onto the higher surface.

White Curbs

One insidious type of edge trap is the white line between two merging traffic lanes. For instance, the on-ramp to a freeway may be separated from the freeway

David L. Hough

You might be tempted to change lanes over that white line, but don't do it. That white line is painted on a low curb that could knock the tires out from under you.

lane by a long white line, providing an acceleration lane. But sometimes the white line is painted on a curb-shaped lane divider. Such curbs form serious edge traps, and they are particularly difficult to see at night. Since we can't always predict whether a solid white line is painted on a level surface or on a divider curb, my tip is to avoid crossing solid white lines at merging locations. Where it is safe to change lanes, the solid white line changes to white dashes.

Slick Edges

Railroad tracks can form great booby traps for motorcyclists, even when the

San Francisco's cable car tracks provide a lot of grooves and shiny steel to cross.

rails are level with the surface. Remember, if the front tire starts to slide sideways or gets captured by a groove, it instantly gets harder to keep the motorcycle balanced upright. Railroad crossings are hazardous when the tracks cross the street at a narrow angle, at a curve in the road, or parallel to your path of travel. Streetcar tracks are especially dangerous, because the rails often run down the middle of a lane or wander from lane to lane. Cable car tracks, with two streetcar rails plus a steel-lined cable slot, such as those in San Francisco, are a special challenge.

The important tactic for negotiating rails is to keep your tires out of the grooves, and when you must cross a rail, treat it as an edge trap. Swing away from it, then steer back across at an angle. Try to get the motorcycle vertical and stable as you cross the rail, even if you have just completed a swerve. Assume that the wood, plastic, or steel covers adjacent to the rails at street crossings are slippery even when dry, and treacherous when wet. In industrial areas, some railroad spurs are used only occasionally, so you shouldn't be surprised by gaping holes and deep grooves near the rails that never seem to get fixed.

X and V Traps

Sometimes you will encounter two railroad or cable car tracks that cross each other or come together in the middle of the street. Such connections form serious X and V traps where a motorcycle tire can slide into the V or even drop into a narrow slot and wedge tight with obvious consequences. When you observe such X or V traps in the street or grooves in the planks, the trick is to pick a path of travel that gets around the traps, or at least crosses them at the maximum angle you can achieve in the maneuvering room you have available.

Railroad spurs in industrial areas can have a lot of nasty edge traps.

Construction Plates

Those giant steel plates construction crews use to cover holes in the street may get polished to a shine, but the edges are just as hazardous as any slick surface. The plates are thick enough to form edge traps. There is an additional reason to stay

It's a good idea to stay away from the edges of steel construction plates.

away from the edges: the plate may be a few inches narrower than the hole in the street or may have shifted under the pounding of truck traffic. Where a normal automobile tire would bridge a 4-inch slot at the edge of a plate, a motorcycle tire might be just narrow enough to drop in for a serious visit.

While it's important to pay primary attention to other vehicles while riding in traffic, a veteran rider knows to maintain awareness of surface hazards as well and to choose a path of travel that puts the tires on the most tractable pavement. When you spot an obvious hazard that you know you'll have to cross, you can simply maneuver your motorcycle to cross it correctly, and continue to focus on traffic.

According to the famous Hurt Report from 1981, only 4 percent of motorcycle accidents were triggered by surface hazards. That's why rider training courses don't waste any time on edge traps. But remember that the Hurt Report was based on accidents in the Los Angeles area. Other cities such as Seattle; St. Louis; or Washington, D.C., have different surface hazards than Los Angeles. So you might want to practice some edge crossing exercises on your own before you get the big test out on the streets. And always keep edge traps in mind when you are riding in an unfamiliar area.

Curb Warnings

One of the reasons riders get snagged by edge traps is that we don't usually get fair warning of the problem. Road contractors are given specific signs for different construction situations. For example, the suggested warning sign for a change in pavement elevation might be Bump. The construction contractor may get reports that a surprising number of motorcyclists have crashed in a work zone, but it won't be clear why the accidents occurred. The common misconception is that it's just a matter of an inexperienced rider or excessive speed. Various warning signs have been tried, including Abrupt Lane Edge, Motorcyclists Use Extreme Caution, and Motorcycles Do Not Change Lanes. If Ralph had seen a sign that said Curbs Ahead, he might have understood the problem. *What do they mean Curbs Ahead? Do they mean curbs along the side of the road or curbs out in the middle of the road? Holy*

Translation: Stay away from the edge of the pavement.

Kawasaki! If there are curbs out in the middle of the road, I'd better be cautious or find a different route!

Riding Practice

Here are some riding exercises you can practice to gain experience crossing edge traps. Be sure to wear your crash padding just in case you haven't quite absorbed the correct techniques yet. Ride a figure-eight path over different edges such as 2 x 4 or 2 x 6 wood that's at least 6 feet long, a low curb, a stiff garden hose, or a large-diameter rope at least 10 feet long, concentrating on positioning your motorcycle to cross as close to a right angle as possible. Use a bit of throttle to drive the front tire up and over the edge.

Running Out of Pavement

It had been a long day in the saddle. I was homeward bound from Denver to Seattle, trying to make time on the superslab. The afternoon had been baking hot and windy across eastern Utah, so when night fell, I kept riding to take advantage of the cool of the evening. The pavement was smooth and so new it was still black. All I could see of the dark pavement was the next 100 feet or so that would momentarily be illuminated by the headlight beam and then quickly pass under my tires. I began to notice road signs lying face down on the shoulder, apparently leftovers from the repaving work. But then something odd attracted my attention: the lights of cars ahead seemed to be wiggling sideways. I blinked my eyes. Maybe I had been too many hours in the saddle.

And then my headlight beam flickered off the end of the pavement into deeply rutted dirt. The paving just ended. With my brain struggling to comprehend

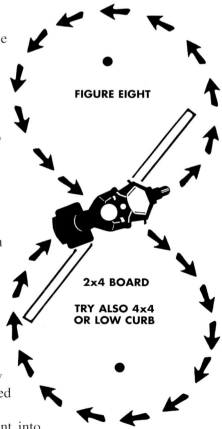

FIGURE EIGHT

2x4 BOARD

TRY ALSO 4x4 OR LOW CURB

Edge trap practice

what was happening, the loaded bike dropped off the edge of the road at 60 mph and plowed into the soft earth, the front tire dodging one way and then the other. Fighting for control, I rolled on the throttle to roost the bike forward. Several hundred feet of black terror later, the front tire again bounced up onto smooth pavement, and I was again cruising through the black night, as if nothing had happened.

Apparently, all four lanes of the freeway had been torn up for repaving, and the construction signs had blown down in the afternoon wind. The wiggling taillights were from drivers ahead plowing through the ruts. As the nightmare played itself again in my memory, anger swelled up at the stupidity of a highway department that would allow repaving all lanes of the same section simultaneously and not ensuring that the work zone was adequately signed. But, calming down, I was thankful I had some off-pavement experience in my bag of travel tricks.

It's easy to think of ourselves as either street or dirt riders, as if our machines rather than our skills defined us. But I've seen some heavy machines sporting proof they have experienced off-pavement missions to Alaska. I've also seen more than a few dual sportbikes dressed with big plastic tanks and shiny adventure-touring cases, but nary a dent, scratch, or speck of dust in the crevices. Obviously, some riders are more concerned about the adventure touring image than getting off the pavement. Back in the good old days, before manufacturers and magazines started labeling bikes by type, we rode whatever we owned, wherever we felt like going.

Now, obviously, street motorcycles are designed with a bias toward hard surfaces. But the pavement doesn't go on forever. There are times when we must ride off pavement, if only through a short detour or across grass into the rally campground. And if you're a serious motorcycling traveler, you should possess sufficient off-pavement skills to handle a few miles of dirt without freaking out.

Dirt

For talking purposes, let's refer to all unpaved surfaces (sand, gravel, clay, grass, dirt, etc.) as dirt. Dirt does provide traction, although in ways different from what we expect of clean, dry pavement. Pavement is static. Dirt moves around dynamically. On pavement, the predictable traction gives us confidence to make precise steering corrections to control balance and direction. On dirt, traction is predictable, but not that firm connection we're used to on clean pavement. When we feel the tires dance around, that's a street feedback that we're about to get down and personal with the ground. The one big difference between street and dirt machines is the tires. It's a lot easier to maintain control on dirt with big fat knobbies that will poke down into the rocks and paddle through the loose stuff. Typical street tires have tread blocks closer together with narrow, shallow grooves. What that means is that riding off-pavement on street tires requires more skill than riding off-pavement on dirt tires. It's harder to balance on little rocky ball bearings or soft sand that doesn't provide that predictable grip street riders are used to. Not only do we need to avoid panic when the tires don't go exactly where we're expecting, we need to master some different control skills.

On dirt we need to master some different control skills.

Traction

If you do suddenly find yourself dropping off the pavement into the dirt on your touring machine with street tires, you can increase traction by lowering tire pressures. Lower pressure means a larger footprint and better conformity to the surface. Dirt bikers sometimes run pressures as low as 8 or 10 psi. But remember that lower tire pressure also increases tire flex, which dramatically increases temperature. So if you do drop the pressure to get through an unexpected sand dune on an Arizona highway, be sure to pump the tires up again before you roll back up to highway speed.

Balancing and Steering

Even though there are tremendous differences in traction between different unpaved surfaces, the same basic techniques apply. On pavement, we balance mostly by steering the front wheel to adjust the position of the contact patch in

relation to gravity and mass of motorcycle and rider. If the machine starts to fall over toward the left, we can countersteer the contact patch more toward the left to get the bike balanced again. On dirt, countersteering still works, but not as predictably or as quickly as on good pavement. In loose or soft stuff, the front tire tends to plow sideways for a while instead of causing an immediate adjustment of balance. Two tactics that are essential to riding off-pavement are shifting body weight on the machine and steering more with the throttle than the handlebars.

Load the Footpegs

You'll see novice riders trying to negotiate loose gravel or wet grass by sitting bolt upright in the saddle and skidding their boots across the ground. Dragging your boot skids is a "survival reaction" to the panicky feel of the tires losing traction, but it doesn't do what you might expect. Next time you're in a position to observe riders negotiating a bit of dirt, you'll notice that the experts stand on the pegs and let the bike work around under them. The novices drag their feet, and the bike gets wobblier. Notice that with feet off the pegs, the rider braces against the handlebars and saddle, rather than against the tank or footpegs. When the novice pushes on the grips without having feet braced against the footpegs, it upsets balance.

The rider of a lightweight dirt bike may use a planted boot to help control the machine in a slide, but on a heavyweight touring machine with street tires, it's smarter to stand on the pegs. If your rubber tires don't have enough traction to keep a loaded Gold Wing upright, why should you think that your leather boots will be able to do any better? What's more, dragging your feet on the ground is an invitation to broken ankles and barbecued shins. If your toe happens to catch on something solid, your foot will be bent back under the footpeg before you can say *Uh-oh.*

High or Low CG?

When a rider is planted firmly in the saddle with feet on the pegs and knees against the tank, the rider and bike move more as a combined mass with a combined

It may seem that standing on the pegs raises the combined CG of bike and rider, but actually it doesn't effect the motorcycle's CG.

center of gravity at about the rider's knees. Now, if the rider stands up on the pegs, doesn't that raise the combined CG? Yes, standing on the pegs, the rider's CG will be higher. But be aware that a low CG on a two-wheeler doesn't necessarily contribute to easier balance. Those skyscraper dual sport machines with big fuel tanks up high can be as controllable in loose gravel as low-slung cruisers, and even more controllable with the rider's weight loaded down at the footpeg level.

On some machines, style gets in the way of ergonomics. For example, the stylish forward-mounted footboards typical of cruisers make it difficult and cumbersome to stand up and unload the saddle. Likewise, the forward-mounted handlebars of some sportbikes make it awkward to stand on the pegs.

The importance of standing on the pegs is that we can more easily lean the motorcycle or shift bodyweight from one side to the other. The motorcycle is carrying the same weight, but separating the motorcycle's mass from the rider's provides more flexibility in controlling balance and lean angles. It is also a lot easier on our spines and kidneys to cushion bumps and dips with bent legs. It isn't necessary to stand on the pegs for miles and miles of hard-packed dirt or firm gravel, but when you are picking your way through a rutted detour or across a bumpy field, standing on the pegs will give you both better control and fewer spine-jolting body slams.

Steering

With reduced traction, countersteering doesn't produce the quick changes of direction the street rider expects. Besides, the front tire is giving a lot of nervous feedback that it's on the verge of washing out, and it probably is. The street response is to strangle the handlebars with a death grip, look down at the gravel just ahead of the front tire, keep the bike absolutely vertical, and let it go wherever it seems to want to go, even if that's off the edge of the road.

The reason for the feeling of falling down while trying to countersteer in soft sand or loose gravel is that the contact patch of the tire expands forward and back-

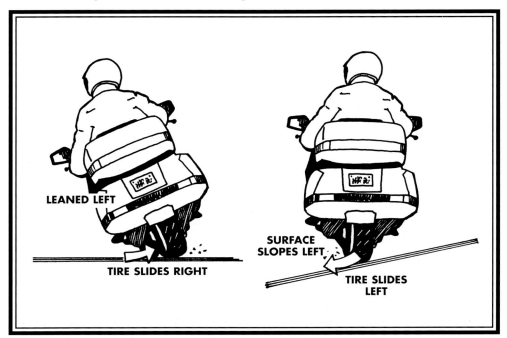

The rear tire tends to slide away from the direction of lean, and that helps steer the bike.

ward, dramatically increasing steering effort. But the quick street-style counter-steering input doesn't seem to result in the bike rebalancing or changing direction. Since countersteering is a lot more sluggish in the dirt, the trick is to use more body English, keep the machine vertical, and steer more with the rear wheel. After all, sliding the rear end sideways is another way of pointing the front end in a different direction.

We can make the rear tire slide by rolling on the throttle, snapping it closed, or by dabbing the rear brake. Consider that when a tire starts to slide, the end of the bike heads off on a tangent or downhill if on a sloping surface. For example, if the bike is in a left turn, sliding the rear wheel will point the bike more to the left.

Cruising Speed

If you've narrowly escaped a crash while slip-sliding through loose gravel spilled on the pavement, you can be excused for thinking that gravel or sand have no traction at all. But the truth is that gravel, sand, and other loose surfaces provide varying traction depending on your speed because even small stones have a resistance to being pushed aside, and the resistance increases with velocity. A gravel road can provide more predictable traction at 40 mph than at 4 mph.

Experienced riders may cruise unpaved roads at considerably higher speeds than novices, not because they are fearless big dogs, but because the correct speed results in better control. Riding too slowly through deep sand or gravel will allow the front tire to sink and plow so badly that you lose balance. At a faster speed, the tire "floats" on top. And don't forget that faster spinning wheels provide increased gyroscopic stability. But, as Chris Scott points out in his book *Desert Biking,* you don't want to get carried away. At speeds in excess of 50 mph it's difficult to react quickly enough to the ever-changing terrain.

Experienced riders cruise unpaved roads at higher speeds because the correct speed results in better control.

On slick surfaces (oily pavement, snow, ice, mud, clay, wet grass, etc.) increasing speed won't help and may just increase the damage should you lose balance. What's important is to keep the wheels perpendicular to the surface of the ground so the tires can sideslip without instantly sliding out from under you. Even if the

David L. Hough

bike seems to have a mind of its own in dirt or sand, keep it moving. Let the bike shift around under you.

Inertia

On slick or loose surfaces, it is important to be more aware of inertial energy and use it to advantage. Increasing speed increases forward energy and that can work either for or against you. Let's say you are on a wet clay detour that descends into a deep gully with a steep uphill climb on the other side. Slowing at the top allows you to let the bike increase speed as you descend without wasting traction on braking. The faster speed at the bottom means increased forward energy to help carry the bike up the hill without the need for more engine power, which would result in wheel spin. If you need to control downhill speed, select a lower gear and use engine compression on the descent, but stay away from that front brake.

Approaching a short section of loose sand or deep gravel, a short burst on the throttle in third gear may be much better than slowing down and attempting it in first gear. When traction is limited, shifting up a gear helps prevent sudden wheel spins.

Braking

On tractable pavement, it's a good habit to use a lot of front brake and very little rear brake. But as traction goes away, we need to favor the rear brake more and use the front brake less. The trick is to apply just enough braking to slow the bike, but not so much that you skid the tires. With today's powerful front disc brakes, even a little may be too much. If you aren't familiar enough with braking to be able to feel when your front wheel is beginning to slide, you're probably better off avoiding the front brake entirely until you get back on pavement.

ABS brakes are great for avoiding fall downs during maximum-effort stops on loose surfaces, providing that you're stopping in a straight line. But the ABS computer may not respond to a sideways slideout, so long as the wheel is still turning. If you attempt to brake while in a gravelly turn, your tires may drift wide without activating the ABS. And of course ABS won't save you from a slideout caused by overenthusiastic countersteering or snapping off the throttle too suddenly.

Riding Practice

Skills improve only through practice. The bottom line is that whatever skills we find difficult are the ones we need to practice. If the thought of riding on loose gravel makes you break out in a cold sweat, the message should be obvious: You need some dirt time. The only way to improve off-pavement skills is to spend some time riding off the pavement. It's not a bad idea for every rider to spend a day at least once each year riding some unpaved back road such as an all-weather forest service road or a country farm road. Remember, when you encounter one of those end of pavement signs, you'll be plowing off into the soft stuff on whatever bike you normally ride. Sooner or later, you should do some dirt time on your favorite traveling motorcycle. But if your only machine is a heavyweight, you probably don't want to attempt any serious off-road excursions, even with knobbies. A big bike can be impossible to extract from a bottomless sandpit without some heavy-duty assistance. If you are concerned about dropping your expensive road burner on some lonesome back road, one acceptable option is to borrow a dirt bike or dual sport machine for the learning phase. Then you can take the heavyweight out later after riding the dirt has become more familiar.

One reason for the increased sales of machines in the 350-650cc range is that plonking around back roads is easier and more fun on a smaller, lighter bike. Riders are learning the advantage of owning both a big-bore road bike, and a mid-size dual sport or off-road machine. You don't really need a 1000cc dual sport to explore a forest service road. A 650 dual sport or even a street bike with dirt knobbies has adequate traction and ground clearance for some real adventure touring.

Here are some techniques to remember while practicing off-pavement skills, especially on a motorcycle with street tires:

- ★ **Plan a path of travel that puts your tires over the best surface.**
- ★ **Shift your body weight and lean the motorcycle to keep the wheels perpendicular to the road surface.**
- ★ **Stand on the pegs in difficult situations.**
- ★ **Steer more with the throttle. Use controlled bursts of power to slide the rear end toward the outside in gravelly corners.**
- ★ **Use momentum rather than engine power to carry the machine uphill or through tough sections.**
- ★ **Start a downhill section very slowly. Use engine braking to keep speed in check.**
- ★ **Stay off the front brake.**

Improving off-pavement skills will do more than help avoid embarrassment when there is a muddy detour or a little wet grass at the campground. Some of us will actually admit that we enjoy exploring roads that are less traveled—even if not hard surfaced. After all, there are more unpaved roads out there than paved ones. A skilled motorcyclist should be able to choose a road without being hampered by a self-imposed limitation of riding on pavement only.

Deer, Oh Dear!

There are a lot of booby traps that the unwary motorcyclist can ride into, including innocuous-looking alleyways, raised pavement edges, railroad tracks, loose

David L. Hough

sand, sunken manhole covers, and white plastic arrows glued to the pavement. Most of those hazards occur in the city. Out in the country on those twisty back roads we love to ride, we can expect some different types of booby traps.

One major trap that can spring on us is a wild animal, especially a wild deer. Deer are so delicate and demure that it's hard to think of them as a hazard. But when we come upon the sickening sight of a dead deer along the highway, we are again reminded of the danger, both to the animal and to ourselves. It's a double tragedy when we hear of a motorcyclist involved in an animal strike.

Yes, it's gruesome, but deer strikes are a real threat on country roads.

Animal strikes are a significant hazard for those of us who enjoy long-distance travel. Statistically speaking, vehicle collisions are the major motorcycling hazard, but as motorcycling experience builds and we get a little smarter, our risks of colliding with a car should decrease. But the risk of animal strikes remains high because animals are so difficult to predict. Wild deer are found all over North America in large numbers, their population is increasing, and they have habits and instincts that put them on a collision course with motor vehicles.

The typical deer strike occurs when the animal suddenly leaps in front of the vehicle, often at night. The vehicle slams into the deer, with deadly consequences. What's startling is the amount of damage even a small deer can do to a speeding vehicle. If the motorist happens to be a motorcyclist, the odds are high that both deer and biker will be seriously injured.

What's so insidious about a motorcycle colliding with a deer is the unpredictability. You may have ridden for hundreds of thousands of miles, proficiently avoiding thousands of left-turners, alley jumpers, edge traps, graveled corners, and decreasing-radius turns. Then, on some easy country ride, a deer suddenly leaps out of the woods into your path, and *Thud!* We don't have reliable statistics on the occurrence and injury rate of motorcycle/animal collisions, because many accidents don't get reported. But animal strikes are a frequent enough problem that we should practice appropriate countermeasures on those rides that take us into deer country.

Deer Instincts

To understand what to look for and what to do about deer, let's consider their instincts and habits. Deer are cautious and prefer to hide among trees. They like munching on tender foliage. So in the summer, expect wild deer in forested areas or riverbeds where the trees and underbrush provide a lot of cover and fresh greens. That lush roadside grass the highway department keeps mowed is a dinnertime favorite. That means you should expect deer feeding along the road's shoulder in shady areas. In the daytime, a deer feeding on the road's shoulder will have its head down, so it may look like a log in the ditch or a mossy boulder or a crumpled cardboard box. When the head comes up, you'll immediately see those large ears, and perhaps a rack of antlers.

It's smart to brake and let deer do whatever they are going to do.

Danger at Night

While antelope, elk, and moose munch away in plain view in the broad daylight, deer are more cautious. Deer seem to prefer hiding in the shadows in the daytime, and feeding at night. That means the risk of deer strikes increases as the sun goes down. It's definitely something to think about when you are considering a nighttime transit on a highway, passing through one of those scenic national forests.

At night, brown deer hide doesn't reflect much light, but deer eyes will reflect a brilliant white from your headlight, similar to a glass reflector. How do you tell if the reflector you see is on a post or on a deer? Easy: the deer eye blinks. If you see a reflector winking back at you, odds are it is a deer, and it's facing in your direction.

Deer Crossing

Why do you think those yellow Deer Crossing signs get put up along certain sections of farmland or scenic forest roads? Would you think the highway department or the Forest Service hires game wardens to count deer migrations across the road? *Wrongo, Big Dog.* What really happens is that the road crew counts dead deer, and when too many carcasses and shattered grills have been found on one particular section of road morning after morning, they put up a sign. The same holds true for antelope crossings in the grasslands of Wyoming and Colorado, and for moose crossings in northern Idaho and Montana.

Deer migration signs should set off warning bells in spring and fall.

Wild grazers such as deer tend to migrate in herds, moving toward higher elevations in the spring, and returning to lower elevations in the fall. They follow age-old migration routes that predate the highway by thousands of years. It's important for touring riders to know that the risks are greatest where the highway crosses the migration areas. Deer migration signs should set off alarm bells in your head in the spring and again in the fall.

Those deer signs are a big advantage to motorcyclists, if the situation registers between our ears. One good step is simply to slow down. Decreasing speed gives you more time to spot an animal, more time to react, and a greater ability to maneuver. *Okay,* you may think, *but how about that pickup truck on my tail?* Well, if you're riding into a deer zone, why not be polite and let the pickup driver go first? By now, you should be able to figure out how to shake a tailgater using some clever tactic other than just screwing on more throttle.

All right, you've spotted the deer sign, momentarily pulled onto the shoulder to let the tailgater on by, and reduced your speed 10 mph to give yourself more time to react. Can we really spot a deer ahead in time to react? And what should we do if a deer does leap out in front of us? Should we just keep riding along at the same speed, or should we attempt some avoidance maneuver?

Evasive Tactics

Okay, let's assume you know you're in deer country, you realize it's the right time of year and hour of the night for a close encounter, and suddenly you spot a pair of ears rising up from the roadside ditch. Should you slow down and then accelerate by as you would for an aggressive dog? Should you prepare to swerve, as you would for a car emerging from an alley? Or should you prepare for a quick stop, as you would for a left-turner?

Unlike an aggressive dog, deer seem to react more to proximity than to sight or sound. A deer may not show much interest in you until you get close, whether your café racer has loud pipes or your tourer is just burbling along quietly. The deer may glance up at you, then nonchalantly go back to munching again. But when you get within 60 feet or so, the deer may suddenly spring into action, jumping first straight ahead, then in a random zigzag wolf-evasion pattern. If it isn't obvious, the deer's first leap is in whatever direction it is facing. That's why hard braking is a smart evasive tactic.

Once the deer leaps into action, there isn't much time left for braking, so smart riders are already prepared to brake when riding into a suspicious area. Some of us brake hard when approaching any wild animal on the shoulder as an automatic precaution. That's a primary reason for shaking tailgaters and keeping some right hand fingers curled over the brake lever in a deer zone or anywhere there are wild animals.

When you suddenly realize that "log" in the left ditch has grown ears and antlers, or one of those white reflectors along the edge of the road starts winking at you at night, or a fawn tiptoes out of the roadside underbrush, my advice is to practice a quick stop. If the deer doesn't leap out in front of you at the last second, great. But when a deer does jump up out of the ditch and clatter around on the tarmac in your path, you'll be glad you got on the brakes early. If you're in the habit of making quick stops, you'll make a power stop automatically, and think about it afterward.

What about swerving? Its tempting to think that you might be able to maintain speed and slip on by or swerve around the deer if it should leap out in front of you. But swerving assumes you can predict which way the deer will leap. The deer's typical zigzag wolf-avoidance running pattern is random.

What about speeding up? After all, the greater your forward energy, the greater your impact force. You may have heard the folk tale of a motorcyclist riding at warp speed through the forest at night, and slamming right through a deer without drop-

You don't want to hit an elk.

ping the bike. Even if that folk tale were true, the rider would have been extremely lucky, not clever or skillful. For every folk tale of slamming into a wild animal without getting hurt, there are several other reports of riders being seriously injured and motorcycles destroyed. And if the winking reflectors you expected to punch through happen to be the eyes of an elk, moose, or bear, the odds lean strongly in favor of the animal.

On the Olympic Peninsula of Washington State in 1997, a rider managed to center punch a wandering brown bear. The bruised bear muttered something about stupid bikers, and meandered back into the woods. The motorcyclist was eventually hauled off in the ambulance and spent the rest of his vacation time in Olympic Memorial Hospital, getting sewn and screwed back together.

Other Wild Ones

Of course wild animals aren't the only four-legged road hazards you'll encounter. Farm animals loose on the road can present a mighty big target. Cows seem to be too dense to be concerned about vehicles, so they generally just keep doing whatever they were doing. Horses are a lot more skittish and excitable and are more likely to bolt in front of a vehicle or kick out at anyone who gets too close. If you come upon a herd of cattle or a flock of sheep being driven across the highway (or even down the highway), don't be too eager to elbow your way through the herd. It's one thing to have a longhorn steer rub up against a fence post—it's a little more thrilling to have a steer scrape his horn down the side of your bike. The drovers will get them off the road as soon as they can.

Livestock on the loose. It's neighborly to notify the owners.

In the West, it's considered neighborly to report escaped beasts. If you see a herd of cattle making a quick getaway over a trampled fence, it's appropriate to find the nearest farm house and report what you've seen. Don't expect the farm hands to get excited. Loose animals are on a par with the tractor getting another flat tire. You may get a chat about the weather (or even a discussion of the relative merits of cruisers and sport tourers) and a cup of coffee before they head out to round 'em up.

Open Range

An Open Range sign is more than a warning that there aren't any fences to keep cattle off the road. Open Range means the animals have the right-of-way. Think of it this way: The highway happens to run through the rancher's farm. The cattle belong there. You're a guest. It's up to you to get through the farm without injuring any of the rancher's livestock. Hit a steer, and you may get to purchase a locker full of beef in addition to some new bodywork for your bike.

In the Rockies, you will see bear, elk, raccoon, porcupine, skunk, and various other critters you might enjoy watching, from a distance. In Texas, it's armadillo. In Louisiana and Florida you may encounter an alligator meandering across the road. Even a raccoon or porcupine is large enough to upset a bike if you hit it with the front wheel, so you probably don't want to try bouncing over any animal if you can avoid it.

Elk and moose are common in Northern Idaho, Montana, and British Columbia. Elk and moose may look stately and reserved, but they are big enough and feisty enough to attack people and motor vehicles, if challenged. In Alaska, British Columbia, and northern states, residents know better than to zoom up behind a moose on the road, blast the horn, and expect it to move over. If you observe a moose trotting down or even alongside the road, remember this: An adult moose is tall enough that the windshield on your sportbike probably wouldn't even tickle his stomach. And a moose is strong enough to flick a fully loaded 1500cc touring bike into the swamp with an easy toss of his rack. The moral is, give large animals a lot of space and a lot of respect.

Moose are feisty enough to challenge you for road space, and big enough to win.

What About Whistles?

There are many different versions of ultrasonic animal alert whistles available. The theory is that the whistle moving through the air makes a high-pitched ultrasonic noise that alerts animals to your approach, warning them to get out of your way. Given the potential for animal strikes, a passive animal warning device sounds like a great idea, eh? But there are a couple of niggling questions. First, the whistle makes noise in frequencies above human hearing so how do you know if your deer whistle is actually working? If a big South Dakota juicy bug lodges in the orifice silencing the whistle, how would you know? And if your whistle is whistling, is the volume really loud enough to reach an animal several hundred feet away? More to the point, let's assume the whistle works and that a deer ahead hears the media. What's the message? Is the noise a collision warning, a mating call, a challenge to fight, or simply an annoyance? Let's assume the deer receives the message as a collision warning. Does that stimulate the animal to run away? And if the deer does decide to run away, is it supposed to make a 180 and run back into the woods, or is it supposed to run straight across the road?

You can find glowing testimonials about reductions in deer strikes after whistles were installed. Just read the deer whistle sales brochures. You'll have to make up your own mind about whether sales brochures are hype or fact. In my opinion, any device that depends on making the other guy get out of your way is probably not the smart approach. My survival theory about motorcycle hazards is that it is you who should always be prepared to get out of the way of the other guy, whether the other guy is a left-turning Accord, or a left-turning alligator. Feel free to bolt on whatever magic talismans you want, including a Back Off mud flap, a pulsating headlight, a string of garlic, a rabbit's foot, or a pair of deer whistles, but the only reliable way to avoid a collision is to get out of the way.

If you want to avoid getting snared by wild animal traps, the keys are the same as for any other traffic hazards: learn to read the situation ahead, adjust your speed and riding style to local conditions, and be skillful at controlling the bike.

Ferocious Fidos

Dogs are allowed to run loose in some parts of the country.

I stopped to talk with the owner of a large dog the other day. I'd been riding along a quiet wooded back road on the way home, when I observed a big yellow Labrador sprinting through the trees on an intercept course with my motorcycle. He'd done this before, jumping off the bank next to the road and trying to make a carrier landing on the deck of the bike. So far he hadn't managed to hit the bike, but it was always a shock to see a big dog flying through the air toward me. I didn't want to play the game anymore. This time I squeezed on a little front brake to heat up the disk, and then did a quick stop just short of where I figured Fido would make his landing. Sure enough, Fido vaulted off a roadside stump, flew through the air at about handlebar height looking for the bike, and made a four-paw touchdown on the pavement in front of me, right where he had calculated I should have been. This particular Fido wasn't really aggressive, just looking for some fun. I figured I could make it up to the owner's door without losing any flesh. Knock Knock.

Hello, is that big yellow Lab your dog? Well, he just about knocked me off my motorcycle, and this has happened before. I'd like to encourage you either to train him not to chase people or tie him up before he causes an accident that results in me being injured.

Well, he's a pretty good dog. He doesn't chase cars. He only chases UPS trucks and motorcycles. We just don't have the heart to tie him up.

Would you mind giving me the name of your insurance agent? I want to make sure you've got enough coverage to pay for hospitalization and motorcycle repairs and lost time from my job if your dog manages to knock me down next time.

That particular community was rural, and letting dogs roam free was part of the lifestyle. There were even reports of dogs forming packs and attacking sheep herds. The pet owners didn't seem to realize that Fido and his pals were playing wolf during the day and returning to their porches at dinnertime to greet the bosses. If you don't ever encounter loose dogs in your neighborhood, you can count yourself lucky. But if you happen to stumble onto a loose-dog community in your travels, you should be prepared to avoid injury to either yourself or the animal.

Over the years I've had a considerable number of encounters with canines and their masters. I've noticed that dogs tend to take on the personalities of their owners. A well-behaved dog usually means a responsible owner. An untrained dog is usually smarter than the owner. An aggressive dog is usually the result of a mean owner. Some dogs chase motorcycles, some prefer fire trucks. Others get a kick out of chasing joggers or snarling at the postman. Whatever the target, most dogs seem to enjoy chasing something. It works, too. If the dog chases a motorcycle, it soon goes away.

If you happen to have a snarling dog closing fast on your shin, it may seem that your biggest problem is becoming lunch. But the actual problem is the probability of dropping the bike. Even a small dog can upset a motorcycle. If you've had any dog encounters, you may have noticed that dogs seem to head for the front wheel. This may be just a misguided attempt at "rounding up" the motorcycle for the kill. Fido may not understand the future consequences of diving under a half-ton bike, but his instincts say it will work. The fact is, he can bring a bike crashing to earth.

Veteran motorcyclists understand the importance of never allowing a dog to get close to the front wheel. Most of the time that simply means being a little smarter than Fido. We don't really know how dogs think, but we can observe their behavior and take advantage of it.

Confrontations

Just like motorcyclists, there are vast differences between dogs. Some dogs are merely playful, others are defending a territory that happens to include the street, and some mistreated or untrained dogs are aggressive enough to be a serious threat to anyone passing by. A vicious dog can be a serious adversary if you

Some dogs are merely playful, others are defending a territory that happens to include the street.

happen to find yourself face-to-face with one. Those snarling teeth and belly growls are the real thing, and a vicious canine can inflict serious wounds. Let's ramble through some ideas about dog behavior and then consider some tactics for not getting bitten or knocked off the bike.

First of all, dogs are sensitive to their territorial boundaries, but they have little ability to reason. They often act out of instinct. An unrestrained dog can have a general turf as large as it wants to defend.

Second, dogs have behaviors that communicate dominance, aggression, fear, and submission. Fortunately, we can read some of this body language to help pre-

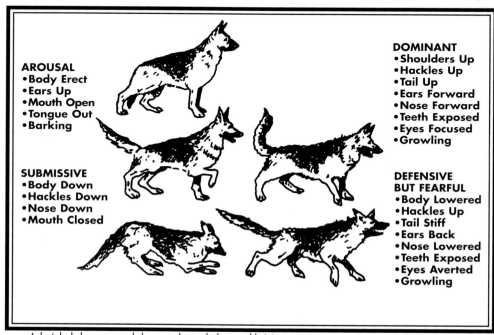

AROUSAL
•Body Erect
•Ears Up
•Mouth Open
•Tongue Out
•Barking

DOMINANT
•Shoulders Up
•Hackles Up
•Tail Up
•Ears Forward
•Nose Forward
•Teeth Exposed
•Eyes Focused
•Growling

SUBMISSIVE
•Body Down
•Hackles Down
•Nose Down
•Mouth Closed

DEFENSIVE BUT FEARFUL
•Body Lowered
•Hackles Up
•Tail Stiff
•Ears Back
•Nose Lowered
•Teeth Exposed
•Eyes Averted
•Growling

A dog's body language can help you understand what mood he's in.

David L. Hough

dict what a dog might do next. If a dog barks a lot with his ears pricked up and his tail wagging, he probably just wants to play. And, if he drops his head low to the ground, with his tail wagging low, he is being submissive. But if he pulls his ears back and tucks his tail in, he is getting apprehensive and could snap at you out of fear.

A dominant dog intent on defending turf will raise his upper body with ears erect, nose high, making himself appear as big and fearsome as possible. If there is a challenge, an aggressive dog plants his feet on the ground, pulls back his upper lip to reveal teeth, points his ears and nose farther forward, stiffens, and raises his hackles (the hair on the back of his neck). He will caution you of his authority by staring you down with unblinking eyes, and warn you of his seriousness with a deep chest growl.

If you understand that an aggressive dog is just defending turf, and if you don't need to be there, consider backing off. If you encounter a large, aggressive dog on the street, you are advised to avoid eye contact, remain quiet, and slink away with head lowered, if possible. Sure, you're a Big Dog rider, and Fido is just a dumb animal, but don't escalate a confrontation if you aren't prepared to lick your wounds.

If you encounter a problem dog more than once, you'll have to decide whether to slink away submissively and never come back, try to reason with the owner, or forget the owner and talk animal control into getting the dog locked up.

Apparently, for fun-seeking dogs there isn't much sport in chasing something that is too easy to catch. The game is to calculate the speed of the approaching vehicle and dash out just in time to intercept it. Dogs typically have very good eyesight and hearing, so Fido often waits in the yard behind a bush or parked car, calculating a perfect intercept that he can reach if he sprints at top speed. When Fido catches you at the intercept point, you might be able to get in a lucky kick with your boot, but the odds are that the dog has better reflexes than the motorcyclist. And if this dog happens to be aggressively defending his territory, it's best to avoid holding out any "fresh meat," even if you think your leathers could protect you against snarling fangs. Besides, attempting to injure the dog makes you the aggressor in the eyes of most owners. The clever approach is to outsmart the dog.

One good tactic for outsmarting Fido is to change speed unexpectedly. Most dogs have a maximum speed of only about 30 mph, so it is easy to outrun them on a motorcycle. If you slow down before entering Fido's turf, he predicts that he can wait a little longer before the attack. Then, just as Fido gets up and starts sprinting toward the intercept point, screw on some throttle and accelerate out of range. Poor Fido gets left in the dust. This is an acceptable tactic for keeping dogs away from the front wheel, given a few caveats. First, you have to spot the dog, which means being aware that there are loose dogs in that community and watching carefully for dogs lurking in the shadows. Second, if you are one of the following riders in a group, this slow/fast technique will make you the prime target. The lead rider will outdistance Fido, but the dog will catch the second rider. Third, if you pull this same trick day after day to outrun a dog in your neighborhood, it won't be long before Fido cracks the code and learns to start the intercept sooner.

. Bob spots Fido, slows down, Fido waits;
. Fido takes chase, Bob accelerates;
. Fido can't get to the intercept fast enough.

Repellents

If you continue to have too many dog confrontations in your community or on your travels, take a tip from your postal worker. Carry some dog repellent with you. Dog repellents are available in small pressurized spray canisters as well as electronic repellents that emit a high-pitched scream that dogs prefer to avoid. To find a source, check with your postal worker, your local utility company, or a kennel equipment supplier.

Some motorcyclists report success in keeping aggressive dogs at bay using ordinary household ammonia. They carry a plastic squeeze bottle of a water-ammonia solution and squirt a trail of the smelly stuff on the pavement as they pass by. Dogs mark their territory by urinating, and urine contains ammonia, so to the dog the motorcyclist is marking the street as his turf. A submissive dog may agree to comply with your demand. But a really tough dog will just urinate over the top of your ammonia as a threat for you to back off, and you'll have to decide how far you're willing to retreat.

Dogs are not a universal problem for motorcyclists. Communities vary in their tolerance for pets running loose, and their laws reflect this. In those areas where pets are allowed to roam, it is assumed the pet is harmless, at least until after the first bite. This means that animal control is probably not going to pick up a dog just because it snarled at you or ran into the street. But we can do each other a favor by working to get problem dogs under control in our own neighborhoods.

It's worth a try to confront a problem dog's owner, but remember that by approaching the owner's house you are invading the dog's territory, which he is defending. If you do feel you can get up to the door without being devoured, consider discussing the problem with the pet owner. It helps if you have done a little research into local animal control laws so that you know what the rules are. And it is also helpful to keep your temper in control. You might try something like this:

Hello, I'm Biker Bob. I live just down the street a few blocks, so I ride my motorcycle past your house every day. Is that big Labrador your dog? What's his name? The reason I stopped is because I thought you would want to know that your dog chases vehicles. He's a nice looking dog, and I'd certainly hate to injure him if he runs out to chase me. I'd really appreciate it if you could do something to restrain him on your own property, so that we don't have to get Animal Control involved. Thanks for your time.

Keep in mind that the owner of a problem dog might be even meaner than the dog. If the owner is a reasonable person who just doesn't realize his dog is a problem, your suggestion may trigger some action. But if the owner responds as aggressively as his snarling dog, or if you don't think you can even get to the door without risking life and limb, the other option is to register a complaint with animal control or the local police department or sheriff's office. Be aware that the legal eagles will want your name and address and will provide that to the dog owner if requested.

Aggressive dogs are sometimes rabid, and a bite can infect you with rabies. Trust me here, you want to avoid getting bit by any dog. The treatment for rabies is no joke. If you should happen to get bit by an animal, don't waste any time. Immediately get medical attention and report the incident to the authorities, who may quarantine the dog until rabies tests are completed. Remember, that first bite also proves to authorities that the dog is aggressive, and animal control can then take steps to either have the dog restrained or put down.

The vast majority of pet owners care for their animals responsibly and keep them out of the street. But during your travels, be prepared for the occasional dog who is undisciplined, or areas of the country where dogs are allowed to roam free. If you can be just a little smarter than the average Fido, you should be able to handle any dangerous confrontations without any pain or expense.

David L. Hough

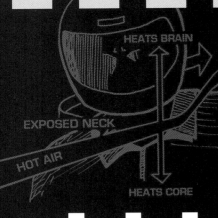

HEATS BRAIN

EXPOSED NECK

HOT AIR

HEATS CORE

SUBJECT TO FLOODING

CHAPTER 6
SPECIAL SITUATIONS

When It Rains

I should have known better than to head up into the Cascade Mountains in early April without putting on my serious rain gear. I was zooming around sloppy-wet logging roads trying to find checkpoints on the Vintage Motorcycle Enthusiasts' Bonehead Enduro, a not-too-serious ride with an emphasis on old guys and old bikes. And bones. All of the checkpoints have bone connotations, such as the snow bone and the mud bone. Anyway, as the day wore on, the northwest drizzle was turning into a steady downpour, and the logging roads were turning to a sloppy quagmire.

It was beginning to remind me of that scene from *Paint Your Wagon*, where the guys are moping around the leaky saloon tent. That scene kept flashing into my mind as I tried to find the road through a steamy, muddy face shield. And instead of Lee Marvin splashing a stagecoach-load of painted ladies down the creek, it was me on my BMW Enduro sidecar outfit, splashing up the muddy roads in a northwest deluge, wearing my adventure touring fabric riding suit without rain gear.

Like I said, I should have known better. I had been commuting to work daily by motorcycle in Seattle weather for many years, and I've traveled enough in wet places to have figured out some serious rain-riding tactics. But the Bonehead Enduro reminded me of how easy it is to be overly optimistic about the weather. When I started out that morning, I didn't know how wet it was going to get. So I just put on my two-piece adventure touring suit, which has a bonded Gore-Tex seam-sealed inner lining.

The truth is, even in Seattle, most of the time it's not raining. When we head out for a ride, we wear riding gear that's comfortable for the day's general conditions based on what it looks like when we fire up the bike. Then if the weather turns miserable later in the day, it's a long, cold, soggy ride home.

Even if you live in sunny Arizona, you'll occasionally get caught in some rain. And if you're from Arizona but traveling to the Oregon coast or western Canada, you'd better plan for some wet days. If you intend to ride cross-country or you live in a part of the world where rain is a regular feature, you'd be smart to carry rain gear always.

Riding in soggy gear is a bigger deal than just feeling miserable. Riding soggy is an invitation for hypothermia to set in. It's cold enough snorting around mountainside logging roads in the rain at 40 or 50° F, but at highway speeds the evaporative cooling of wet riding gear can chill you to the core within a few miles. And if you are becoming hypothermic, your thinking and muscle control are going to suffer. A couple of extra seconds reaction time can easily mean the difference between a close call and a trip to the ER.

So, let's think about being prepared for when it rains. First, let's consider some of the mechanics of both traction control and keeping dry, and then I'll offer some common sense rain-riding tactics.

Traction Control

Once you've had your two-wheeler do the moon walk on a rain-slick off-ramp, you can be pretty paranoid about a fall down every time you see the slightest pitter-patter of rain. It's important to realize that wet pavement has areas of relatively good traction as well as a few slippery areas. That's a clue that the slickness is caused by

When it first starts to rain, you can actually see the slippery goo floating away.

something more than just rainwater. The truth is that clean, wet pavement has something like 80 percent of the friction of clean, dry pavement. Of course, the critical word is clean, and pavement rarely is. Passing vehicles drip all sorts of lubricants on the surface, including diesel oil, antifreeze, chassis grease, brake dust, and rubber particles. Note that antifreeze is so slippery that liquid-cooled race bikes must use only water in the radiator.

In addition to those slippery vehicle droppings, people toss, dribble, and spit a variety of lubricants out car windows, including cigarette butts, hamburger wrappers, french fries, ice cream, pizza, soda pop, and used diapers, to name just a few. That road debris doesn't simply evaporate. Most of it gets squished into particles and mashed into the pavement. A little moisture mixed with those particles can create a slippery goo that really reduces traction. That's why the road seems so treacherous after just a little mist or morning dew: it's the slippery goo, not just the water.

Now, think about this: the only really good pavement cleaner is a steady downpour that lasts long enough to float that accumulated slimy stuff into the gutters. That offers us two lessons: First, the longer it's been since a good rainstorm, the slicker the pavement is likely to be when it finally does rain. If it's been dry for a while, you can actually see the slime floating away. Second, the pavement is slickest when it first starts to rain, before enough water has fallen to flush away the slippery stuff. Just a little sprinkle or some morning mist may leave the road slippery hours later. Those lessons are especially important for riders who live in dry climates.

Once the road gets washed clean, both asphalt and concrete paving can have decent traction in the rain, with some obvious slick exceptions. Shiny spots such as plastic arrows, steel plates, grated bridge decks, and railroad tracks are treacherous when wet. Loose objects such as leaves and flattened cardboard are even more hazardous when damp. Use more caution when following commercial trucks or transit busses, both of which are notorious for oil leaks. A vehicle with leaking seals continues to dribble a fresh coating of oil on top of rainwater. That's a good reason to ride in the wheel tracks of other vehicles, rather than in the center of the lane.

Hydroplaning

Water escapes from under a tire by squishing out sideways along lateral grooves in the tread. A good rain tire has deep angled grooves that point out toward the sides of the tread. The good news is that motorcycle tires have a relatively long, narrow contact patch compared to auto tires, and a narrow contact patch can more easily push the water aside. The bad news is that today's wide-profile motorcycle tires (which handle so much better in the dry) are more likely to hydroplane over standing water.

Roughly speaking, the typical low-profile radial car tire will start to hydroplane (lift up on top of the water) in a 1/2 inch of standing water at about 60 mph. The wider your tires, or the deeper the water, the more likely they are to hydroplane at the same speed. That's something to consider when you're thinking, *Hey, maybe I could fit a 170/50-17 on the back instead of that old-fashioned 140/80-17.*

And while we're talking tires, remember that a worn tire has shallow grooves that won't eject as much water from the contact patch. One of the advantages of a new tire is deeper grooves, and therefore a higher hydroplaning threshold. Different rubber compounds also have different traction characteristics, but that won't make any difference if the tire is hydroplaning.

It's also important to keep your tires pumped up to correct pressures. Tires actually flex a lot more than you might think, and form ripples or waves as the tires rotate against the ground. An underinflated tire can form a ripple in the tread that traps water and increases the risk of hydroplaning. An overinflated tire is less likely to trap water, but the tread isn't as resilient so the tire has less traction. A properly inflated tire has a better chance of pushing down through the water and maintaining a grip.

Water Ingestion

Don't worry about your engine "drowning" from too much water being thrown around in the airstream. Water is vaporized during intake and turns to steam during the heat of combustion. And steam can actually help increase horsepower. But solid water doesn't compress, and if the engine swallows enough water while running, it will lift the cylinders right off the block or collapse the pistons. So, don't ever try to splash through a puddle that is deeper than your carburetor intakes.

Water is more likely to affect electrical and ignition systems. Corroded connectors or cracked coil insulation are more likely to cause electrical failures when wet. It's important to have all those little rubber boots intact and snug around spark plug wires, for example.

Keeping Dry

When it rains, one big priority is to keep warm, which starts with keeping your body dry. The traditional way to keep dry is to add a layer of waterproof rain gear over you're clothing. That's still a reliable approach to rain riding, especially if what appeared to be a little mist in the morning turns into an all-day gully washer. We've got a lot of different styles, features, and qualities of motorcycling rain gear from which to choose.

Serious rain gear, what I should have worn on the Bonehead run, is what I wore while commuting through Seattle winters: Norwegian fisherman style bib pants and hooded jacket, plus boot and glove covers. For traveling, bring rain gear that packs small and light. In general, a one-piece rain suit packs up smaller than a two-piecer. But unless you have double-jointed shoulders, you'll also discover that a one-piece rain suit is more of a struggle to get into while standing under a freeway overpass. It's a lot easier to slip your boots through the bulbous legs of oversize fisherman-style bib rain pants and then put on a separate jacket.

It may seem strange, but if you choose a water-resistant fabric suit for commuting,

The PVC fisherman's two-piece suit is heavy and bulky to carry but easy to get into. The bib pants don't leak and the tall collar extends inside the helmet. A neck warmer insulates the neck.

David L. Hough

A lightweight one-piece rain suit can be a struggle to get into while standing alongside the highway in a downpour.

you'll probably be happier with a one-piece, step-into style because you'll be putting it on and taking it off inside a building rather than alongside the road. For touring, you may find it more practical to have two-piece gear and multiple layers that you can add or remove as the weather conditions change.

When I first got the fabric adventure touring gear, I wondered whether a breathable membrane suit would keep me dry without added rain gear. The question was answered on a trip to Great Britain when the sky opened up and I was caught on the M25 Motorway wearing just my adventure touring outfit. There really wasn't any

Some fabric suits are ideal for commuting and water-resistant enough for serious travel without additional rain gear.

place where I felt safe pulling over, and the next rest area was almost 20 miles away. The bottom line is that I didn't get soaked, although the pockets filled up with water through the unsealed zippers. The point is, today's adventure touring riding gear is water-resistant enough to weather a few wet days without adding an additional layer of real rain gear. And for those smart enough to stuff their maps in a clear plastic bag, even leaky pocket zippers aren't a serious problem.

Whether you prefer leathers or fabric suits, an outside layer of rain gear will keep your jacket and pants drier, which reduces much of the evaporative cooling effect. On the Bonehead, I was getting chilled because the wet fabric on the outside of the suit was drawing heat out of my body.

For cold or wet weather, I wear a windproof, waterproof neck triangle that seals off the opening between my jacket collar and my nose. And to keep icy water from dribbling down the back of my neck, my rain jacket has a tall collar that extends up under the back of my helmet. That's a custom modification. I buy a hooded rain jacket, and then snip off the top of the hood.

Although some leather gloves include rain covers and others have water-resistant linings, the only way to really keep your hands dry is to add a waterproof layer over your leather gloves. One tactic that works is to buy some XXL-size unlined rubber work gloves that you can wear over your leather gloves when it rains.

Rubber boot covers will keep your boots dry, once you figure out how to slip them on over your soggy leather boots. The trick is to pull a plastic baggie over your boots first, then the rubber will slip right on. The alternative I prefer is fabric boot covers that wrap around my boots and secure with hook and loop strips.

Riding Tactics

At the first patter of raindrops, the temptation is to crank up the gas and beat it out the other side of the cloud. That's a standard practice to get through desert thundershowers but not wise for riding around cities. Remember, the road is most slippery when it first starts to rain after a dry spell, especially in and around big cities where traffic is ever-present. So the smarter tactic in heavy traffic is to take a break for a few minutes and let those bumper-to-bumper drivers slip, slide, and bash into each other while the accumulated goo gradually washes away. A half-hour break is a wise precaution, giving you a good reason to warm up and put on serious rain gear if it looks like it's going to be more than a light shower.

Scrutinize the Surface

Remember my discussion about those trucks and busses leaking fresh oil? It's most likely that during rain showers any oil will dribble down the center of the lane, but oil also spreads downhill on cambered curves. During rain showers, watch for any beading up or rainbow sheens that indicate oily areas, and keep your tires out of the slippery spots, especially when approaching intersections and in turn lanes.

While rounding a curve or a cambered freeway ramp, try to stay in the uphill wheel track, and reduce your speed to reduce lean angle. Adjust your line to cross railroad or streetcar tracks at an angle as close to 90° as practical, and maintain a steady speed and direction when crossing any such slippery areas. Those black plastic planks laid next to railroad tracks can be as slippery as the shiny rails. Try to keep your tires away from painted lines, plastic arrows, manhole covers, and loose objects such as leaves. Expect brick streets and wooden bridge decks to be especially slippery when wet.

Those plastic planks laid next to railroad tracks can be really slick in the rain.

Smooth Is Good

We probably won't have to remind you to reduce speed to make up for the reduced traction of a smooth surface. It's also important to avoid any sudden changes of speed or direction that demand more traction. Even if you feel your tires let go for a moment, avoid that sudden disastrous instinct to snap off the throttle or jam on the brakes. If the bike can recover, it will. Don't do anything to make the situation worse.

Keep the Wheels Perpendicular

For really slippery areas such as steel plates, place more of your weight on the pegs and try to keep the bike leaned so that the tires are perpendicular to the road surface. That way, if the tires do lose traction momentarily, the bike can slide sideways a bit without immediately falling down.

Use Both Brakes

On rain-slick pavement, your braking technique must be modified. You can use more rear brake than you use on dry pavement for the same bike loading because there is less weight transfer to the front, and therefore less traction for braking on the front. In the rain, you have less total traction available for braking, but you can share braking almost equally between front and rear.

Brake in a Straight Line

When slowing or stopping on wet pavement, try to brake in a straight line. For example, when approaching a sharp turn, use both brakes to decelerate with the bike vertical, then get off the brakes before you lean. If you realize you are going to cross a slippery area such as a plastic arrow while braking, momentarily ease off the brakes as your tires cross the plastic.

Get on the Brakes Early

When approaching an intersection where you may have to stop, apply both brakes lightly to get the disks dried off and warmed up. The stainless steel alloys used in most disk brake systems are beautiful in the dry, but some have embarrassingly low friction when wet. It may take a revolution or two to squeegee enough water off the disk to get full braking effort. If you panic at the delayed braking reaction, the tendency is to squeeze the lever harder, which then results in the wheel locking up as the disk suddenly dries off and grabs. If you should overbrake on the front, release the lever and squeeze more gently. If the rear tire starts to slide during a straight-line stop, just stand on the pedal and slide it to a halt. The solution to such problems is to ease on the brakes earlier and be a little less aggressive.

In the wet, ride brakes lightly to keep the disks squeegeed off.

Don't Get Zapped

If you are riding into a thunderstorm that's generating some good lightning strikes, you'd be wise not to place your body between the electrically charged cloud and the earth. Riding on rubber tires won't save you from getting zapped by a lightning bolt. Preferably, get inside a sturdy building or at least wait under an overpass. Don't stand in the open under tall objects. A lot of golfers have been fried standing under trees clutching shiny metal anodes.

Out in the Desert

Out in the desert away from civilization you don't have the same problem with road contaminants, but there is a bigger potential problem: flash floods. In Arizona and New Mexico, you'll see monstrous steep-sided ditches carved across the landscape, sometimes 20 feet deep and 80 feet across. These are washes created by sudden thundershowers. The sunbaked soil can't soak up the water fast enough, and large torrents of muddy water race across the landscape for miles, tearing out soil and roads in their paths.

A touring rider from Iowa or New Jersey riding under a blue Arizona sky may not appreciate the effect of that thundershower 20 miles away, which has created a flash flood that is now roaring across the desert at speeds in excess of 50 or 60 mph. Experienced desert riders understand the importance of not zipping over a hill until they can see what's on the other side. They want to know that a dry wash really is dry. And if you do encounter a flooded wash across a desert highway some day, don't be foolish enough to attempt to ride through the water. Even if you don't get swept away by the current, there may be a big hole carved where the pavement used to be.

Out in the desert, it doesn't have to be raining for a sudden wall of water to come roaring across the road.

Alternate Motorcycles

A lot of riders are paranoid about sliding out and dropping their two-wheelers on slick surfaces. If you learn and practice the techniques already discussed, fall-downs should be few and far between. Today's tires have a lot more traction than you might give them credit for. But if the fear of falling is taking all the fun out of motorcycling or if you intend to commute or travel in lousy weather conditions, you might consider looking into sidecars. Three-wheelers can slip and slide without falling down. Speaking for myself, I was glad I took the old sidecar rig on the Bonehead Enduro instead of a two-wheeler. I may have been cold, soggy, exhausted and covered with mud, but I didn't have to be concerned about falling down.

When You're Hot, You're HOT

I had started the day at a campground in Wyoming and intended to make a fast transit across Nebraska on my way to southern Missouri. Thunderclouds over the Black Hills of South Dakota kept the temperature pleasant most of the morning. But as I dropped south into Nebraska, the temperature soared, and a strong southwest wind howled across the prairie, blasting me with hot, dry air. By noon, I started to

Keep yourself hydrated on long, hot trips.

get a headache, then my legs began to cramp, and a few miles later I began to feel sick to my stomach.

Late for lunch and low on fuel, I looked for a restaurant and a gas station, but there was only a "convenience" station at the junction where I needed to turn off. So I filled the tank, bought two cans of ice-cold soda, and planned to find a nearby park where I could make my own sandwich. I was thirsty enough to down both sodas on the spot, but the station was dirty and congested with cars, so I went looking for a wayside where I could get out of traffic and into some shade.

A few miles down the road I found a state park. I felt exhausted, my head was throbbing, and it was all I could do to park the bike and drag myself to a picnic table. As I unzipped my jacket and started to gulp down the first can of cold pop, my stomach cramped so badly I almost blacked out. I doubled over with my head down on the picnic table, feeling as though some invisible ghoul were plunging a knife into my belly, but I had no energy to fight back.

I managed a few sips of the soda, then some water, and as I slowly recovered, I mentally kicked myself for not listening to the signals my body had been sending for the last hundred miles. Those leg cramps were a message: *We're running low on water, bunkie.* Thinking back, I hadn't had anything to drink since a couple cups of coffee at mid-morning. The leg cramps, the headache, the nausea—yeah, all the classic symptoms of heat exhaustion. I'd been too focused on covering the miles, and not focused enough on hot weather riding tactics. Heat exhaustion had sneaked up on me because it was hot, but not one of those triple digit scorchers that really gets my attention.

I remembered a ride I had taken south over the Siskiyou Mountains from Oregon to California that turned into a scorcher. Up at 4,000 feet, it was chilly enough. But 100 miles later, descending into the Sacramento Valley was like riding into a broiler oven. By the time I reached Oroville, the temperature signs were flashing 118° F, and I had another 150 miles to the rally site at Mariposa. To continue that ride, I needed to go into desert survival mode.

On that trip, I kept the full riding gear on, including riding pants, jacket, insulated leather boots, gloves, and a knit neck "cooler," which I saturated with water

David L. Hough

from a squeeze bottle. As quickly as the fabric dried out in the blast-furnace wind, I would flip the face shield open, squeeze a gusher of water down my chin, and slam the face shield shut again. Whether riding or stopping for more ice water, other people stared at me in disbelief. Peering out of their air-conditioned cars, or sitting in an air-conditioned restaurant, they just couldn't grasp the concept of someone being outside in 118° weather, bundled up in heavy clothing.

Back at the park in Nebraska, I reminded myself about how the human body reacts to even tiny changes in temperature of the core organs. The human body won't tolerate much of a drop in core temperature (*hypo*thermia) or more than a couple degrees rise in core temperature (*hyper*thermia) without taking drastic action. When you're hot, you're HOT. The tactics the body uses to deal with heat stress include sweating, vasodilation, increasing heart rate, and reduction of blood pressure.

Sweating

Sweat (perspiration) evaporates on the surface of the skin and clothing. The process of evaporation actually cools the surface of the skin, transferring heat from the body to the air. While sweat contains a few chemicals, it's mostly water. Run low on water, and your body will start complaining. It's important to keep replenishing the water you've lost through sweating. Drinking should do it—about a pint of water every hour.

Vasodilation

As one's core temperature heats up, blood vessels enlarge to circulate more blood (and therefore transfer more body heat) toward the skin. If air temperature isn't much higher than body temperature, evaporating sweat helps transfer the extra heat to the air. Of course if the sweat evaporates too quickly and the skin dries out, it begins to absorb heat from the air, and the increased blood flow from vasodilation just pumps more heat back to the core.

Heart Rate and Blood Pressure

The heart responds to rising core temperature and vasodilation by increasing the heart rate to keep filling those enlarged blood vessels. The heartbeat can be 50 percent to 70 percent faster than the resting rate. If the body (or core temperature) continues to heat up, blood flow is shunted away from muscles and brain in an attempt to carry heat to the skin, and blood pressure drops.

When our bodies are struggling to get rid of excess heat, we're going to get messages. Our arms will get tired and our leg muscles will cramp. We'll get headaches, our stomachs will churn. We'll start to feel dizzy and may even black out. These various symptoms are warnings, our bodies' attempt at trying to tell us to do something other than keep on hammering through the hot air until the bike runs out of gas.

Heat Cramps

Muscle cramps caused by heat usually affect the legs and lower abdomen first but can also affect a motorcyclist's arms and shoulders. Heat cramps are a symptom that the body's water supply and electrolytes are running low. It's similar to the water evaporating out of your bike's battery until there isn't enough power to crank the engine anymore.

You don't want to ignore heat cramps because they're not going to get better until you drink water. Take a break, find some shade, massage the cramped muscles to relieve the spasms, and take sips of water. If the cramps don't subside, the recommended first aid dose is 1/2 teaspoon of table salt per half glass of water every 15 minutes for 1 hour.

Heat Exhaustion

If you don't pay attention to those headaches and cramps and just keep on riding, you may get to heat exhaustion before you get to your destination. You just run out of energy as a result of that lower blood pressure and shunting of blood away from the brain and muscles. You may not recognize heat exhaustion because it's normal to feel hot and tired during a long, hot, windy ride. And note that you can lose all your energy without a significant rise in body temperature. Symptoms of heat exhaustion include headaches; dizziness; nausea; momentary fainting; muscle cramps; tiredness; weakness; profuse sweating; pale, clammy skin; and near normal body temperature.

If you didn't drink some water for those cramps, that's a high priority now that you've started to become weak. Find someplace where you can get off the bike and into the shade, preferably into an air-conditioned room. First aid books suggest adding a little salt to the water, same dose as for heat cramps. Remove your riding gear and wet down your skin. Pour a glass of water down your neck or onto your head. Wet your shirt. The evaporating water will actually help your body get rid of some heat.

If you feel faint, lie down before you fall down, and elevate your feet above your head to increase blood flow to the brain. And if there is vomiting, you're in worse shape than you thought. Call the emergency number and explain the situation, or pull over at the next fire station and ask for help. It may be necessary for you to go to a hospital for an intravenous salt solution. Get out of the sun and stay out of the heat for 24 hours. If the symptoms have gotten this far, don't plan on getting back on the bike for at least a day. Your body needs some time to recuperate.

Heatstroke

I've seen motorcyclists who ignored all the symptoms of heat exhaustion and eventually just sat down in the sun with dazed looks on their faces. One British couple on the Mojacar Tour to Spain had already been several days on the road under a blazing sun, hadn't taken any liquid since breakfast tea that morning, and were quickly falling into the incoherent stage of heatstroke. Fortunately for these riders, someone else saw the symptoms and organized help in time to get medical aid. They were in bed for a week, slowly getting their bodies to function again.

If the body's core temperature continues to rise, the body's temperature regulating mechanisms begin to shut down. Sweating stops, the heart beats faster, the victim becomes confused, then incoherent, and then comatose. The symptoms of heatstroke include incoherence; blanking out; hot, red, dry (no perspiration) skin; rapid pulse; and elevated body temperature (skin feels hot to the touch, temperature may climb as high as 106° F).

Heatstroke is a medical emergency. Without immediate medical care, the person can die. If you recognize these symptoms in yourself or a riding buddy, get into some shade, out of riding gear, and cooled down by any means available. If possible, get the victim into an air-conditioned room, and immediately seek emergency treatment. Yes, this is a life-threatening emergency.

While you are waiting for the medics, you can apply ice wrapped in a towel, sponge water or rubbing alcohol on the victim's skin, fan air over him or her, or do whatever you can to help cool down the victim. Your target is to get the body temperature below 102° F. Do not give the victim any stimulants or alcoholic beverages.

Running Cool

When you're riding in hot, dry climates, the tactics for avoiding heat problems are simple: drink a lot of water, insulate your skin from the hot air, and use evaporative cooling. Plain old tap water is fine, if you can stand the taste and the local bugs. Bottled water is better and available most everywhere in the world in 1-liter plastic bottles. Exercise drinks containing electrolytes are acceptable, unless you have high blood pressure. Carbonated soft drinks are better than nothing, although it would be smarter to get plain water without large doses of salt, sugar, or chemicals. Alcoholic drinks such as beer are unwise because alcohol not only increases heartbeat, depresses the pump function of the heart, and degrades judgment, but it actually dehydrates the body.

Insulate Your Skin

People from cooler climates have learned to layer their clothing so they can remove clothes piece by piece to cool down. So as the day warms up, a motorcyclist thinks about taking off his or her riding pants, then the jacket. If the temperature continues to climb, the rider becomes really hot, so off comes the shirt, and the blue jeans get swapped for shorts. But guess what? The rider can get even hotter. Why doesn't baring more skin cool the rider down? Think about this: when air temperature rises above 99° F, bare skin just soaks up more heat from the air. You can't give off heat to air that's hotter than you are. If you expose your skin to air that's hotter than you are, the heat flows in one direction—from the air to your body.

Once air temperature climbs above 99° F, you keep your insulation on and the vents closed. That's why I wear my leather gloves and insulated riding boots in the summertime as well as in the winter. My feet are down in the airstream that's first been heated up by the pavement, and then heated some more by the engine. Are my feet hot? Sure, but not as hot as they would be if I were wearing thin boots or shoes that exposed my ankles.

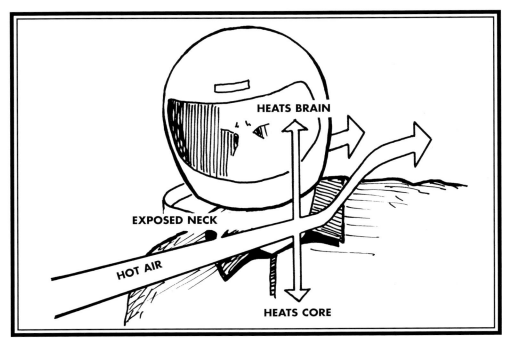

If you expose your neck to hot air, your blood absorbs the heat and pumps it to your brain and body core.

Evaporative Cooling

Before leaving the park in Nebraska, I change my neck protector for a knit neck cooler and wet it down. The water bottle is filled and stowed in the front of the tank bag where I can reach it while riding. Remember how sweat works. Evaporating water absorbs heat from the skin and transfers it to the air. Motorcyclists can augment sweat by wetting down clothing. The most important area is the neck below the ears because that's where large arteries are most exposed to the airstream. A wet cotton bandanna around your neck will help cool down your core temperature, although you will need to wet down the bandana every few minutes. A knit neck band works even better, since it will hold more water.

I've tried those tubular neck "snakes" filled with water-absorbing crystals. They work reasonably well for walking, but for me they aren't efficient enough for motorcycling. The crystals hold water so well that it evaporates too slowly. For motorcycling on a seriously hot day, I need a lot more evaporation, and I need it positioned over the carotid arteries under my ears, not loosely around my neck.

The bad news is that evaporative cooling works well only in dry climates. When the humidity is already high, neither perspiration nor the water in your shirt can evaporate. No evaporation; no cooling. But of course there is always shade, so the best bet may be simply to take more breaks in humid climates and to look for alternate tactics.

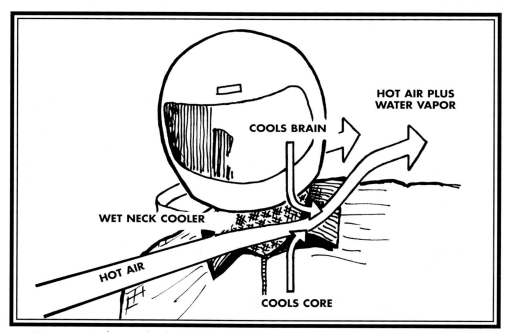

Water evaporating from a neck cooler absorbs heat from the neck and transfers it to the air, even if the air is hotter than the body.

Alternate Tactics

In Arizona, it's standard practice to nap until midnight and cross the desert between midnight and dawn. In California, you can usually find cooler air by heading for the mountains or following the coast. Mountains and coastal roads are nonexistent in states such as Kansas or Iowa, but you can take advantage of the typically cooler morning air. Get up at dawn and get your riding in before the sun starts to warm things up again.

Crossing Nebraska, now in my desert survival mode, I make a point of taking

David L. Hough

more frequent breaks, drinking more water, keeping my gear zipped up and my neck cooler saturated. The heat and the wind abate as the sun sets, so I decide to keep riding after dark to cover some miles in the cool of the evening.

The next time you're making a long transit on a hot day, remember my little flirtation with heat exhaustion. Trust me here, motorcycling is a lot more fun when your body temperature is steady in the green band, and your electrolyte level is up at the full mark.

Dang Wind

Cruiser Carla finally saved up enough vacation to take that big cross-country trip, and today she is heading west on Interstate 90 across South Dakota. Last night there was something on the television about high winds across the plains, but she was too tired from yesterday's ride to get the message. This morning, the breeze is kicking up little whirlwinds in the parking lot, but the sun is warming up the air, and it looks like another good day to lean back on the cruiser and motor off toward the horizon again.

Carla likes the feel of her cruiser. The low seat allows her to reach the ground with both feet. The forward mounted footpegs give her room to stretch her legs. She has added a windshield on the front, and has her gear stacked up on the back of the saddle and strapped to the sissy bar. For the first hour, there are a few disconcerting wind gusts, but the sky is blue, the cruiser is thrumming along sweetly, and she continues to enjoy the freedom of the road.

Carla takes a break at Mitchell to see the famous Corn Palace, and when she comes out to get back on the bike, she realizes the blue sky is rapidly disappearing behind dark clouds. Back on the superslab, the wind has shifted to the southwest, and the gusts are getting stronger and more frequent. A few miles down the road, gusts suddenly slam into the bike from the left front, and Carla can barely hang on. The bike slows as if she had jammed on the brake and points off toward the shoulder. The leather fringe on her jacket whips against her neck. The wind takes her breath away, and grit blows into her eyes behind her sun glasses.

Crossing the bridge at Chamberlain, a malevolent gust suddenly hammers into the bike, slowing it and pushing it toward the railing. Carla's heart jumps into her throat as she struggles to lean the bike upwind. Then, as the gust suddenly passes, she is barely able to keep from shooting over into the oncoming lanes. For the next

hundred miles, she can't shake the image of a bike and rider slamming head-on into an 18-wheeler and cartwheeling off the bridge into the Missouri River.

The ride has ceased to be fun, but she forges ahead anyway. By the time Carla has battled her way to Wall, her eyes are stinging and watering, and she is scared, fatigued, flayed, windburned, dehydrated, and angry. To top off her frustration, the engine sputters onto reserve earlier than expected. And when she parks the bike at the gas station, a gust slams into the bike and pushes it off the sidestand before she can catch it. *Dang wind!* Carla screams into the gale. *I hate wind!*

Most of us can empathize with Carla. Motorcycles can be tricky to control in crosswinds, especially in gusting crosswinds. We try to keep the motorcycle balanced, but the gusts suddenly blow it sideways and then just as suddenly let up. It's a constant battle to stay between the lines, we're being assaulted by blowing grit and our fuel mileage suffers. Is there some method to riding in this windy madness, or do we just have to tough it out?

Sometimes riders contribute to the problem without realizing it. The fringe on Cruiser Carla's riding jacket is stylish, but it flails around in the wind, adding another annoyance. Her sunglasses are cool looking, but can't keep grit from blowing into her eyes. Carla likes her cruiser because of the image and the low seating position, but the forward-mounted footpegs make it more difficult to quickly make steering adjustments. Stowing her gear on the sissy bar is handy, but that also creates a "sail" high above the center of gravity. Let's consider how different motorcycles react to wind and how the motorcycle ergonomics relate to ease of control.

Sails

A bike with a lot of sail, a tall windshield or a large fairing, for example, is more susceptible to crosswinds. The shape and location of the sails is just as important as the size. Remember, a motorcycle tends to lean around its center of mass. Wind pushing on the area below the CG has little effect, but wind blowing on the sail above the CG can have considerable effect.

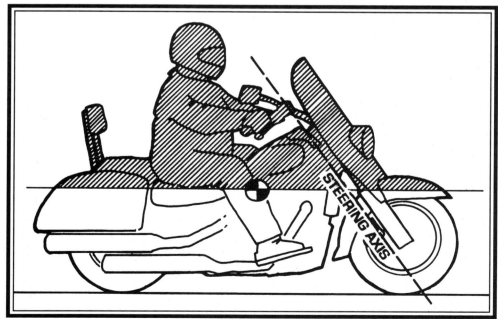

The relative position and shape of the windshield and fender affect how the bike reacts to crosswinds. A fork-mounted sail forward of the steering axis can actually help countersteer the bike upwind.

Obviously, wind pressure on a frame-mounted windshield would push the bike downwind. But a fork-mounted fairing, windshield, or fender can produce a different result because wind pressure on sails attached to the front fork can apply a steering force to the front wheel.

Steering controls lean angle, whether it is our hands pushing on the grips or the wind pushing on the front fender. The relative position and shape of sails attached to the front fork, including fenders, fairings, and windshields, have an effect on how the bike handles in windy conditions. For example, a large fork-

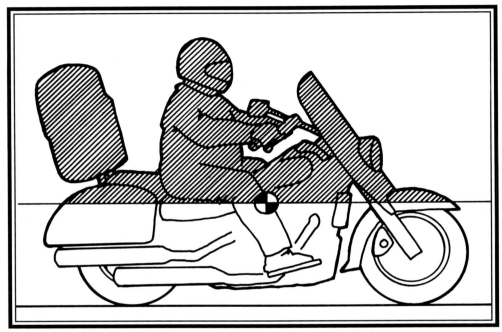

Wind blowing on the sail above the CG pushes the bike over. Baggage up high adds a lot of sail.

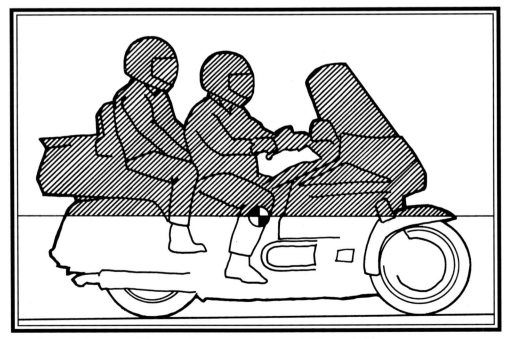

The combination of fairing, tail trunk, and passenger creates a large sail high up on the bike.

David L. Hough

mounted windshield angled back steeply might steer the machine into more of a downwind lean. A front fender with a lot of sail ahead of the steering axis might actually steer the machine upwind.

Saddlebags mounted no higher than the machine's CG will be less likely to push the bike downwind than bulky sails such as a sleeping bag strapped up high on a sissy bar, or a duffel strapped on a rack over the taillight.

Bare bikes can theoretically be as stable as a bike with a fairing, except that the wind tugging at the rider's arms will impart some unintentional steering input. For instance, a strong gust from your right can push your elbows toward the left, resulting in countersteering the bike into even more of a left lean. A large frame-mounted fairing acts as a sail, pushing the bike downwind. A passenger seated on the back of the saddle also adds to the sail. The combination of a frame-mounted fairing; large, boxy tail trunk; and a passenger creates a large sail high up on the bike, making some big touring machines harder to control in gusting crosswinds.

Ergonomics

The way the machine is designed, dictating how you sit on it and reach for the controls (the ergonomics), also has a dramatic effect on how well you are able to control the machine. For best control in difficult conditions, the rider should be seated on the saddle with torso leaning slightly forward, arms slightly bent at the elbows, hands grasping the handlebar grips at a natural angle, and body weight supported over the footpegs. The footrests should be located beneath the rider's center of gravity, both to allow holding knees against the tank for stability, and to enable shifting body weight from one peg to the other. What we're describing here is essentially a dual sport posture, or perhaps a very conservative sport touring posture.

Cruiser-styled machines with forward-mounted footpegs and high handlebars (like the one Carla rides) may look cool, but the ergonomics are far from ideal for windy conditions. Even sportbikes can be difficult to steer if the handlebar position is too far forward, or if the bars are too narrow or too low. The upright seating position on a typical touring bike may be comfortable for the long haul, but the sit-up ergonomics can also make it more difficult for the rider to make the quick steering inputs that are needed to counteract a wind gust. It isn't just the style of the bike at issue, it's how the individual rider fits a particular machine.

Consider that the ergonomics determine which muscles are used to lean the bike. Quick, powerful steering input requires quick, powerful muscles, like those in your arms.

To understand this concept, lean your torso forward in your chair with your feet flat on the floor. Stretch both arms straight forward as if you were reaching for some imaginary handlebars mounted too far forward. Reach out far enough that your elbows are locked straight. Now, turn your imaginary handlebars a little to the left, and then a little toward the right, and think about which muscles are doing the work. With your arms locked straight, you must use your back and stomach muscles, right? And you're probably bracing with your legs, too.

Now, pull your imaginary handlebars toward you just enough that your elbows are bent, and try steering left-right again. With your arms bent, you can steer with your arm and shoulder muscles, which happen to be quicker and more accurate than the larger muscles in your stomach, back, buttock, or legs. The bottom line is that ergonomics make a big difference in your ability to control the bike.

Whatever your favorite machine, if you find it difficult to control it in windy conditions, take a serious look at both the sails on your bike and the ergonomics. If you have trouble countersteering, or if your shoulders or back always ache halfway through the ride, consider how you might modify the bike to fit you better. And if your current machine can't be adjusted to fit you, the message should be obvious.

Rider Skill

Even if the machinery, loading, and ergonomics are perfect, a rider's balancing and steering technique has a lot to do with accurate control. Riders who consciously countersteer have better control and are less frustrated in windy situations than riders who merely think lean, or who try to steer with their knees or feet.

When riding through strong winds, you must lean the bike into the wind, which may require a forceful push on the grips. For example, with a strong but steady crosswind from your left, pushing on the left grip will lean the bike left (upwind). If the bike drifts too far downwind, you need to lean it even more toward the wind. Pushing a little harder on the upwind grip will lean it over more and point back toward your desired line. Of course, when the wind suddenly decreases, or changes direction, you will need to quickly countersteer to whatever angle is needed to maintain your line of travel.

When riding through crosswinds, you may get some strange feedback from the front wheel. It may require more pressure on the grip than during a curve since the contact patches are way over on one side of the tires even though the machine is traveling straight ahead. Just concentrate on countersteering to make the motorcycle go in whatever direction you wish, and let the tires swerve around under you. Many of us have ridden for miles through strong, steady crosswinds with the bike leaning over at a startling angle, controlling the bike by pushing firmly on the upwind grip.

Gusting Cross Winds

The most difficult situation is with strong, gusting winds. Suddenly a gust slams into the bike, pushing it off on a tangent toward the shoulder or into the opposing lane. What's needed to counteract gusts is to lean the bike into the wind quickly. And the way to lean a bike quickly is to countersteer forcefully, the same tactic you'd use to initiate a quick turn or swerve around an obstruction. To lean the bike left, push on the left grip. To lean right, push on the right grip. When you get hit by a stronger crosswind gust, just push a little harder and be prepared to push on the other grip to straighten up again as the gust passes.

Since we can't see the air, it helps to have some understanding of what wind does around other vehicles and structures. Oncoming trucks can push a powerful bow wave toward you, or suddenly block the wind as they pass. Be especially wary of large vehicles that pass upwind of you from the opposite direction.

I might also note that Cruiser Carla's wind troubles grew worse toward afternoon. That's because wind typically gets stronger and more turbulent as the earth warms up. There are many locations in North America where a strong wind is expected every summer afternoon. For example, in the Columbia River Gorge between Oregon and Washington, the cool coastal air rushes inland to replace the hot air rising over the deserts. For the wind surfers, it's heaven. For motorcyclists, it's somewhere else. The narrow steel-grated bridges cross the river at right angles to the wind direction. In such locations, wise riders plan the transit earlier in the morning, before the wind gets serious.

Body Armor

Obviously in gusting wind conditions there is an increased possibility of an accident, so smart riders zip on their best armor. But don't forget that getting irritated or frustrated can distract you from road hazards. Wear sensible riding gear that covers all skin, and keep everything zipped and buttoned closed. Wear your earplugs, because the wind velocity when riding into a headwind generates noise levels way up into the injury range. Most importantly, wear eye protection that keeps wind and windblown grit out of your eyes.

Know When to Fold 'Em

You don't have to like wind, but you can gain the confidence that comes from knowing you can control the bike under most wind conditions. We mention most, because sometimes winds are so violent that it is unwise to continue riding. I can recall dropping down off a pass early one spring, to find myself headed straight into a sinister silver-streaked cloud moving across the valley ahead. Suddenly, a snarling sleet squall hammered the bike so hard the tires were starting to slide into the other lane. I made a quick downwind U-turn, sped back to a road maintenance area I had just passed, laid the bike on its side in the lee of a gravel pile, and hunkered down until the squall moved on. Between Texas and the Great Lakes, motorcyclists must be aware of the extreme hazard of tornadoes. Should you observe a funnel start to form, you should immediately seek shelter beneath some heavy structure such as a highway overpass.

Homework

The homework exercise for gusting winds is to practice countersteering (push steering) all the time as you ride along. Approaching a curve to the right, consciously push on the right grip. Changing lanes toward the left, push on the left grip. Or, if the ergonomics of your machine have you leaning back and pulling on the handlebars as you ride along, try pulling both grips toward the direction you want to go. For a right turn, pull *both* grips toward the right. If you practice countersteering every time you ride, you'll lean the bike into sudden wind gusts without having to think about it.

Freezing Your Gas on the Pass

I couldn't believe how cold it was for a desert ride in Southern California. Up on the Angeles Crest highway, only 30 miles uphill from sunny Pasadena, my dual sport sidecar rig was crunching into packed snow and black ice. I'd missed an important turnoff on the Los Angeles-Barstow-Las Vegas dual sport ride and had continued on the highway far enough that I didn't want to go back and try to find the off-road route. I didn't realize we'd have to follow the crest highway another 50 miles at elevations above 6,000 feet before we could get back down to the desert and connect with the dual sport route again.

The moral of this tale is that even in balmy Southern California, with warm breezes wafting through the palm trees down at sea level, you can find yourself in winter conditions just by gaining a little altitude. Now, whether you are heading out on an April tour from Amarillo, a September trip from Seattle, or just itching for a December spin in Duluth, my advice is to be a little smarter than I was up on that Angeles Crest highway. Let's consider some of the implications of cold weather riding.

Being on a sidecar rig gives you options such as climbing above snow level.

Turning Back

There is a lot of wisdom in knowing when to turn around. Ascending the Angeles Crest highway, we were passed at warp speeds by a rider carving corners on a Ducati. But at the first sign of frost in the shadows, the Ducati rider wisely turned around and zoomed back downhill. Being on the sidecar rig, we had additional options, so we continued. But if I had run into sleet up there, I would have turned around also. It's not smart to keep motoring ahead into worsening conditions if you have a choice.

Before you continue rushing off across the landscape into worsening conditions, pull over alongside the road, shut down the engine, and squander a few minutes focusing on the situation.

On the other hand, if you're in the middle of a cross-country trip when you're caught in a winter storm, the only sensible option may be to continue ahead. Say you're making a transit across Utah. The next warm restaurant is 40 miles away in Salina, and the last one was 60 miles back in Green River. That front is going to run over you whether you stop, retreat, or continue, so you might as well keep moving toward Salina. Now, one of these days you're going to find yourself in this situation, and I want you to remember this: Before you continue rushing off across the landscape into worsening conditions, pull over alongside the road, shut down the engine, and squander a few minutes focusing on the situation. Okay, it's cold and the wind is howling. Get out the map. Huddle down in the lee of the bike, warm your fingers on the engine, take a look at the map, and make a decision. Is it wise to keep going, or should you beat a retreat? If the only option is to keep going, what extra insulation can you add under your riding gear? Remind yourself of the symptoms of hypothermia.

The Human Heating and Cooling System

To understand the tactics for protecting the body, let's remember how the human heating and cooling system functions. The body "burns" food to generate heat, and pumps warmed oxygen-rich blood throughout its system. Blood near the skin surface gives off heat to the air. The lungs absorb oxygen from the air and expel warm water vapor and carbon dioxide. The body automatically adjusts blood pressure, blood flow, and breathing rate to maintain an almost constant temperature of the central core (the heart, lungs, kidneys, and other central organs) regardless of outside air temperature. If the core temperature begins to increase or decrease, the system quickly attempts to correct it. A core temperature that is too cold is called hypothermia. Only a couple of degrees below normal temperature can be life threatening.

Hypothermia

When the body senses a drop in core temperature, the response is to shut down blood flow to the extremities, starting with fingers and toes. If necessary to save the vital core organs, the system will sacrifice fingers and toes to frostbite. What isn't so obvious is that the head is an extremity, too. Large arteries along both sides of the neck carry warm blood to the head. So when the heating system decreases blood flow to the extremities, there's also less blood (and less oxygen) going to the brain. The bottom line is that as you become hypothermic, your woozy brain may not be able to recognize what's happening.

For motorcyclists, the hazard is that a chilled, oxygen-starved brain starts making silly mistakes. At first, maybe it's just stopping the bike without putting a foot down, or cruising off the road onto the shoulder, then laughing giddily at the result. It should be obvious that in a hypothermic state, a rider can make serious or even fatal control errors such as crossing the centerline or going wide into a power pole. If you really begin to chill down, it may seem perfectly sensible to run off into a field, lean up against a tree, and go to sleep.

Insulate the Neck

One of the most important defenses against hypothermia is insulation of the head and neck. The major blood flow to the head means it can radiate a lot of heat, unless it is insulated. Insulating the neck slows down heat loss from those big arteries, and provides warmer blood to the brain. Neck insulation is vitally important to a motorcyclist because our heads and necks are hanging out in the windstream.

David L. Hough

You can lose up to 50 percent of your body heat from your head and neck if you don't add insulation.

The crushable EPS liner in a helmet is similar to a foam ice chest and helps insulate the head. But it's important to close off that gap between collar and helmet. Luckily for me up on the Angeles Crest, I was already wearing one of my favorite neck protectors: a windproof Aerostich Wind Triangle. Other riders prefer a synthetic fleece (Turtle Fur) neck tube, a heavy bandanna, or a balaclava that covers both head and neck. Whatever your choice of neck insulation, don't leave home without it.

Electric Heating

A fellow moto-journalist described his electric jacket liner as a quantum leap in cold weather riding gear. One reason an electric vest is so useful is that keeping the chest (and core organs) warm keeps more blood flowing to the extremities. Okay, I admit it. For years I was reluctant (or perhaps not sufficiently motivated) to buy an electric vest. After that chilly ride up on the Angeles Crest, I finally caved in. I've now got an electric cord hanging out of my suit, too.

However, I consider electric heating only a supplement to insulation, not a replacement, especially for trips into more remote areas where there aren't any warm restaurants to duck into. A little electrical failure can leave you freezing. For example, several years ago, Ironbutt rider and *MCN* contributor Mike Kneebone had a charging failure on the return trip to Fairbanks from Prudhoe Bay, Alaska, in freezing weather. To keep the engine running, he had to unplug all non-essential electronics, including the electric vest. His knees are still knocking.

Crash Padding

While I was up on the Angeles Crest at 7,000 feet, a motorcyclist on an old BMW Airhead eased by heading the other way with a full load of touring gear. On the black ice and snow, he was riding very cautiously and managing to keep the bike upright—at least while he was still within our view. But on such slippery conditions, there's a thin line between vertical and horizontal. Considering the risks of a fall-down, I'm sure he was glad to be wearing durable riding gear. If you have a choice in your cold weather crash padding, go for armor that's shock absorbing as well as abrasion resistant.

Rest Breaks

If you know you're going to be on the road all day in miserable weather, plan frequent rest breaks to warm up and refuel your body. The weather doesn't have to be freezing—you can become hypothermic at 50° F. It's not a bad idea to stop once every 2 hours or once every hour in really bad conditions. Get into a heated room, have a snack, and drink one or two glasses of water. Remember that the body burns food to make heat and gives off water vapor through breathing, so you need to replenish your water even if you've just ridden through a thunderstorm.

Hot soup is good for cold rides because it provides both nourishment and liquid. Coffee or tea is acceptable but go through the body faster than plain water. Definitely avoid alcoholic beverages. When you take a break, remove or unzip enough outer insulation to allow your body to soak up room heat, and move around to get blood circulating to the extremities again. Spend long enough inside to get warmed, refueled, rehydrated, and your body core cranking out heat again. That may take half an hour or longer if you've spent a long time in the cold. If you're still shivering, that's a sign your body core is bordering on the cold side. You need some additional warm-up time before continuing your trip.

Survival Tactics

If you know you're really freezing your gas up on the pass but there are no warm indoor facilities available, don't just keep riding until you pass out. Take steps to conserve heat while you're still shivering and still thinking. For instance, on my chilly ride, I could have stopped the bike out of the wind and huddled around the hot engine to soak up some heat. I could also have taken a better look at the map, thought seriously about how far I had to go, and decided whether to continue or make a U-turn.

Got some dirty socks in the saddlebag? Wear 'em over your thin gloves. Wrap a spare T-shirt around your neck. Put on your rain gear for a little added insulation. Buy a newspaper, and stuff it inside your jacket. If you're riding the freeway, stop at the rest areas and use the MPW (the Motorcyclist Power Warmer—otherwise known as a hand dryer). If you spot a Laundromat, take a break while your gear is cooking in a dryer. The point is don't just keep riding and hope you'll survive—take steps to conserve that important core heat while your brain is still functioning.

Yes, It's an Emergency

Frostbite and hypothermia are nothing to sneeze at. If you or your riding buddies appear to be confused, can't seem to stay awake, or start making silly riding mistakes, that's a sign hypothermia is setting in. Other symptoms include irritability, slurred speech, loss of attention, lessening of pain, and stiff muscles. The symptoms are similar to being intoxicated. Shivering is a good sign—it means your body is still trying to generate more heat. When shivering stops in cold conditions, you're in trouble. You may start to feel very relaxed and peaceful, with a reduction in muscle coordination and judgment.

When you recognize the symptoms of hypothermia in yourself or in others, take action. Get emergency assistance immediately. Hypothermia is a life-threatening emergency, even if the victim hasn't lost consciousness or crashed the bike yet. The top priority is getting the victim warmed up. If you're in an exposed outside location, get the victim off the bike and out of the wind, cover him or her with whatever insulation is available, and get a volunteer to share body heat. As soon as possible, get the victim into a warm room where the body core temperature can gradually return to normal.

Don't be bashful about flagging down a passing vehicle and asking for help. Yeah, we know you want to be independent out there, but when you're hypothermic, you can't just tough it out. Got a CB radio? Get on the horn and explain the situation. You may find truckers more sympathetic to your plight than other drivers.

Be cautious about applying external heat since you or the victim may not be able to feel burning temperatures. Remove wet clothing. Pat the skin dry, and wrap the victim in blankets if you have them, and cover the feet and head. Provide warm liquids such as soup, broth, or warmed milk to help restore the body's core heat. Avoid alcohol. It may take several hours for the body's core to regain normal temperature.

I remember a rainy ride years ago when I felt "funny" and finally recognized the symptoms of hypothermia. I made a U-turn, and rode back to the nearest motel where I could get a room, crank up the heat and huddle in blankets. Two hours later, I was barely getting over fits of uncontrollable shivering. Had I continued much farther, I might have become too confused to understand what was happening.

Keeping the Plastic Side Up

All right, let's assume you understand all about body protection, and you've got the gear and the tactics to avoid hypothermia. The next question is, how do you keep the plastic side up? On slick surfaces, the tires don't have as much resistance to sliding sideways. You know it's a thin line between a little slip-slide and an instant slam-dunk onto the ice. One of the advantages of a motorcycle is that you can put your tires over the most tractable surface. If the wheel tracks are polished ice, you can usually improve traction by moving over onto the shoulder, or riding between the wheel tracks.

On an icy road, look for the best traction such as that crunchy snow over at the edge.

Most of the same traction management tactics for dry pavement also apply to slippery roads. Ride as smoothly as possible, avoiding any sudden steering, throttle, or braking changes. Even at slower speeds, follow cornering lines that maximize the turn radius and minimize lean angle. For really slippery roads, slow down to an appropriate speed for the radius of curve and angle of camber. If you ride too fast for a flat curve, centrifugal force will pull the bike to the outside. If you ride too slow for a banked curve, gravity will pull the bike toward the inside. Speed is correct when the wheels are perpendicular to the road surface.

You can lessen the risk of falling on slippery surfaces by placing more of your weight on the footpegs rather than on the saddle. With your weight supported on the footpegs, you can lean the bike to keep the tires perpendicular to the road surface. That way, even when the bike slides sideways, it's less likely to slam onto its side. You may be tempted to put your feet down to help stabilize the bike, but if your tires don't have enough traction to hold the bike upright, your boot soles probably won't be any better. And if you do fall, it will be less painful if your ankles aren't in the way.

Remember, bridges stay frozen longer than the ground.

For a slippery downhill section, slow to a crawl, stay in a lower gear, and use both brakes lightly.

David L. Hough

Be aware that bridges freeze sooner and stay frozen longer than adjacent pavement, because the cold air can refrigerate the bridge from underneath as well as from above.

Approaching a downhill section, slow to a crawl at the top, stay in a lower gear, and drag both brakes lightly to hold back speed. If the tires start to slip, release the brakes and let speed increase. Riding uphill, approach a little faster at the bottom, then ease off the gas and let forward energy carry the machine up.

You can also increase traction by letting some air out of the tires, dropping pressure from, say, 35 to 20 psi. Soft tires are less likely to skid. Just remember to pump them up to normal pressure again after you get off the slick stuff.

The Third Wheel

If you tend to get motorcycle withdrawal symptoms from not riding during the cold winter months and think you can successfully stave off hypothermia and frostbite, maybe it's time to think about a sidecar rig. A sidecar outfit can slip and slide in circles without any major penalties such as falling down. That's a big reason motorcyclists who choose to ride during the winter months are likely to add a sidecar outfit to their stable of machines. But if you're thinking seriously about a sidecar, be aware that a motorcycle/sidecar combination is not just a regular two-wheeled motorcycle with this big *thing* on one side, but an entirely unique three-wheeled vehicle with different operating characteristics.

Night Owls

Remember old Paul Revere, pounding through the streets in the middle of the night? Wouldn't you think that Paul would have been smarter to do his fast riding in the daylight? Well, he had a schedule problem. The enemy was coming. He had to ride at night. At least he was riding a horse. Sometimes we motorcyclists choose to ride at night. We need to cover some miles and there isn't enough daylight. Or maybe we want to cross the Arizona desert at night rather than during the day beneath the scorching sun. Let's consider some tactics for night riding.

Stay Alert

The very first problem with night riding is that most of us have our bodies programmed for sleep at night. Unless we change our programming, it is extremely difficult to keep our eyelids propped open while staring into the darkness and listening to the hypnotic drone of the engine.

One way to change our body schedules is to change our sleep timing. For example, let's say I want to be at a rally in the next state by Saturday noon, and I can't leave until after work on Friday. Rather than hit the road immediately after work when I am already fatigued, I could go home, have dinner, and take a nap for a couple of hours. That not only gives me a fresh start, but allows me to avoid the evening traffic rush as well. Taking a nap before leaving on a trip eats up some time, but it may make the difference between being able to keep going at 3 A.M. or being too fatigued to continue.

Perhaps the most important night-riding tactic is to take frequent rest breaks. I make a point of stopping about every 60 miles, or once each hour. When I pull over for a break, I don't just sit on the bike and nod off; I get off and take a jog or do some exercises to get the juices flowing again. As a practical technique, stopping for a coffee break at a restaurant provides a good cue for a subsequent stop at a rest area. If you don't drink coffee, drink a couple glasses of water. Later, your bladder will make you an offer you can't ignore.

Even with some pretrip shuteye and frequent exercise breaks, my body sometimes rebels and refuses to stay awake any longer. I oblige by crashing on a picnic table at some reasonably safe rest area and catching a few z's. I don't take off my riding gear because it provides insulation. Usually, I wake up within half an hour or so, and can then continue. If there are suspicious-looking persons hanging around a rest area, I get just enough exercise to refresh myself and keep moving. If the situation seems reasonably safe, I lock the bike and put the ignition key in an inside pocket to discourage thefts. Some night owls just pull over and take a nap in the saddle.

The Eyes Lose

When riding at night, we need to maximize the view ahead to give us time to react to problems. Human eyes have some interesting characteristics that can get us in trouble, and we're not talking just about winking at the Sheriff's daughter. Be aware that every eye has a small blind spot, usually off to one side of center. It's something that can be measured during a good eye exam. Fortunately, the blind spot of your left eye doesn't overlap the blind spot of your right eye, so both eyes together can cover the whole field of vision. But, consider that a bug splat or a scratched face shield in a critical area can totally blot out a portion of the view. That's one good reason to keep your head and eyes moving, and your face shield clean.

Our vision also tends to fade as we get older, and most of us age another year about every twelve months. One common problem is floaters that drift around on the surface of the cornea and interfere with clear vision. As the years go by we may become near-sighted or far-sighted and need corrective lenses. Then we may discover that our reading bifocals have the wrong focus distance for reading our motorcycle instruments. If you have trouble reading the instruments, you might consider some special bifocals just for motorcycling.

Some people gradually lose peripheral vision, start to form cataracts, or lose the ability to distinguish colors. Because vision is so important to a motorcyclist, it is smart to have vision checked every couple of years, preferably by an eye physician (ophthalmologist) who is trained to spot problems as well as dispense lens prescriptions. If you know you have more trouble seeing at night, that's a good reason to avoid night riding altogether.

The eye can adjust to bright daylight by closing down the iris. But the vision receptors in the back of the eye also adjust chemically to the average light intensity. And that chemical change takes a while. Our eyes can't instantly adjust as we go from bright light to darkness to bright light again. This is most obvious to me during a night ride when I walk out of a brightly lit building and stumble blindly over a curb while my eyes are adapting to the dim nighttime level. That's one reason some veteran truckers wear sunglasses in restaurants at night, and why experienced night riders wait a few moments in the dark before riding away.

David L. Hough

Blinding Lights

Consider what happens when someone takes a flash photo of you while you're staring at the camera. The flash of bright light overwhelms vision for 3 or 4 seconds. The same thing happens when you ride from bright daylight into an unlit tunnel or at night when another vehicle goes by in the opposite lane. But what do you do when you're cruising down a narrow road and an oncoming vehicle approaches with its lights blazing at you? As the other lights approach, your eyes begin to adjust to the higher light level, and then when the vehicle passes, it takes several seconds to adjust back to low light again. In the meanwhile, you're almost blind.

FOCUS ON FOG LINE

As the other vehicle gets close, temporarily shift your focus to the white fog line along the right edge of your lane.

The trick is to avoid focusing on bright lights. Instead, as the other vehicle gets close, temporarily shift your focus to the white fog line along the right edge of your lane. The vision receptors in your peripheral vision may be temporarily overwhelmed, but your important central vision is saved for the dark road you need to see after the vehicle passes. If you haven't tried this before, it may be unnerving to look away from that other vehicle hurtling by you, but your peripheral vision is able to track movement and lane position, and your focus on the fog line helps you maintain your lane position. If you stare at the oncoming lights, you'll be temporarily blinded. It is far more important to be able to see that narrow bridge or that deer along the road in the critical seconds after the car goes by.

One other odd characteristic of human eyes is that color relates to distance perception. In other words, you might be able to accurately judge the distance from you to a green light, but not to a red light. As it happens, it is more difficult to judge the distance of a red light. Since taillights are red, it pays to occasionally count out your following distance in seconds, rather than assuming your eyes are giving you an accurate reading of distance. At night, you should avoid following another vehicle closer than 4 seconds.

Deer Strikes

Wild deer are a major nighttime hazard in many parts of the country. Deer often travel at night, feeding on the tender mowed grass on the shoulder of the road. Deer have no instinct to run away from bright lights hurtling toward them, but they do have an instinct to leap away from any predator that gets too close.

You won't see much of a deer at night except the eyes. Deer eyes reflect head-lights, looking similar to those white reflectors on roadside posts, except for one important difference: deer blink their eyes. When you see a reflector ahead that suddenly winks off and on again, it's probably an animal, and whatever it is, you don't want to hit it. Get on the brakes and practice your best quick stop, allowing the deer to leap wherever it wishes.

Keep on Truckin'

Commercial truckers keep on truckin' day and night. And these nights, truck traffic is more aggressive than ever. It is likely that today's big 18-wheelers will run a lot faster than you are willing to risk at night, which means you may be getting passed frequently. It is awfully easy for the trucker to lose track of a tiny two-wheeler in the mirrors, especially if the biker isn't helping. Give truckers a better chance of not squashing you by staying out of their blind spots and moving along fast enough when approaching hills that they don't need to pass you. When a trucker does pass you, it's difficult for the driver to see where you are in relation to the trailer. To give you some idea of what a truck driver can see in his mirrors, let's consider two day-time photos. Notice that the lead bike right alongside the cab isn't visible at all from the cab. The second bike is visible in the daytime, but consider what it would look like at night. At night, the driver can see the motorcycle headlight, but can't really gauge where the bike is in relation to the end of the trailer.

It is polite to flash your high beam once or twice as a signal that the end of the rig has cleared you, and it's okay for the trucker to pull back in the right lane. If the

Here are two motorcycles positioned alongside a typical tractor/trailer rig.

David L. Hough

From the cab, the driver can barely see the second bike.

trucker appreciates the courtesy, he will flash his running lights as a thank-you.

Night riding is one good reason to run with your CB radio on. Jabbering back and forth on the radio is a good way to stay alert. Just as importantly, the truckers you are talking to are more likely to be aware of you and cut you some slack. You might even hear some important information such as there's an accident ahead, your taillight has burned out, or your left saddlebag lid is open.

Drunks, Crooks, Creeps, and Weirdos

Remember that the most dangerous hours to be on the road are between 11 P.M. and 2 A.M., especially on weekends. Those are the hours when drinkers are heading home from the taverns. Your risks double during these hours. If you are making a long transit at night, be especially wary of cars and pickups in the outskirts of towns and cities. Drunk drivers tend to be erratic, wandering out of the lane, making sudden steering corrections, or suddenly jamming on the brakes for no apparent reason. Give the drunks a lot of room. If you're wired for communication, do the rest of us a favor and report the vehicle before someone gets killed.

Nighttime seems to bring out the creeps and weirdos. Some people are just looking for a confrontation. Psychologists suggest that about 1 out of 10 people are at least borderline unstable. Now and again, you may encounter an aggressive person who picks you as a potential victim. There is no lack of criminal behavior around. We all know to pull the key out of the ignition when going to the restroom, and to lock the forks while having coffee. But there are scams to watch for other than getting your bike ripped off. More than one rider has come out of a restroom to find a leather jacket has disappeared or the tent bag is missing.

As a general rule, don't flash the contents of your wallet near strangers or pay for anything with bills larger than a 20. I have had a $50 bill magically turn into a $20 bill while I was fumbling with my helmet and gloves. There is little you can do to recover from such scams once you allow them to occur.

While I am still rolling into the parking lot at a rest area, gas station, or restaurant, I scrutinize the people and vehicles already there. If I don't like the "smell" of the situation, I keep rolling through and look for a different place to take a break. For example, I would avoid a group of young men hanging around a car with others inside, especially if all eyes turn to check me out as I ride in. These kids may be friendly, but I don't need to find out. I avoid eye contact and just disappear.

One night at a quiet restaurant, a weirdo several seats away began to make insulting remarks about bikers. I was the only one within earshot wearing riding gear and carrying a helmet. I simply pretended I hadn't heard, avoided eye contact, finished my coffee quietly and confidently, paid my bill with a stone face, and departed. This guy was obviously looking for an argument or a fight, and I wasn't interested.

On the road, I maintain separation from other vehicles. I never allow someone to pace me in an adjacent lane, especially if anyone inside appears to be checking me out. I move out of the way of tailgaters, and I make a point of not cutting closely in front of other vehicles when I pass them. When I become aware of someone invading my space, I immediately take evasive action; changing lanes, dropping back, accelerating, or using a truck as a blocker.

Punching Through the Dark

Obviously, it helps to have some big candlepower punching through the darkness to illuminate the deer, potholes, and tire carcasses you might otherwise not see in time. If you're going to do any serious night riding, consider upgrading your lights. Replace a standard filament bulb with a 55 or 60 watt halogen bulb. If you already have halogen, think about increasing the wattage to 80 or 100, or add a driving light wired through a relay into the high beam circuit. Obviously, there are laws about such things. Check on legality before bolting on any extra lights, keep your headlight adjusted, and dim your brights courteously for approaching traffic. You don't want to find out the hard way that the guy you just blinded is driving a patrol car and that your new blue driving lights are not legal.

Over the years, I've had headlights suddenly fail at night. From personal experience, I can confirm that it's a little scary when your headlight suddenly quits while you're rounding a curve at night. Usually there has been some hint of a problem earlier, such as the headlight taking a second

Reflective patches on the back and legs of your riding suit can help other drivers see you at night.

to come on after the ignition is turned on, or both high and low beams occasionally coming on together. If your bike exhibits electrical problems, it would be smart to fix them before heading out on an all-night transit.

Don't forget about the rear end of your bike. Many motorcycles have only a single bulb for both taillight and stoplight. Either filament can burn out while you are riding along, and you won't know about it. As a test, park your bike on a dark street with the lights off and walk back for a look. Observe what happens when other vehicles pass by. That's what following drivers would see with your taillight burned out. If your bike looks a little gloomy back there, you might think about adding extra tail or clearance lights or at least additional reflectors. Does your jacket and helmet have

reflective patches on the back? Would it help to wear a reflective vest over your leather jacket at night? At least give other drivers a good opportunity to see you at night.

Body Care

Considering the increased hazards of night riding, it makes sense to wrap yourself in a good crash suit. If tonight is your turn to go sliding down the tarmac on some spilled diesel oil, you'll be a lot happier if you're wearing your best abrasion-resistant duds and a high-quality, full-coverage helmet when it happens.

Even during the summer, nighttime temperatures can be surprisingly chilly. Don't forget to wear insulation under your crash padding, slip on your neck-warmer or balaclava, and plug in that electric vest. There are enough problems to deal with while riding at night—you don't want to get hypothermic too.

One final note: It's always smart to avoid alcohol while riding a motorcycle, but it is critical at night. Not only does alcohol degrade your judgment, hearing, and muscle control, it also upsets vision, including the ability of your eyes to focus and adapt to changing light levels.

Obviously, the risks of riding increase after the sun goes down. If you have any reservations about being a night owl, just say no. Take a day off work and make that rally transit in the daylight or have an early snooze at night and get up at dawn to start that desert crossing. If you have a choice, choose daylight. If Paul Revere were around, he'd probably agree. Come to think of it, if Paul had had a good motorcycle instead of a horse, he could probably have warned all the troops and been in bed by sunset.

White Line Fever

Riding the white line between traffic lanes is a subject that motorcycle experts tend to avoid. First, white lining (lane splitting) in North America is acceptable only in a couple of states, and tolerated in and around a few congested cities. Sharing lanes is commonplace in countries such as England, Italy, and South Africa, but it's

David L. Hough

taboo here in most of the U.S. Second, riders who haven't experienced or observed skillful lane splitting typically have a built-in resistance to the subject, and any discussion seems to generate a pile of hate mail.

If you think the practice of motorcyclists squeezing between columns of cars on the freeway is completely stupid, dangerous, and unnecessary, you're not alone. Many riders live in areas where lane splitting is neither legal nor tolerated, and the whole idea may seem wrong. But lane splitting is a tactic used daily by many motorcycle officers, couriers, and commuters in congested cities where commuter traffic is so clogged that weaving through the stalled cars on a skinny motorcycle is the only way to get across town in a reasonable time frame. As congestion gets worse, you are more likely to see lane splitting by local motorcyclists, whether or not it's legal.

You may not have thought about white lining, and you may not want to. If lane splitting is illegal or socially unacceptable in your part of the world, and you don't ever intend to ride into a congested city where lane splitting is a possibility, the following discussion will not interest you; it will probably just increase your blood pressure. But if any of your future travels might take you into cities such as San Francisco, Los Angeles, or San Diego; or if you are planning a foreign trip that will take you to any of the major European cities, white lining is a tactic you should be prepared for.

Dangerous? Illegal?

Is white lining dangerous? Is it illegal? Let's deal with the danger issue first. Of course lane splitting isn't safe! Squeezing between moving cars and trucks with your legs in a position to get crushed is definitely risky. But before you reject white lining as just a foolhardy stunt pulled off by a few nutty Californians, consider the risks of getting knocked down by inattentive tailgaters while creeping along in stop-and-go freeway traffic. Is placing yourself directly between two larger vehicles ever safe?

For example, let's assume you are dribbling along in stop-and-go traffic in line with the cars. After thrumming your fingers on the brake lever for 5 minutes, traffic finally starts to move out, you roll on the gas, and then the brake lights come on again. Meanwhile, Crusher Cathy behind you in her big wheel SUV with the FOBYFO plates is closing fast on your taillight, and there's no escape.

In other words, if you are faced with the decision between creeping along in bumper-to-taillight traffic or white lining, the odds aren't necessarily better staying in line. It's a lot more difficult for Crusher Cathy to rear-end you while you're easing down the white line. While I'm not aware of any formal traffic studies that would shed some statistical light on the relative risks of creeping vs. lane splitting, a Santa Barbara BMW club did an informal poll of some local California Highway Patrol (CHP) officers, who confirmed that there were a lot more rear-end accidents than lane-splitting accidents involving motorcycles. You'll have to draw your own conclusions about the relative risks for you.

I'm not going to go out on a limb and suggest that lane splitting is a risk reduction advantage for everyone. I will suggest that proficient urban traffic warriors can split lanes without dramatically increasing the risks by following several ironclad rules. First, lane splitting must be both legal in the eyes of the law and tolerated by local drivers. Second, traffic must be moving slowly enough that surrounding drivers can't quickly change lanes. Third, the rider must have both sufficient mental skills to predict the movements of all surrounding drivers and control skills to accurately position the bike within inches of other vehicles, make sudden swerves, or manage quick stops with no warning.

Is It Legal?

You may have heard that white lining is illegal in your state or legal but only if you don't ride faster than 20 mph above surrounding traffic or only if all other vehicles are stopped. When we talk about what's legal, we need to remember that most of the traffic laws on the books were created well before Hitler commissioned the Volkswagen and are equally outdated. Some states cover the issue by making it illegal for two vehicles to share the same lane. Few states define *lane splitting* or *white lining.*

Since California represents a large percentage of the nation's motorcyclists, and because Los Angeles and San Francisco are well known for lane splitting, let's see what California laws say about lane splitting. Hey! there's nothing in the California vehicle codes about lane splitting. It's just not in there. The reality is that various existing laws potentially apply to what we (and the police) know as lane splitting. With no specific laws about splitting lanes, the responsibility falls on the individual police officer to find some code that can be used to keep you in line.

One handy law often used by the CHP is the Basic Speed Law, which states, "No person shall drive a vehicle upon a highway at a speed greater than is reasonable or prudent having due regard for weather, visibility, the traffic on, and the surface and width of, the highway, and in no event at a speed which endangers the safety of persons or property." (California code 22350)

That's a pretty handy law. Think about it: Since the wording includes "reasonable or prudent," that means Officer Ollie can make a judgment call. Even if you are well within the posted speed limit, Ollie can cite you for riding at a faster speed than surrounding traffic if in his judgment you weren't being prudent. And if you tick someone's mirror while trying to zip between two creeping cars, you could also be cited for "endangering the safety of persons or property."

California codes don't specify what is meant by "reasonable and prudent," so it's left up to the officers to interpret the law. A spokesman for the CHP suggested that when lane splitting you should go no faster than 10 mph over surrounding traffic. However, a general consensus among CHP motor officers hints that riding 20 mph faster than other traffic is "reasonable or prudent."

The second law often used by California officers refers to laned roadways. "Whenever any roadway has been divided into two or more clearly marked lanes for traffic in one direction, the following rules apply:

(a) A vehicle shall be driven as nearly as practical entirely within a single lane and shall not be moved from the lane until such movement can be made with reasonable safety.

(b) Official signs may be erected directing slow-moving traffic to use a designated lane or allocating specified lanes to traffic moving in the same direction, and drivers of vehicles shall obey the directions of the traffic device." (California code 21658)

Consider part a. It obviously encourages you to drive (ride) entirely within one lane or the other, but it doesn't say it's illegal to ride a motorcycle half in one lane and half in the other. More importantly, it gives the officer a judgment call over whether he thinks you moved out of one lane (or the other) "with reasonable safety." Changing lanes too often would be easy to construe as not using "reasonable safety."

The third law that can be applied to lane splitting is Turning Movements and Required Signals. "No person shall turn a vehicle from a direct course or move right or left upon a roadway until such movement can be made with reasonable safety and then only after the giving of an appropriate signal in the manner provided in this chapter in the event any other vehicle may be affected by the movement." (California code 22107) In other words, in traffic you are required to signal before moving out of one lane, and your signal (in the form of either a hand signal or a turn signal lamp) "shall be given continuously during the last 100 feet traveled by the vehicle before turning." (California code 22107) Of course, signaling doesn't make sense when splitting traffic, but Officer Ollie could cite you for failure to signal or for making more than one "lane change" within 100 feet.

To clarify the legal issues and police attitudes surrounding white lining, I stopped in at a district CHP office in the San Francisco Bay area. Two officers gave their unofficial interpretations of the laws plus their own personal advice. Officer A, who had no motorcycle experience, suggested that while lane splitting wasn't technically illegal, he felt it was never safe or prudent under any circumstances. Officer B, a motorcycle patrolman, believed that lane splitting was reasonably safe and prudent, providing that the motorcyclist used some common sense.

Think about that. If Officer A caught you lane splitting at 20 or 30 knots faster than traffic, he would probably cite you on all three counts. But tomorrow you might find yourself following Officer B on his police bike down the same white line at an even faster pace. The obvious conclusion is that whether or not you get cited for splitting lanes depends greatly upon the situation, the officer, and how you react to being stopped. Give Officer Ollie some lip, and you might morph a warning into a triple whammy ticket.

In some states (Florida, Washington, and New York, for example) it is illegal for two vehicles to share the same lane. In Washington, splitting lanes is rare. In New York, an increasing number of bikers flaunt the law and split lanes anyway. After all, how is a cop in a squad car going to catch a lane-splitter on a fast bike?

Most everywhere in North America except in California, lane splitting is considered illegal and is not expected and not tolerated by other motorists. Don't assume that lane splitting is legal somewhere just because you see some other motorcyclist doing it. What really counts is how the local police prioritize traffic problems. If you have any question about the legality of sharing lanes, call your state or city police and ask.

When Is Splitting Prudent?

Okay, let's get down to the nitty-gritty. Let's say your trip takes you into San Francisco, and you're motoring south on Highway 101 toward the Golden Gate Bridge

Lane splitting is least risky when traffic is so dense and moving so slowly that drivers can't make sudden lane changes.

at 7:30 A.M. All the lanes are full of cars and trucks creeping along a few feet a minute. In most states, motorcyclists can use the diamond, or high occupancy vehicle (HOV), lane, so that's the place to be. Even if the diamond lane is slowing down, it still makes more sense to stay between the lines as long as traffic is moving. But some cities don't have HOV lanes, or the HOV lane ends at a critical junction and all lanes become a continuous sea of cars, creeping along a few feet a minute, or even stopped for several minutes. Well before the bridge, the HOV lane ends. You can creep along with the cars, wearing out your clutch, or you can slip over onto a white line and keep moving. Other motorcyclists are doing it. It's your call.

Lane splitting is least risky when traffic is so dense and moving so slowly that drivers don't have room or maneuverability to make sudden lane changes. Let's be clear about this: if traffic is heavy but still jogging along at speeds of 30 to 40 mph, that's not the time to be splitting lanes. Other drivers can (and often do) jump from lane to lane, and you should never assume they see you coming in their mirrors, or that they will signal before yanking on the steering wheel.

In the Los Angeles basin, some bikers are zipping along the white lines 30 or 40 mph faster than moving traffic. Never mind that such antics are an advertisement for arrest—the point is that weaving through moving traffic really increases the risks of getting sideswiped by a driver who suddenly decides the next lane is the place to be.

If you do decide to split between traffic lanes, here are some suggestions:

DOs

★ **Maintain your awareness of the pattern of movements of vehicles ahead, especially those that are constantly changing lanes for no apparent reason.**

★ **Watch the head and eye movements of drivers ahead and to both sides of you to predict what they may do next.**

★ **Keep your speed down, cover your brakes, and apply the front brake lightly when approaching an erratic driver to reduce your braking reaction time.**

★ **Use more caution approaching interchanges and merging lanes.**

★ **Split between the lanes farthest left, not the right lanes where vehicles are more likely to merge.**

★ **Put your tires on either side of shiny lane markings such as those white plastic botts dots or glued-down plastic strips.**

★ **Monitor your rear view mirror for other, faster-moving riders or motor officers.**

★ **Watch for extended mirrors on trucks or vehicles towing trailers.**

★ **Politely move back into one lane if the lanes narrow or are blocked by wide vehicles.**

DON'Ts

★ **Don't try to force your way between vehicles if you think you can't get through without bumping a mirror or scraping a bumper.**

★ **Never position yourself between another vehicle and an off-ramp.**

★ **Don't move outside the lines defining the far left and far right of the roadway, except in emergency situations. Don't even think about splitting over the yellow lines into oncoming traffic (at least not in the U.S.).**

Urban Commuter Weapons

If you find yourself wandering north into Los Angeles traffic at 7:30 A.M. on your 1500 UltraTourer (complete with hard bags, engine guards, highway pegs, and double CB antennae), you can forget lane splitting. A motorcycle with full size hard bags is too wide, and it's too easy to bang into another vehicle. Rather than inch along in com-

Don't try to split lanes unless you have the right machine to fit through the slot.

muter traffic risking a rear-ender, why not make a side trip to the coast highway or have a leisurely breakfast at San Juan Capistrano? If you don't need to be in the big city at the same time as everyone else, why expose yourself to the frustrations and dangers of bumper-to-bumper traffic?

On the other hand, if you are making the same commute every day, why not consider a motorcycle that's a more ideal urban weapon? A narrow V-twin machine always makes a good commuter bike. What's more, you don't need 1000cc's to haul one human body through traffic, and you might not want a shiny temptation parked on the street all day. For commuting, consider a dual sport machine of 350cc to 650cc. Single-cylinder engines provide a narrow profile, a lot of low-end grunt, excellent economy, and less plastic to get scuffed or broken. The lightweight translates into easy handling.

The bottom line is that lane splitting by motorcyclists is becoming a fact of life in an increasing number of congested big cities, where too many vehicles try to share too little road space. But don't let anyone pressure you into lane splitting if it isn't legal in your area, if you aren't comfortable with your skill level, or if you aren't willing to accept what you perceive as an increased risk. Where the climate allows, a sharp motorcyclist on a narrow two-wheeler can carve through congested traffic and shave hours off an otherwise frustrating commute without significantly increasing the risks.

Keep your speed down. This rider is sailing by so fast, he's just a blur.

ROAD CAPTAIN

ONE
SEC.

TWO
SEC.

FORMATION
RIDE

Sharing

SHARING

the Ride

THE RIDE

RIDE CAPT
(parked

RIDER CAUSING PROBLEM

TOO SLOW   KEEP MOVING

RIDERS
EXPOSED
TO TRAFFIC

CHAPTER 7
SHARING THE RIDE

Batches of Bikers

Given my choice of traveling alone or in a group, I'd prefer to travel alone. When I'm cruising toward the horizon all by myself, life is much simpler. I only have to make decisions for one person. I can change plans instantly without having a roadside conference. When I'm ready to go, I just go. If I want to stop, I just stop. If I run out of gas, I—wait a minute! Who's going to help me if I'm all by myself? What's more, even if I don't have a bike problem, it gets kind of lonely after a while. When I peer over the rim of the Grand Canyon to absorb the awesome view or stop at an overlook with Mount Rainier gleaming in the twilight, I feel like sharing the experience with others.

I can remember some great group rides. Back in the "good old days," I used to lead the Puget Sound Motorcycle Tour, a three-day ride-to-eat bash where socializing was a big part of the fun. The final tour in 1976 had 120 participants. I've also had some great canyon rides with small groups of proficient riders, and I can remember a few spectacular rally parades where there were thousands of riders in one never-ending formation. The flip side is that I've also had some group rides that were dangerous, frustrating disasters. I suppose my preference for traveling alone isn't so much that I don't like groups, but that I'm cautious about joining groups that aren't organized well.

Daffy Don

I remember a small group of friends led by a rider who turned a day ride into a nightmare. Daffy Don didn't tell us where we were going or offer any advice about riding style or speed. Daffy didn't do hand signals or check his mirrors or use a radio. Taking off from a stop sign, he would peel out in front of a line of cars, leaving the rest of us riding over our heads trying to catch up. When Daffy instantly decided to make a fuel stop, he dove across two lanes of oncoming traffic without signaling, abandoning the rest of us in the left lane of a busy highway, hoping we wouldn't get run over by passing 18-wheelers. After a couple of hours of that nightmare, I purposely missed a turn and got lost from the group. Looking back, I wonder what took me so long.

Boss-Man Bill

By comparison, I remember a different group I joined for a ride through the mountains and canyons north of Los Angeles. Boss-Man Bill explained where we were going and maintained a pace in traffic suitable for the least experienced member. Bill also explained that once we turned off onto the narrow, twisty canyon roads, each rider should ride at his or her own pace. The more aggressive riders could zoom on ahead, enjoying the curves. Average riders could motor along enjoying the scenery. And the slower riders could bring up the rear, riding at their own pace. The key to keeping the group a group was that at critical intersections, Bill patiently held everyone up until the slowest rider caught up. That way, no one felt pressured to ride faster than their skill level just to avoid getting lost, and we could all socialize together at the rest stops. The difference between the two groups is that Daffy Don had no idea of how to lead a group. Boss-Man Bill had an excellent understanding of group riding dynamics and set some simple rules that allowed everyone to enjoy the ride without creating dangerous or frustrating situations.

The Ride Captain

Most of us have gone for a ride with two or three companions, although we may not have recognized them as group rides at the time. If you haven't had the humbling opportunity to lead a batch of bikers yet, you will, even if it's just one other machine. Whether the group is large or small, the ride will go better if you follow some common sense rules. Let's review some of the dynamics, consider some techniques for leading a formation ride, and evaluate some alternate ways to move a group of motorcyclists down a road.

Let's say you are asked to lead a club ride with a potential for twenty bikes. Hold it! Don't run away just yet. We'll talk you through it. You'll be the leader, or ride captain, but you should arrange for another experienced rider (or Tail-End Charlie) to bring up the end of the group. Now don't just fire up the engine and zoom into traffic just yet. First, here's a trick question for you: If you immediately pull out onto the street and accelerate up to 55 mph, how much time will pass before Charlie, who's nineteen bikes behind you, starts to move? Well, if there aren't any other vehicles on the road and the riders manage to follow you exactly 2 seconds apart, Charlie will be sitting in the same spot for 38 seconds. At 55 mph, you'll be 3,078 feet down the road before Charlie even eases out the clutch. What's more, if you maintain 55 mph, each following rider will have to go faster than 55 to catch up with you. If Charlie throttles up to 110 mph, he can catch up to the group in maybe 30 seconds. If Charlie is willing to risk only 80 mph, it will take him about a minute and a half to catch up, assuming you hold 55 mph. So you shouldn't be surprised if he's approaching meltdown long before the lunch stop.

Think of a group of motorcycles like a train with the cars hitched together by 10-foot bungee cords. That's why the sharp ride captain pulls out slowly and creeps along at 30 mph or so until Tail-End Charlie finally gets rolling. As the captain, you can either watch in your mirrors or listen for Charlie on the CB if you are wired for radio. Once the entire group is rolling, you can pick up the pace to cruising speed. To avoid holding up other motorists, it's wise to maintain at least the speed limit or the average speed of traffic if the road is busy. You don't want to encourage other motorists to attempt passing the group two or three bikes at a time.

When approaching a slower speed zone, the clever captain decelerates the group well before the speed sign, so that as the first bikes arrive in the slower zone, Charlie has also slowed and isn't having to stand his bike on the front wheel to avoid jamming it into someone's muffler.

The Formation

You've probably seen motor officers (and also big bad bikers) riding side-by-side in two columns. The side-by-side formation looks really impressive but limits both riders' maneuvering room. Even motor cops have had accidents where one bike has bumped into the one beside it. A staggered formation allows more maneuvering room.

In a staggered formation, you ride in the opposite wheel track from the rider

That group of riders coming down the hill are in pretty good staggered formation.

ahead of you. That is, if he's in the left wheel track, you take the right wheel track. The staggered formation moves the same number of bikes in the same road space as a side-by-side formation but allows machines in either column to temporarily move sideways to avoid a hazard such as a car door, pothole, or edge trap. The staggered formation also provides a slightly better view of other riders. If you follow 1 second behind the rider in the other wheel track, that puts you 2 seconds behind the rider directly ahead of you. Two seconds is the minimum distance to provide a space cushion while keeping the group as compact as possible. If everyone pays attention, it is easy to establish and maintain a staggered 2-second formation. It's the captain's choice to ride in the left or right wheel track. I prefer leading from the right track, which provides a better view of the formation to oncoming motorists.

The bad news is that we must be prepared for a Daffy Don to join the group. When you are signaling *start your engines,* Daffy will probably still be nattering with that chickie-babe on the pink cruiser, with his helmet and gloves left inside the coffee shop and his keys in an inside pocket.

During the ride, you can expect Daffy to constantly be drifting over into the wrong track with following riders all doing the lane samba trying to reestablish the staggered formation. If we know Daffy, he will drop back an extra 8 or 10 seconds, just enough to allow a following car to pass and cause the last three riders to miss the green light. And of course, Daffy will expect you to find a gas station in a few minutes, because he only fills up after his bike has gone on reserve, and that won't occur for at least another 5 miles. Don't think you can ignore him—he'll roar up through the formation to tell you when he's ready.

When It's Time to Go, GO!

My suggestion for ride captains blessed with a "Daffy," is to make it clear at the riders' meeting before the ride that you expect everyone to conform to the group. Explain your expectations for the ride, along with any rules you think would help. For instance, you might suggest that if any rider in the group can't maintain a 2-second following distance, it is acceptable for following riders to pass. Describe where the group will be stopping and where the ride is expected to end. Make it clear that when the group stops for fuel, everyone is expected to top up their tanks and drain their bladders.

When it's time to go, GO! When I was directing tours, I would post some odd start time, such as 8:17 A.M., and then leave exactly at 8:17 A.M. to make it clear that I wasn't kidding. Leave Daffy running around in circles back in the parking lot if he's not ready and keep the rest of the group moving when Daffy runs out of fuel during the ride. Don't let the Daffy Dons of the world ruin the ride for everyone else.

Getting Through the Green Light

When you're leading a group through controlled intersections in traffic, it is unlikely you'll get everyone through before the light turns red. There is a temptation for following riders to speed up and run the yellow to stay with the group, and riders at the tail end may panic and run the red, too. Explain at the start that riders are expected to obey all traffic signals, and that you will slow down as necessary to let everyone catch up.

In practical terms, with a series of signal lights the leader will get stopped as often as the tail end riders, and everyone will pass through all the intersections at about the same rate. I've been in some big groups where "escort" riders pull over to block the intersection and let everyone run the red light, but I don't recommend that tactic unless the escorts are on-duty cops. The real legal eagles tend to look askance at motorcyclists taking the law into their own hands.

All you usually have to do in a group ride through the city is keep speed in check as you leave town to give everyone a chance to catch up before you roll the group up to cruising speed. Once in a while you may have to creep along in the slow lane or even pull the group off the road to wait for riders caught at a long light. With a group of only five or six riders, it is easy to find a place to stop, and to get rolling again, but with groups of thirty or more, it is best to keep going at a slower speed and let the stragglers catch up.

Don't even think about stopping a group on the shoulder of a busy highway just because one rider has a problem. I've seen some extremely dangerous screwups where a whole gaggle of bikes has come to a screeching halt along a busy freeway because one rider dropped a glove. Yes, I'll admit to having been a "Daffy Dave" now and again, running the tank dry or having a flat tire. But I'd encourage you to avoid the embarrassment yourself, whether a leader or a follower.

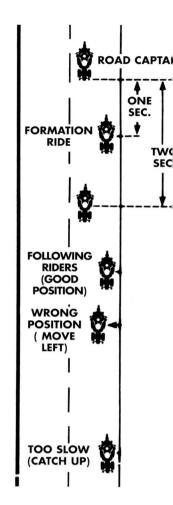

To avoid being a Daffy Don yourself, stay in your wheel track, and maintain your 1 second distance behind the rider ahead of you.

Communication

Even if you're just going for a ride with three or four friends, it's a good idea to have a riders meeting just before taking off to explain where you're going, what sort of formation you'll use, the meaning of various hand signals, the CB channel you'll be using, and what to do in case of a breakdown. That also establishes in everyone's mind who the leader, or captain, is. If you've made up route sheets, this is the time to hand them out. You, as captain, might also suggest that you be informed if anyone needs to split from the group, so you won't have to waste time looking for a "stranded" rider.

Clubs who ride together on a regular schedule often find it useful to have CB radios. The captain can explain what's coming up next, and Charlie can report what's happening back at the tail end. For example, Charlie can whine that he's had to stop with Daffy, whose dry battery has finally expired, and would the next participant with a radio kindly drop back and assume the Charlie job?

Signals

Hand and light signals are quick ways to communicate, whether or not you have radios. I once happened to pull into line behind a group of Gold Wing riders during our state's Governor's Run, and was privileged to observe their impressive group skills. The ride leader maintained a slow enough speed to allow the others to quickly catch up as they pulled onto the road. Once rolling, all riders maintained exact position and following distance in a nice staggered formation. At the sight of a pothole, the leader flashed his stop light twice, and all the others passed the warning signal back. Where the road narrowed, the leader held up one finger, and everyone shifted smoothly into single file. Through a twisty section, the riders cornered briskly at the same pace. Where the road widened again, the leader held up two fingers, and the group immediately changed back to a staggered formation. To change lanes on an urban arterial street, the leader positioned the group next to a space in traffic and signaled. Charlie immediately signaled, and the whole group moved over as one. Their ride truly was a performance.

Getting Stopped

Okay, you got the group rolling, you've managed to herd everyone through eighteen signal lights and twelve intersections without losing Daffy or causing an accident, and it's been a pleasant ride. Now, how do you get a long string of motorcycles stopped and parked for lunch without creating a traffic hazard? The most important consideration is having a parking area that's big enough for the whole group to ride into. You don't want to get half the group off the road, and leave the other half stranded out there in traffic like sitting ducks. The best scenario is when the group has space to motor into a parking lot and park side-by-side to conserve space. Riders should pull up to the left of each rider ahead, so that everyone can immediately back into the parking space without waiting. When your group pulls into a parking lot, don't try to be creative. Follow the parking drill with everyone else. Don't ride up behind the next rider, but pull alongside to the left, and immediately roll your machine back into the parking space. Creative parking decisions tend to slow down the process and leave tail-end riders still trying to get off the street. With a little experience, the whole group can get parked quickly, which helps move everyone off the road efficiently.

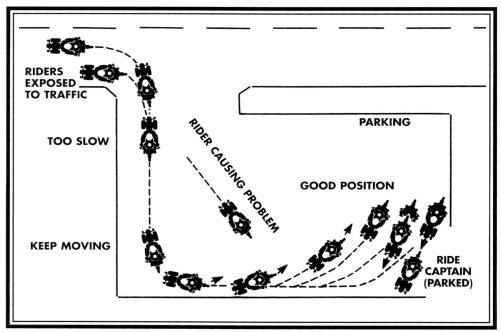

RIDERS EXPOSED TO TRAFFIC

TOO SLOW

KEEP MOVING

RIDER CAUSING PROBLEM

PARKING

GOOD POSITION

RIDE CAPTAIN (PARKED)

Locate a parking area that's big enough for the whole group and don't leave the last riders exposed to traffic.

The larger the group, the more important it is to have specific stops arranged. When I lead groups of eighty to one hundred riders, I ride the entire route prior to the tour, both to identify specific problem areas such as construction zones and to find suitable parking areas. If I'm planning to stop for lunch with more than a dozen riders, I also either make arrangements for a meal or call ahead to give the restaurant an opportunity to have enough help on hand. Keep in mind that if you are making arrangements for a really big group, you'll need a lot of help to direct traffic.

A large group takes a lot of organization.

Back in the Pack

Group rides are a lot more enjoyable when the leader is more like Boss-Man Bill and less like Daffy Don. If you've never ridden in a group, make a point of staying close to the ride captain rather than at the back of the pack. It's a lot easier to maintain speed and position if you are no more than two or three bikes from the front. Fill your tank and empty your bladder before the scheduled departure time. When the leader puts on his helmet and gloves, get your key in the ignition and get ready to roll.

Once underway, maintain the requested interval and lane position. Try to avoid drifting back and creating a big hole in the formation. If someone ahead suddenly wakes up to being in the wrong track and moves over, every following rider should immediately reestablish the proper staggered formation. Watch the leader for hand signals. When riders ahead give warning signals, pass the signal back down the line. If another rider has a problem and pulls over, stay with the group and keep rolling unless the leader also pulls over or asks that you stop to help. It's Charlie's job to deal with the problem.

Alternate Ways to Move a Group

When we think group ride, we usually imagine a long string of bikes in formation, but there are other ways to move a group down a road. One technique I have used is printing up route sheets that detail the route and schedule. It's relatively easy to make up route sheets by snipping pieces out of an official state tourist map or printing maps from the Internet and adding schedule information alongside. Poker runs and mystery tours are different forms of a group ride, where everyone does their own navigating and rides at their own pace.

Group Rides

There are forms of group rides where everyone rides at his or her own pace and does his or her own navigating.

★ **Gypsy tours** are multi-day events during which riders travel to different towns along a route made known to the participants, usually by a route sheet.

★ **Mystery tours** typically have checkpoints where a rider receives a clue and information that helps him or her get to the next checkpoint.

★ **Poker runs** have checkpoints where each participant draws a card, which is added to the rider's list of cards to determine a "hand" by the end of the ride.

Try It, You Might Like It

If you've been avoiding group rides like the plague, consider joining up once in a while as part of your skill improvement program. Maybe you'll even discover some fellow enthusiasts you enjoy riding with. If none of the ride captains measures up to your standards of group leadership, maybe you'll just have to be the ride captain and show them how it's done. But remember, riding in a group once in a while doesn't mean you can't go droning off toward the horizon by yourself when you feel like it.

The Second Rider

I've ridden motorcycles in some scary situations. Once, crossing Nebraska, I faced two converging tornadoes. In Colorado during a torrential downpour, I sprinted into a restaurant a few seconds ahead of a lightning bolt. In a canyon in the French Alps, I barely managed to swerve out of the way of an Austin mini driver in a four-wheel drift around a blind turn. I've narrowly avoided a moose collision in British Columbia, been surrounded by longhorn steers in Utah, chased by baboons in South Africa, and blinded by freezing sleet in Oregon. Been there, done that, got the Scary Ride T-shirt.

But the scariest rides of my life were those rare occasions when I had to thumb a ride on the back of someone else's bike. *Hey! There aren't any handlebars back here—what am I supposed to hang on to? Where's the brake lever? I can't see where the bike is headed! I don't know which way we're going to lean. Uh-oh, I think I'm slipping off the back! Slow down!*

Most motorcyclists I know ride solo most of the time. Sure, there are couples who ride two-up on every trip, but most riders seldom carry a passenger. So when we do ask someone to share the bike, we may forget to explain what he or she needs to know or forget ourselves that the additional load will require different riding tactics. Let's review some of the basic concerns for carrying passengers.

David L. Hough

The Safety Briefing: Informing the Passenger

When you board an airplane, you assume the pilot knows what to do, but the passengers may need some coaching about whether the flight will arrive in time for connecting flights, and whether it includes breakfast. First-time passengers may need some coaching about things like emergency exits, toilets, and seat belts. When you have a passenger lined up to ride on the back of your saddle, it's part of your job to provide the necessary riding gear, explain how to climb aboard, discuss what to do when the bike leans, and suggest how to communicate at speed. After a few rides, passengers will know what's expected.

For a novice passenger, you should explain the need for riding gear that is warm and durable, including a heavy jacket, leather boots to prevent burns on hot exhaust pipes, gloves to protect the hands, a helmet to protect the brain, and goggles to protect eyes. You don't need to bring up the possibility of rain if the weather that day looks sunny. You should discourage your passenger from wearing any potentially harmful clothing such as a long, floppy scarf, which could wrap around a helmet in a crosswind; a long cowboy coat, which could snag its tails in the rear wheel; boots with dangly things that could catch on a footpeg; or spiked heels, which could melt onto the mufflers.

For first-timers, it's also helpful to explain that you will saddle up first and get the bike balanced, and then the passenger can stand up on the left passenger peg and swing onto the saddle. Mention that motorcycles lean into corners, leaning over is normal, and the passenger should lean with the rider. There are a number of other little points you could cover such as the passenger keeping feet on the pegs when stopping and that you will do the hand signals, thank you. New passengers want to do the right thing and will probably appreciate some coaching.

When you have a passenger lined up to ride up on the back of your saddle, it's part of your job to provide the necessary riding gear, explain how to climb aboard, discuss what to do when the bike leans, and suggest how to communicate at speed.

Handling Changes

What's most important for the rider is that a second person on the bike not only increases the weight but also relocates the center of mass and adds sail to the rear of the bike, and those changes affect the rider's control of the machine.

David L. Hough

Acceleration, braking, and cornering tactics all change, not just because of the additional mass and where the weight is loaded on the bike, but also because the second rider's weight can shift around.

Quick Stops

For example, consider what happens during hard braking. There is more total mass to stop, so you can expect a somewhat longer stopping distance. With more weight on the rear wheel, more rear braking can be used in a quick stop or on slick pavement. On a machine with integrated brakes, you won't notice much difference, except that it takes harder braking and more distance to stop quickly. More weight means increased traction, so you might think the limiting factor would be brake efficiency. But what you will discover when you try a quick stop is that the passenger slams forward during hard braking, limiting how much brake effort you're willing to apply.

Once when riding with my wife on the back, I observed what appeared to be a brown log in the left ditch. But as we got closer, the "log" suddenly raised up its antlers, leaped up onto the pavement, and clattered into a U-turn. I immediately applied the brakes, but my wife wasn't prepared for a quick stop and slammed into my back, pushing me forward onto the tank. Even though she is a relative lightweight, I had to modulate the brakes well short of maximum, just to keep from being pushed into the handlebars. We managed to miss the deer by inches, but the lesson to me was clearly that I must always allow more stopping distance when carrying a passenger. Remember, the passenger can't see ahead as well as you can, doesn't know when you are going to suddenly squeeze the lever, and during a stop doesn't have much to brace against accept you.

If you regularly carry a passenger, you might consider practicing quick stops with the passenger aboard. Some training sites allow passengers to be carried during the practice exercises. The typical drill is for the rider, you, to take the course with no passenger, and then repeat the same exercises with a passenger the next day. Passengers may find it helpful to listen to the classroom presentations, too. It helps them understand why you're doing what you're doing, and why you must concentrate so much on traffic and surface hazards.

Acceleration

When accelerating, you have more control over the situation because you can roll on the gas smoothly to help the passenger stay put. Heavyweight touring machines with top boxes and passenger backrests provide a relatively secure perch for the second rider, but many machines don't offer much in the way of passenger handholds. Those silly straps that manufacturers used to stretch across the middle of the saddle were supposed to be grab handles for passengers, but only lawyers could figure out how human beings might brace against a quick stop with their hands between their knees. Some machines provide solid grab handles around the rear of the saddle, but it is still difficult to hold on if the bike is accelerating quickly.

Just remember that your passenger may not have much except you to hold onto. You can suggest that they grasp you lightly around your waist. If your passenger gives you a little squeeze while riding along in a beautiful sunset, the message is probably, *Gee, Honey, I'm glad you brought me along.* But if your passenger suddenly strangles you in a bear hug as you roll on the gas, it's probably a sign you are getting a little too aggressive with the throttle. If you want to enjoy the company of a second rider, you've got to make him or her comfortable, which really means riding more conservatively than if you were all by yourself.

Cornering

When you are carrying a passenger with little motorcycle experience, don't be surprised when they panic as you lean the bike over into the first sharp turn. Of course it will be your turn to panic if the passenger manages to lean toward the outside while you're trying to get the bike leaned over toward the inside. The wise rider takes corners sedately for the first hour or so to allow the novice passenger some time to adapt to this leaning business and for the rider to adapt to cornering with the additional mass.

If your bike already has limited leanover clearance, don't be surprised when the bike starts making sparks while cornering with a passenger. That's because the additional weight of the second rider compresses the rear suspension more, reducing leanover clearance. You can reduce the touchdown problem by following a larger radius cornering line, by reducing entry speed from that of solo riding, and by rolling on the throttle more as the bike is leaned over. But if your machine makes sparks too easily, that's a message to get the bike jacked up off the pavement a little more.

First of all, check your tire pressures. When carrying extra weight, your tires need extra pressure. Typically, the tire chart for your bike will suggest 3 to 6 psi more pressure in the rear tire. If you've already been lazy about checking your rear tire pressure, you could easily be 10 pounds under "passenger" specs.

While you're checking the bike, take a close look at the rear suspension. The springs on your shocks may have been on the weak side right off the showroom floor, and most springs sag a bit as the mileage builds up. If you have an agile and cooperative passenger, you can check the shock preload by measuring the travel with a tape measure. With the bike unladen, measure the spring length. Then measure again with both rider and passenger weight on the machine. Ideally, the springs should compress only about halfway to the limit with the full load supported on the wheels.

If the shocks are close to bottoming out just sitting there, jack the spring preload to maximum, and check again. If that doesn't get the preload back into an

David L. Hough

acceptable range, it's time for stronger shock springs. Shock suppliers usually can provide either similar-looking but stronger springs or dual rate springs. There are also specialty shocks with multiple springs for a wider range of preload adjustment and spring spacers for front forks. The suspension specialists are always willing to offer advice. Talk to your parts person, or call the aftermarket suspension people directly. Be prepared with the model number and year of your bike, and the weight you intend to carry, including rider, passenger, and typical baggage.

Hills

Hills can provide some surprises, too. Consider where a passenger's weight is positioned on the bike. Typically, the second rider is sitting over the rear axle. On level pavement, that means the rider's weight isn't applying any load on the front wheel. But when the front end is pointed downhill, more of the passenger's weight is transferred to the front wheel.

When you are braking on a downhill section, the weight shift forward will increase front wheel traction. Obviously, the brakes have to overcome the forward energy of both riders and machine. What's less obvious is that when pointed downhill, the weight of the riders is being pulled downhill by both forward energy and gravity. And kinetic energy increases dramatically with increased speed.

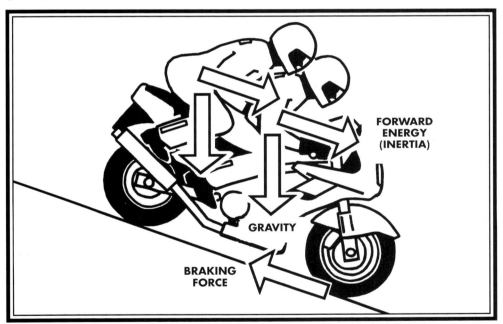

When braking on a downhill section, the brakes have to overcome both forward energy and the downhill pull of gravity.

If you're approaching a steep downhill turn, you don't want to delay braking until the last second and then find you can't get the bike slowed to an acceptable entry speed for the corner. More than a few riders of heavy touring machines have made sight-seeing excursions into the weeds when they discovered they couldn't get the overloaded bike down to speed on the available pavement.

When pointed uphill, it's a different ball game. Remember, if the passenger is perched over the rear axle on the level, then on an uphill slant the passenger's weight may actually be centered behind the rear axle. And the rider's weight will also be shifted toward the rear wheel. That's why a bike with a passenger aboard wants to do a wheelie when you're trying to get started uphill.

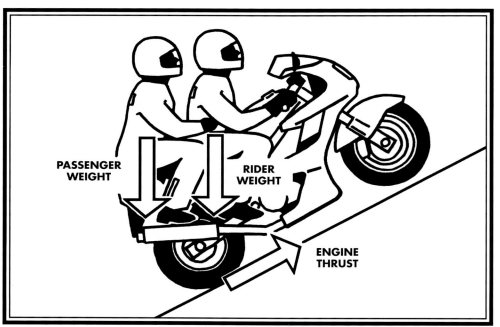

With a passenger aboard, the bike may do a wheelie as it's starting uphill.

The wheelie problem can be even worse when there is a heavy load carried behind the passenger. If you find yourself in a situation where the front wheel starts to float as you ease out the clutch, try to get some weight shifted forward. You can try standing on the pegs and leaning up over the tank, but that's not easy when balancing the bike with a passenger. If you encounter this situation more than occasionally, you should take steps to unload the rear of the bike, one way or the other.

For instance, consider what you're carrying in the top box or saddlebags. Perhaps heavier objects could be moved to the front of the saddlebags or to a tank bag. Maybe you don't really need to carry that set of $1/2$-inch drive sockets strapped over the taillight. Or maybe it's time for a bike with a longer wheelbase.

Even if the bike doesn't show any air under the front wheel when the bike is climbing uphill, be aware that the weight shift rearward unloads the front tire, and that decreases traction. In an uphill turn, the front wheel has more of a tendency to drift wide.

You can help maintain front tire traction in uphill corners by entering at a slightly higher speed than in a comparable level corner so that the machine's forward energy continues to pull it uphill. Remember, rolling on the gas tends to lift the front end, so you don't want to roll on just where you're also leaned over. If the machine's inertia can carry it uphill, you won't have to roll on the gas in mid-turn. That's a good tactic when riding by yourself, but when carrying a passenger it is much more important.

Carrying a passenger, the front tire has reduced traction in uphill turns.

David L. Hough

Carrying Children

If you're suddenly faced with the dilemma of choosing between children and a motorcycle, the obvious win/win situation is to take the kid along on the ride. The problem with that is that children younger than perhaps nine or ten years old tend to be unequipped physically or mentally to stay put on the back of a motorcycle at speed. The potential problem for the adult rider is that even a minor injury to a child from motorcycling will probably spell the end of the ride for another sixteen years or so. Statistically speaking, very few children under age twelve are injured in motorcycle accidents, but if you're the unfortunate parent or grandparent holding onto the handlebars when a kid gets hurt, you're going to receive more trouble than you bargained for.

A variety of imaginative approaches have been invented for carrying children on the back of motorcycles, but none of them are foolproof. The most obvious hazard is that the child can fall off. So there are belts with passenger handles for a child to hold onto, and belts that strap the child to the rider. Providing a belt with handles for the child, you'd have to assume the child can stay awake and hang on tightly enough to stay put during any aggressive maneuvers. If the child is belted to the rider, and the bike goes down, the child gets dragged along with the rider. Either way, there is the potential for injury.

The safer approach to carrying children is to go for a sidecar outfit. Not only is it unlikely a child will fall out of a sidecar after falling asleep, but in the event of an accident the child has some protection by the sidecar body and chassis. Most importantly, a three-wheeler is much less likely to take a spill if the tires lose traction on a surface hazard, so there is much less risk of anyone taking a tumble.

If you're faced with the dilemma of making a choice between children and motorcycling, maybe it's time to look into a sidecar.

If you aren't quite willing to risk carrying a child on your two-wheeler but you're willing to learn how to drive a three-wheeled motorcycle, maybe it's time to look into a sidecar. Be aware that driving a three-wheeler is an entirely different experience from driving a motorcycle but fun in its own way. There are no statistics available from the insurance industry, the federal government, or the motorcycle industry in the U.S. that give us any conclusions about the lowered risk of sidecars, but veteran sidecarists believe outfits are inherently less risky than two-wheelers. If you're a parent facing the motorcycling vs. child dilemma, you'll have to make up your own mind.

Whether you're intending to carry an occasional passenger or your significant other wants to go along on every ride, the experience is bound to be more fun if everyone understands what's needed and if there aren't any hazardous surprises. If your life has been getting a little boring recently, I highly recommend a ride on the back of someone else's saddle to gain a little experience and a lot of feeling for what it's like to be the second rider. After that, you'll probably appreciate a conservative rider who takes off gradually, stops smoothly, and corners uphill or down without any unplanned sight-seeing excursions off the road.

Let's Get Loaded

A few decades ago, while on a gypsy tour of Northern California, our group was temporarily delayed by a road construction project. Since the road would be closed for an hour or so, most of us took advantage of the break to do laundry and bike maintenance. I was standing around "kicking tires" with Hawgbone Hal. Hawgbone was snorting about the extra "junk" his "old lady" felt were necessities on a motorcycle tour: hair dryer, travel iron, portable radio, high-heeled shoes. I understood his concerns. The amount of weight a motorcycle can carry is limited. My wife and I had wondered whether we should bring our heavyweight rain gear in addition to the load of camping gear and clothing. We were already pushing the weight limits on our Moto Guzzi Ambassador. And Hawgbone had a homemade top box the size of a steamer trunk on the back of his Harley-Davidson.

While we were waiting for our significant others to finish the laundry, Hawgbone decided it would be a good time to adjust his drive chain. From the bottom of his monster top box, he started extricating tools, including a full set of 3/4-drive sockets, an impact driver, a large-size locking pliers, a monster adjustable wrench, a selection of drift pins, and a hydraulic jack. My jaw dropped open. Peering over his shoulder, I could see he still had a three-jaw bearing puller, a serious ball-peen hammer, and a full set of combination wrenches in there.

Here I'd been concerned about an extra 5 pounds of rain gear—and this XXL-size rider had brought along an extra 50 or 60 pounds of serious tools! I don't know what the suggested weight limits were for his H-D, but Hawgbone was so far over any reasonable limits he gave new meaning to the term "gross."

If you ride a sport or sport touring bike, you'll have to work hard to exceed the gross vehicle weight restriction (GVWR) for your machine. Sportbikes don't provide a big enough platform to attach much luggage, and a heavy passenger probably won't become a regular on a tiny "pillion pad." You, your tank bag, and your throw-over saddlebags will probably be within the limits, even if you are 6 foot 6 inches and 240 pounds. But, if you often carry a second rider plus a pile of camping gear, you can be close to the limits. And if you or your passenger are packaged in the XL or XXL sizes, you may be well over the GVWR for your bike, even with empty saddlebags.

Gross Vehicle Weight Restriction

Motorcycle manufacturers determine the maximum weight they'd like to see you carry on a specific machine. *Gross weight* is the total load of motorcycle, passengers, fuel, and gear, as weighed when riding across a truck scale. The permissible gross weight, or GVWR, is determined by such things as frame and wheel strength, steering geometry, suspension damping capacity, braking systems, and tire load ranges.

Carrying Capacity

The GVWRs are a quick way to compare different motorcycles, but GVWRs aren't the bottom line. You need to subtract the "wet" weight of the motorcycle from the GVWR to get the maximum load you, your passenger, and your gear can share. The wet weight includes battery, fuel, oil, and fluids, but not passengers or baggage. For example, the GVWR of the 1996 Harley-Davidson FXDS Convertible is listed as 1,086 pounds. Subtract the wet weight of 675 pounds, and that leaves you a carrying capacity (CC) of 411 pounds. That 411 pounds is the maximum load for you, your passenger, and your gear, including the hair dryer, tent, hydraulic jack, and whatever else you intend to carry on board.

When you add a second rider, 411 pounds gets used up quickly even though it may sound like a lot of carrying capacity. Without getting too precise, let's say my weight is, ah, around 200 pounds wearing leathers and helmet, and my wife is maybe 135 pounds. So we add up to 335 pounds. Subtract that from the carrying capacity for the bike, and we can strap on an additional 76 pounds. If we stuff 20 pounds of clothing into each saddlebag, we can pile on another 36 pounds of camping gear, tools, etc. before we exceed the limits set by Harley-Davidson.

FXDS Convertible, GVWR	1,086 lb.
Minus wet weight	675 lb.
Maximum carrying capacity	411 lb.
Big Dave	200 lb.
Little Diana	135 lb.
Clothing	40 lb.
Other gear	36 lb.

Get out Your Calculator

For comparison, let's check the carrying capacity for a few other bikes.

MACHINE	GVWR (lb.)	CC (lb.)
1996 Kawasaki ZX-7R	915	397
1997 Honda Valkyrie GL 1500C	1,133	412
1996 Suzuki DR650SE	770	412
1996 Suzuki GSX-R750	870	419
1996 BMW R1100RT	1,080	458
1997 Kawasaki Concours	1,118	500

Just looking at motorcycles parked next to the curb, you'd think the giant-killer Honda Valkyrie would be the champion weightlifter, eh? Does it surprise you that the little Suzuki 650 dual sport has the same CC as the Valkyrie? Or that the Concours can carry 100 pounds more gear than a 7X-7R?

We're not trying to step on anyone's toes here but just point out the significance of comparing the GVWR and carrying capacity numbers when you go shopping for a bike, especially if you intend to do a lot of long-distance touring, two-up or with heavy camping loads.

How Much Can I Overload?

Obviously, as Hawgbone Hal demonstrates, you can overload a machine and still keep it more-or-less under control. But you'll have to accept some responsibility for exceeding the limits. First of all, overloading will affect reliability. Hawgbone has to adjust his drive chain more frequently because that chain wasn't designed to handle the full-throttle power required to push an overloaded machine up steep hills and through gnarly detours. His wheel bearings, fork sliders, shock absorbers, and brakes all are stressed more than the designers had intended. Second, overloading affects handling. Hawgbone barely managed to keep his groaning machine from wallowing into a mud bath as we struggled through a detour. And after we got through the dirt, the bottomed-out machine would make sparks if leaned over even modestly in the corners.

So—big deal, you may be thinking. *We can live with a little less cornering speed, and a few more jolts, right?* Obviously, the springs will sag more under a heavy load, eating up ground clearance in the corners and bottoming once in a while on sharp bumps. The ride might turn into a big deal if the corner ahead happens to be one of those decreasing-radius killer corners, where reduced ground clearance makes the difference between staying on the pavement and taking an excursion through the underbrush.

What's more, suspension helps maintain traction. Shock and spring suspension systems are designed to maximize traction with the shock absorber piston in the middle of the suspension range. What we mean by *maximize* is that the tires can keep a constant grip on a bumpy road. If the tires can't get down into holes or up over bumps quickly enough, they can't maintain constant traction. For instance, if the shock piston is already down at the end of the cylinder when the wheel hits a bump, the wheel can't absorb the jolt. The wheel can only try to lift that end of the bike. The resulting shock can bounce the tires right off the pavement, reducing traction to zero for a moment. So we're not talking just bouncing kidneys here. We're talking bikes levering themselves off the pavement, tires losing traction, and maybe even axles or shock rods bending or the frame cracking. We could go on, but you probably get the idea that GVWR and CC are important numbers we shouldn't ignore.

Staying Within the Limits

There are several techniques for staying within the weight limits. First, pay enough attention to the carrying capacity when buying a motorcycle to be confident it will handle the loads you expect it to carry. If you weigh less than 250 pounds and primarily ride alone and with maybe just a tank bag of extra gear, you won't have to worry about the limits. Even small machines such as the Honda 250 Rebel have CCs in excess of 300 pounds. But if you and your passenger add up to some impressive weight and your style of motorcycling leans toward long-distance touring, you ought to be more concerned about the GVWR than the horsepower and torque charts. *Motorcycle Consumer News* includes GVWR and carrying capacities in motorcycle reviews to help readers make informed decisions. You'll also find the GVWR on the machine, usually on a decal under the seat.

Prioritize, Downsize

When you are getting ready for a long trip, it is easy to take too much. Wise trip advice: Take twice the money and half the gear. One tactic for piling less gear on a bike is to prioritize. Make a list. Or, even better, put everything you think you must have in one pile on the floor. Put the items you think you might need in a second pile. Put the nice-to-have-along items in a third pile. Of course, if you will be carrying a passenger, each rider will have separate piles of gear. Now take a good look at those gear piles, starting with the must-have pile. What can you reduce in size and weight? You might consider spending some time in an outdoor store looking at compact, lightweight solutions to tents, sleeping bags, and cooking utensils. If you'll have a second rider aboard, compare the items and see if you can eliminate duplicates. For example, maybe toothpaste is a must-have item, but you may not need to carry two economy-size tubes. And do you really need two full 35mm SLR photo outfits with 600mm telephoto lenses, or can you get along with one little shirt-pocket range finder camera? Does a weekend trip require the six-person stand-up-to-put-your-pants-on tent, or can you make do with a cramped little two-person tent? If you can reduce the size and weight of the items in the must-have piles, you may have room for a few more might-need and nice-to-have-along items.

When you have pared down the gear, weigh the load on the bathroom scale. Don't forget to include any extra tools or spare parts. You should have some idea of the carrying capacity of your motorcycle. If you are stretching the limits, you can forget the nice-to-have-along things and start paring down the might-need piles. Of course the next question is, how are you going to pack it all on the bike?

Packing the Bike

When you begin stacking everything on a bike, where you pack it is important. Loading extra weight far from the motorcycle center of gravity will contribute to sluggish handling. You could tie a big suitcase on the back, hanging out over the taillight, but saddlebags are a better location for heavy objects, because they are closer to the bike's CG. A tank bag is an excellent place to carry weight but be smart about what you put in it because you may have to get up close and personal with whatever is in the bag should an accident occur.

Big touring machines often have a capacious box over the rear end called a touring case, top box, or scoot boot. You may also have big chrome racks attached to the top of the saddlebag and top box lids to which you can tie even more gear. Hold on, though. If you check the suggested weight limits for bags, boxes, and racks, you may find the limits surprisingly low. One familiar chrome rack for Honda Gold Wings lists a 3-pound limit. What the manufacturers are trying to tell you is to keep the weight down even if the volume is large. Load heavier objects in the saddlebags, lighter things in the top box, and only the lightest gear strapped on the bag racks.

Tie One On

If you're a novice motorcycle traveler, consider how you're going to package the load to carry it on the bike. You don't want to have your underwear falling off on the freeway or getting soaked in a rain shower. If you don't want to install hard bags, take a good look at the various fabric bags on the market. Whatever system you choose, be sure it can be secured in place and doesn't get tangled in the running gear or sag down onto the mufflers.

If you're traveling without a passenger, the rear half of the saddle is a good location for larger, heavier gear because the bike is designed to carry passenger-sized loads there. When I'm riding by myself, I often lash a heavy fabric duffel bag over the back of the saddle. Other travelers prefer an upright pack, which secures over their sissy bar.

The standard device for holding loose items on a motorcycle is the elastic bungee cord. I've learned to dislike bungee cords because of their bad habits and limitations. For example, a long bungee stretches as the bike goes over a whoop-de-do, allowing something on the bottom of the pile a chance to slip out. I'll leave it to your imagination to consider what happens when the hook on a loose bungee strap gets snagged by a wheel spoke.

Flat straps don't stretch, so you need to have straps of the correct length with suitable buckles to attach them. One smart design for straps is to sew a long closed loop in one end, which can be secured around a frame tube without the need for any paint-scratching hooks.

No offense, bungee snappers, but I've gone back to an earlier technology: rope. A rope can be tied around a frame tube or rack. It won't stretch out when you go over a bump. It can be tied around itself. A piece of rope coils up easily and stows without snagging everything in sight. It's cheap. And you only need one length of rope rather than a collection of different lengths. I prefer 1/4-inch braided nylon ropes about 6 feet long. Okay, you have to know how to tie knots. If that's a technological problem for you, find an old Sea Scout manual or sailing handbook and learn the ropes. Personally, I think it's easier to tie knots than unsnarl a rat's nest of bungee cords. If you do go for rope, don't stop at the twine counter. Get rope that is at least 3/16 of an inch in diameter, preferably nylon, and definitely not polypropylene, which is too stiff to hold knots. It's great for a water ski towrope but not for holding gear on a bike.

Luggage

If your motorcycle didn't come with factory luggage, you may want to add some bags. The most obvious choice is throw-over fabric bags. But hard bags (usually cast plastic) have several advantages over fabric. Hard bags can be rigidly mounted to the machine so they don't sag into the mufflers or flap in the wind. They are reasonably water resistant and are usually equipped with locks to help keep your stuff secure. The disadvantages of hard bags are the extra width on the motorcycle and the difficulty of removing luggage if it is permanently installed.

The Europeans have focused more on removable (quick detach) luggage systems to provide the security of hard bags with the ease of being able to grab everything off the bike and hustle it up to a hotel room. Quick-detach bags also make maintenance much easier. Quick-detach luggage systems usually depend upon a clever bag carrier that attaches to different motorcycles with different brackets. If you don't like what your dealer has available, check out the European luggage.

Quick-detach hard luggage is an ideal approach for long-distance touring.

Wind Turbulence

As you add gear to your bare bike, be aware that it all affects wind turbulence. Unless the luggage has been tested by the manufacturer, you are advised to avoid speeds above 85 mph, whether it's hard luggage, throw-over fabric bags, or duffel bags that are secured with bungee cords. Generally, the closer you can tuck everything in toward the bike, the less wind turbulence you'll encounter. The 85 mph maximum speed is a precaution against turbulence that could cause the bike to wobble. But when carrying passengers or adding accessories, consider that anything on a bike carried above the center of gravity will act as a sail in crosswinds. That's something to remember when you are thinking about stacking a tall load behind the sissy bar or strapping bulky sleeping bags on the top box rack.

Remember: Take twice the money and half the gear.

Sidecars

When you hear the word *motorcycle,* do you picture in your mind a cruiser, a sportbike, a heavyweight tourer, a dual sport, or a dirt bike? Whatever the style of motorcycle that comes to your mind, it's probably a two-wheeler. Sure, you may have seen a sidecar outfit somewhere, but it may not have occurred to you that sidecar outfits and trikes are motorcycles too.

Adding a sidecar allows the whole family to go motorcycling together.

Mainstream motorcyclists tend to look upon sidecar outfits with both curiosity and disgust, cracking jokes about training wheels, and old guys, and questioning out loud why anyone in their right mind would screw up a perfectly good motorcycle by attaching a third wheel. Of course automobilists often wonder out loud why anyone in their right mind would ride a two-wheeler, so maybe it's just a matter of prejudice. To be sure, sidecars have some negative points. Dragging a car around eats up horsepower; makes the bike handle strangely; and adds extra stresses to the frame, suspension, and wheels. To add insult to injury, attaching a sidecar will probably void your new bike warrantee. Considering all that bad news, why do so many motorcyclists take the big plunge?

One practical reason for a sidecar is to carry passengers in greater comfort and safety. When you're young and free, kids are someone else's problem. But when kids arrive in your family, there is an immediate crisis of the bike vs. the children. A caring parent realizes there is really no safe way to carry small children on the seat of a two-wheeler. So what are the options? Some parents ignore the risks and pack the kid on the back of the saddle. Others sell the bike or let it gather dust until the kids grow up. Some parents leave the kids with a sitter and accept the guilt of motorcycling without them. Adding a sidecar allows the whole family to go motorcycling together, without taking any unnecessary risks, accumulating any guilt, or letting the bike gather dust.

Another practical reason for a sidecar outfit is stability. The threat of dropping your speedy two-wheeler on a streak of diesel oil or patch of loose gravel is a very real concern. In northern climates, motorcyclists tend to put away the bike for the winter because it's just no fun trying to keep a two-wheeler upright on a slippery road. The addition of a sidecar provides a way to keep on motorcycling even when the roads are slippery wet or icy slick. One recent trend is toward dual sport sidecar rigs with high fenders and knobby tires for exploring unpaved back roads or participating in off-road events such as the famous Los Angeles-Barstow-Las Vegas desert ride.

The addition of a sidecar provides a way to keep on motorcycling even when the roads are slippery wet or icy slick.

For those with physical limitations, a sidecar holds the bike up when stopped. And a lot of aging riders discover that a third wheel can prolong their motorcycling long after their legs have become too wobbly to hold up a bike. Remember, you are growing older at a rate of about one year every twelve months. When the day comes that you are reluctant to take the bike out because you're concerned about dropping it, you're ready to stop chortling at sidecars and start looking for one.

A sidecar can also be handy for carrying bulky loads of camping gear or even larger objects. I've had occasion to carry a side of beef, a five-drawer file cabinet,

David L. Hough

A lot of riders think of sidecars as old-guy bikes, but it's more a matter of risk than age. When you can't afford to fall down anymore, it's time for a hack.

a steel wood stove, a load of lumber, and several stacks of firewood on a flatbed sidecar. There are even commercial firms that vend ice cream and coffee from special sidecars. The utility of the breed is legendary.

But in spite of all the practical reasons for sidecars, the simple truth is that a lot of motorcyclists get into three-wheelers just for the entertainment value. It's fun to motor through a neighborhood on your outfit and have people smile and wave. People who would normally sneer at a motorcycle will accept a motorcycle with a sidecar attached and may even exchange pleasantries with the driver. It's especially pleasing to take some dyed-in-the-wool motorcycle-hater for a ride in a sidecar, and watch his or her expression change from a smirk to a grin, or to take some silver-haired octogenarian for a spin, and see her eyes sparkle for the first time in years.

Most importantly, some of us enjoy challenges. Once we've learned about two-wheelers, we're ready to try something different. Sure, a sports car would be fun, but it's not a motorcycle. A sidecar outfit is an extension of motorcycling. You're still out in the breeze, hanging onto handlebar grips, and rolling on the throttle. Sure, it's a big challenge to figure out how to handle these strange, off-center vehicles that are like no others, but it's worth the effort.

Yeah, but It Doesn't Lean Around Corners

Riders who have limited themselves to two-wheeled motorcycles typically are concerned that not leaning around corners would take all the fun out of riding. Over the years, various sidecar outfits have been built with connections that allow the motorcycle to lean, even with a sidecar attached. You might wonder why these "leaners" aren't more popular. The answer is that driving a rigid outfit is just as much fun as riding a two-wheeler, but in a different way. It's a real kick in the pants to hang off and slide an outfit around a sharp turn or drift down a gravel road without the fear of taking a tumble.

One point to remember about sidecars is that you don't have to give up your two-wheeler just because you learn how to handle a hack, too. It's possible to attach a sidecar to your only bike, and disconnect it for solo rides, but the most practical solution is to have a bike set up permanently as a sidecar rig, and in addition have a two-wheeler for those occasions when you want to enjoy leaning into curves. A sidecar gives you a good reason to have more than one type of motorcycle.

Sidecars Are too Slow for Me

Yes, if you compare a 1949 sidecar outfit to a late model motorcycle, it's going to look awfully fragile and slow. If you compare a 1949 automobile to today's cars, it will look ridiculously slow and clunky, too. There are all sorts of sidecars available, from antiques all the way to three wheeled exotica with low-profile tires, center hub steering, steerable sidecar wheel, three-wheel drive, ABS, and electric windshields. Some of the European sidecar rigs corner with the best of today's two-wheelers, without the risk of falling down.

There are even a few sporting three-wheelers on the drawing board, such as the Pegasus, with performance that is equal to a sports car but with the appearance of a sidecar rig. Hannigan sidecars developed a Tri Car with an offset left rear wheel like a trike but with an integral body on the side like a sidecar. The T-Rex from Canada is a symmetrical low-slung three-wheeler based on the drive train of a Suzuki motorcycle. Once you let your imagination go, it's possible to build a screaming three-wheeler, if performance is your thing.

A prototype of Pegasus Vigilante three-wheeler. No, it's not in production yet, but think of the fun you could have.

A Little History, Please

Sidecars have been around almost as long as motorcycles. Gottlieb Daimler and Wilhelm Mayback built the first "motorcycle" in Germany, back in 1884. By 1895, three-wheelers were being built in France. Within a few short years, there were hundreds of different motorcycle manufacturers around the world, and just about all of them offered sidecars, or at least included sidecar lugs on their frames, so the owner could easily attach a car.

David L. Hough

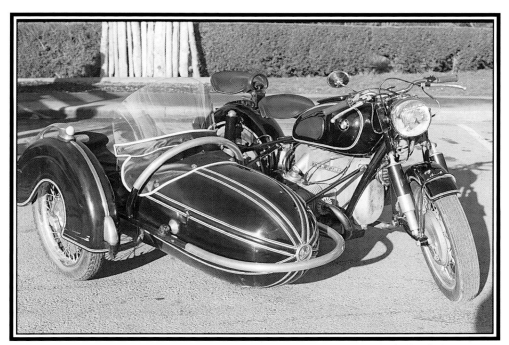

Classic sidecars from Germany, such as this Steib S500 attached to a modified BMW, are much sought after by collectors.

Back in those "good old days," men might straddle a bike wearing breeches, but women wore dresses. If you wished for female companionship on the ride, you needed to bolt up a "chair." (The reference to chairs isn't that odd, since some early sidecar bodies were constructed of wicker, using the same technology that was used for furniture.) But, at the end of World War II, everyone seemed to fall in love with the automobile, and sidecars began to disappear into dusty wood-

EML sidecar kits from the Netherlands include not only the sidecar but also special wheels, frame reinforements, leading link front suspension, and all the other bits and pieces to build a contemporary outfit.

sheds and museums. There were still a few sidecars on the road in the 1950s, but the Japanese manufacturers designed only two-wheelers, and the rest of the world followed that lead. By 1970, even BMW had changed to designs that no longer included provisions for sidecars.

Over the years, only Harley-Davidson in the U.S., and a few small manufacturers in Russia, the Ukraine, China, and Czechoslovakia continued to produce motorcycle/sidecar combinations. But that didn't stop inventive sidecar enthusiasts, who found ways to attach a sidecar to every imaginable type and size of motorcycle, whether or not the motorcycle manufacturer approved. So sidecars never disappeared and are now actually gaining in popularity. Today, there are hundreds of different sidecars available, both from manufacturers in the U.S. and from countries all over the globe. Small firms in Europe and Great Britain continue to build high quality sidecars and components such as leading link front ends, reinforced frames, and special wheels.

Where Do I Start?

Buying and attaching a sidecar can be a confusing and complex business for the first-time sidecarist. "Hacks" are just rare enough that genuinely knowledgeable experts are few and far between. Worse yet, there is a lot of faulty information floating about. Even your local motorcycle dealer or mechanic may know nothing about sidecars and may not know where to go for help. Some motorcycle dealers are sidecar friendly, but the majority of dealers today seem to be focusing on high-performance two-wheelers, off-road quads, snowmobiles, and personal watercraft. They just don't know enough about sidecars to offer any advice. If you don't want a new 180 mph sportbike, how about a new jet ski, or maybe a motocross bike for the kids?

Your best bet is to find a dealer who specializes in sidecars, or locate a sidecar club where experienced hackers can show you the ropes. Before you make any decisions about what you think you'd like, why not attend a sidecar rally and look around at the different rigs? You'll find most sidecarists are gregarious and willing to offer helpful advice. You might even get a demonstration ride. Sidecar gatherings tend to be family affairs, and motorcyclists arriving on two wheels are perfectly welcome to join in the fun.

Building an Outfit

Building a sidecar rig is a lot like a treasure hunt. You can't just run down to your local motorcycle dealer and pick out a rig you like. The sidecarist must be ingenious, curious, and persistent to solve all the riddles and find all the pieces. You really need to find a sidecar specialist, even if that means a trip to another state. Sidecar installation specialists either know where to find the needed bits and pieces or can custom-fabricate whatever special clamps or adapters are needed to attach the sidecar of your choice to the motorcycle you have selected for sidecar duty.

If you're thinking about attaching a sidecar to your current motorcycle, bear in mind that the sidecar should be matched to the motorcycle in size and weight. If you found a good deal on a lightweight sidecar at a swap meet but your bike is a heavy-duty cruiser, the combination might be a poor match and you won't enjoy a poor-handling rig. In very general terms, the sidecar itself should weigh approximately 30 percent of the bare motorcycle.

Attachment

Attaching a sidecar isn't as simple as dropping a trailer onto a ball hitch. The connections between the motorcycle and sidecar must be strong enough to handle the stresses of cornering and braking. The standard approach to sidecar attachment is four mounting points, two along the lower frame rail of the bike and two at the top. To facilitate alignment, the frame ends usually have threaded adjusters or sliding tubes that clamp in position.

Some sidecar manufacturers focus only on specific motorcycles so that they can build a foolproof kit to attach their sidecar to one particular model or family. For example, Liberty Sidecars focuses on specific models of Harley-Davidson only. The result is an installation with factory fit and finish. Ural America markets complete Russian-built motorcycle/sidecar outfits that are ready to drive.

One good approach for the novice is to buy a used outfit from a sidecarist who is stepping up to a more exotic rig. That provides a completely assembled vehicle to learn with. Later on, you'll be in a better position to decide what you really want. You can find used sidecar outfits in the back of *The Sidecarist* and *Hack'd,* and there are usually outfits for sale on display at motorcycle and sidecar rallies.

When you're looking at other people's sidecar rigs, you might wonder why some have strange front ends, different wheels, steering dampers, and other such modifications. Such modifications are usually made to improve handling. For example, changing to a leading-link front suspension not only provides a stronger design than a telescopic fork but also reduces steering effort. You don't have to modify your motorcycle to pull a sidecar, but some changes make a tremendous difference in handling.

The first important lesson about sidecars is that attaching a third wheel to a two-wheeled motorcycle produces a different vehicle with very different dynamics. Sure, it's the same motorcycle with the same license plate, but having a tricycle footprint changes the way it handles. And that can be a real mental shock for the experienced motorcyclist who expects to take a sidecar rig for a spin without any training.

Learning to Drive

If it isn't obvious, there are a number of special skills involved in piloting a hack, and it may take a few errors before the correct skills settle in between your ears. If you haven't driven a rig before, it makes a lot of sense to practice some specific exercises away from traffic and fire hydrants before you take an outfit out on public roads. Once the novice sidecarist acquires the new skills, an outfit magically gets a lot easier to control. And in case you're wondering, it is relatively easy to switch back and forth between a two-wheeler and a three-wheeler, just as you can switch between a car and a bike.

Remember that two-wheelers must lean to turn, and leans are initiated by countersteering. To turn left, you steer right. A sidecar rig doesn't have to lean first before turning. So to turn a rig to the left, you just point the front wheel toward the left. For motorcyclists with years of practice steering two-wheelers, steering a sidecar combination tends to confuse the brain until it switches off the two-wheeler balancing habits. That's one reason a veteran motorcyclist may initially dislike the feel of a three-wheeler and why it's a good idea to do a few practice laps before hitting the street.

To make life on a sidecar outfit even more interesting, left turns are different from right turns, accelerating and braking cause different steering reactions, and the driver must know how to steer the rig on two wheels as well as three. The lesson here is that your two-wheeler skills don't count when you climb on a three-wheeler. When you attach a sidecar, you're a sidecar novice.

What about MSF Rider Training Courses?

Most rider training sites offer two standard motorcycle courses, the *Motorcycle RiderCourse/Riding and Street Skills (MRC/RSS)* and the *Experienced RiderCourse (ERC)*, but neither is applicable to sidecars or trikes. Both of these courses were developed exclusively for two-wheelers. Some states are just beginning to offer three-wheeler training courses.

USCA Sidecar Safety Program

The United Side Car Association *Sidecar Safety Program (SSP)* has developed training programs for both novice and experienced sidecarists. The Sidecar Safety Program is independent of the Motorcycle Safety Foundation (MSF), although many SSP instructors are also MSF-certified.

A book is available, *Driving a Sidecar Outfit,* that includes both theory and practice exercises. It is a complete do-it-yourself text, including the curriculum used to train sidecar instructors. Sidecar courses are rare, and if you hear of one, don't hesitate to take it. If you're thinking seriously about driving a rig, (or even if you're mildly curious) why not get your own copy of *Driving a Sidecar Outfit?*

Information

The United Side Car Association publishes a magazine, *The Sidecarist,* that is mailed to all members of the organization. *The Sidecarist* provides information about rallies and other events, plus reports about travel, safety, and new products. One handy feature is the Classifieds, which list used sidecars and outfits for sale by owners.

Hack'd magazine is a quarterly publication devoted entirely to sidecars. Each issue is huge, stuffed full of stories, technical information, and commercial advertisements.

The Sidecar Industry Council (SIC) is an association of sidecar manufacturers, importers, dealers, and installers. The SIC can provide current information about sidecar specialists.

Internet Information

The USCA and SIC maintain an Internet site (at www.sidecar.com) that includes general information about sidecars, listings of sidecar events, links to various sidecar retailers and training courses, and a forum where you can ask questions. The SIC page provides links and information about sidecar manufacturers, importers, and installers.

Trikes vs. Sidecars

Motorcycle-based trikes are similar to sidecar outfits in many ways and handle much like a sidecar rig of comparable size. The most popular type of trike today is built by replacing the single rear wheel of a big bike such as the Honda Gold Wing with a two-wheel rear axle/differential. A trike corners as well as a typical sidecar rig with surprisingly good tip-over resistance. A trike shares the stability of a three-wheeled footprint but carries a passenger motorcycle-style behind the driver, which can be either a plus or a minus, depending on the passenger. But a sidecar outfit provides greater passenger protection, providing a better view ahead without having to peer around the rider, definite plusses for children. A sidecar outfit can carry three passengers or even two adults and two children.

Trikes based on motorcycles such as the Honda Gold Wing are a recent phenomenon, but three-wheelers are nothing new.

A trike provides symmetrical handling, which can be a plus for a driver who is considerably overweight, but a sidecar provides a means for carrying a wheelchair. A trike with a heavy automobile-type differential and large wheels tends to bounce more because of the greater unsprung weight. Because of its independent suspension, a sidecar outfit typically has a less bouncy ride but demands somewhat higher skill to drive due to the asymmetrical handling.

Both trikes and sidecar outfits are licensed as motorcycles in most states. The cost to convert a motorcycle to either a trike or a sidecar rig is approximately the same for a package of equivalent quality.

The old British Morgan was a good handler because the two front wheels provided excellent tip-over resistance.

Not the Bottom Line

We wouldn't want you to believe that this is all you need to know about sidecars. The need-to-know list is about twice as long as for other motorcycles, and we've barely scratched the surface. Now, if all this stuff about building a strange-handling vehicle, sliding the tires, and riding around in the wintertime leaves you colder than a frozen mackerel, you probably aren't cut out to be a sidecarist.

But if something we've said has triggered your imagination, let it simmer for a while. It seems to take most future sidecar pilots about three years before the third-wheel virus sets in. Use caution when looking at three-wheeled motorcycles or talking with sidecar or trike enthusiasts. The third wheel virus is contagious, and there is no known cure.

The End of the Trip

Similar to a motorcycle journey, this book heads off across an intellectual landscape, allowing the curious traveler to file away new memories, and, hopefully, triggering some fresh ideas. We started this *Proficient Motorcycling* trip by facing the risks of motorcycling openly and honestly, and we've wandered through a whole range of topics that have offered the possibility of becoming a smarter, more skillful motorcyclist. It's up to you to put the information to use, ignore it, or update it with what you discover from your own motorcycling experiences.

It may be the end of the trip, but it's only the start of the journey toward becoming a proficient motorcyclist. One final suggestion to make that journey more fulfilling is to share your knowledge with other less-experienced riders. You may discover what I've learned, that discussing motorcycle dynamics around a campfire or scribbling diagrams on a coffee shop napkin or writing articles to help others learn is an important part of the process. You'll always get back more than you give.

Now the trip is finished, the book has a back cover. Or perhaps we've just come full circle, back to the place where we started and ready to head out in a different direction. Thanks for the ride.

—David L. Hough

Resources

Organizations

Sidecar/Trike Education Program
Evergreen Safety Council
401 Pontius Avenue N
Seattle, WA 98109
(206) 382-4090
(800) 521-0778

Sidecar Industry Council
SIC President
P.O. Box 8119
Van Nuys, CA 91406

United Side Car Association
USCA Membership
130 S. Michigan
Villa Park, IL 60181
(708) 833-6732

USCA Sidecar Safety Program
SSP President
93 Thunder Road
Port Angeles, WA 98362

The Sidecar Industry Council and the USCA jointly sponsor a Web site at www.sidecar.com

Books and Magazines

Code, Keith. *Twist of the Wrist: The Motorcycle Racers Handbook.* Los Angeles, Calif.: Code Break, Inc., 1983.

Hack'd magazine
P.O. Box 250
Chandler, IN 47610-0250
(812) 825-3931

Motorcycle Safety Foundation Staff. *Motorcycling Excellence: The Motorcycle Safety Foundation's Guide to Skills, Knowledge, and Strategies for Riding Right.* North Conway, N.H.: Whitehorse Press, 1995.

Scott, Chris. *Desert Biking.* North Conway, N.H.: Whitehorse Press, 1995.

Driving a Sidecar Outfit. Port Angeles, Wash.: USCA Sidecar Safety Program, Inc., 1997. To order, call Whitehorse Press at (800) 531-1133.

Reports and Statistics

The U.S. DOT Bureau of Transportation Statistics (BTS) collects highway accident and fatality data through its Fatal Accident Reporting System and General Estimates System. The data first appeared on CD-ROM in 1996, and now much of the information can be found on the Internet at www.bts.gov. To order the information by phone, leave a message at (800) 853-1351. The BTS services are paid for by federal taxes.

The *Motorcycle Accident Cause Factors and Identification of Countermeasures,* January 1981—Final Report (aka the Hurt Report) is available to the U.S. public through the National Technical Information Service (NTIS), 5285 Port Royal Road, Springfield, VA 22161 (Web site: www.ntis.gov/ordering.htm). The essential data is in Volume I. The NTIS reference number is PB 81-206-443. However, the HPRL finds that the NTIS copies are of poor quality. The HPRL furnishes a higher quality, 425-page copy for $30.00. To order, contact the HPRL at:

Head Protection Research Laboratory
6409 Alondra Boulevard
Paramount, CA 90723-3759
(562) 529-3295
Fax: (562) 529-3297
E-mail: info@hprl.org

For more vehicle statistics, you can find enough numbers to make your head swim on the BTS *Traffic Safety* CD-ROM, which includes software to view and print the data. To order, contact the BTS at:

Bureau of Transportation Statistics
400 Seventh Street, SW
Washington DC 20590

BTS stats by phone:
(800) 853-1351

CD-ROM and products:
(202) 366-3282
E-mail: info@bts.gov
Web site: www.bts.gov

List of Abbreviations

ABS: antilock braking system
BTS: Bureau of Transportation Statistics
cc: cubic centimeters
CC: carrying capacity
CG: center of gravity
CP: contact patch
DOT: Department of Transportation
ERC: Experienced RiderCourse
GVWR: Gross Vehicle Weight Restriction
HOV: high occupancy vehicle lane
HPRL: Head Protection Research Laboratory

MCN: *Motorcycle Consumer News*
MRC/RSS: Motorcycle RiderCourse/Riding and Street Skills
MSF: Motorcycle Safety Foundation
NHTSA: National Highway Traffic Safety Administration
NTIS: National Technical Information Service
SIC: Sidecar Industry Council
SSP: Sidecar Safety Program
SUV: sport utility vehicle
USCA: United Side Car Association

Glossary

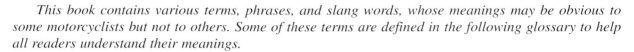

This book contains various terms, phrases, and slang words, whose meanings may be obvious to some motorcyclists but not to others. Some of these terms are defined in the following glossary to help all readers understand their meanings.

balaclava: a knit cap for the head and neck

big dog rider: an experienced and aggressive motorcyclist known for feats of daring and skill, such as riding at high speeds on public roads, without apparent fear of accident or arrest

binders: brakes

blind corner: a turn in the road that is partially hidden by visual obstructions such as trees or an embankment, making it so that a rider cannot see the road's path (surface hazards, other cars, etc.) around the rest of the turn

blind turn: see blind corner

body English: a method used by motorcycle riders to help control lean angle or direction independent of the handlebars by moving body position on the motorcycle

bow wave: a wave of water pushed ahead of a tire, similar to the wave pushed ahead of a boat moving through water

camber: sideways angle or slant of the pavement

canyon bites: serious accidents that occur while riding fast on twisty roads that are often found in canyons of mountainous areas

centerstand: a ladderlike stand that pivots down from the center of a motorcycle frame to support the motorcycle vertically with the rear wheel off the ground

contact patch: the spot in which the tire of a bike is in contact with the road's surface

countersteer: to turn the handlebars so the contact patch shifts in the opposite direction from that which the rider wishes the motorcycle to lean

countersteering: a method of controlling and balancing a bike as it initiates a turn in which the handlebars are momentarily turned in the opposite direction the rider intends to go

crash padding: a motorcyclist's protective clothing, especially abrasion-resistant and impact-absorbing riding gear and helmet

dicing: 1: taking the risk of racing one or more riders, usually on public roads **2:** riding a motorcycle in dense traffic

dive: to quickly change direction such as suddenly leaning the bike into a tight turn

edge traps: the raised edges of bumps or cracks in a paved surface that can catch a motorcycle's tire and cause the bike to lose balance

endo: pitching the rear of the motorcycle over its front, end over end

fairing: an aerodynamic shell covering the front of some motorcycles to reduce wind drag, provide wind protection for the rider, and enclose the machinery with a stylish skin

fairing pocket: a small compartment in the fairing, usually found in the sides of the fairing, alongside the fuel tank

flickable: unstable; taking very little effort to move between an upright position and a lean

fog line: the edge of the pavement

foot-skids: a rider's boots that are extended to the ground while the bike is in motion

formation ride: a motorcycle road event in which participants maintain their relative position in a group while riding down the road

four-wheel drift: sliding all four wheels at high speed

full chat: riding at top speed for the rider's skill level and road conditions

gypsy tour: a motorcycle road event, usually several days in duration, in which the participants travel through the countryside and stop at a different destination each night

hacker: a sidecar driver or enthusiast

hanging it out: riding aggressively, increasing the possibility of injury; continuing to ride when weather and traffic conditions are not safe; riding faster than skill level and/or without proper safety gear with the potential for losing control of the bike and slamming exposed body parts onto the pavement

high side flip: when a sliding rear tire suddenly regains traction while the motorcycle is leaned over, causing the motorcycle to violently snap from the leaning side to the other side (the high side)

low side: the left side in a left turn or the right side in a right turn

low sides: when the motorcycle loses balance and falls onto the ground on its low side

mystery tour: a motorcycle social and travel event in which participants stop at checkpoints to unravel a clue and solve the mystery of where the tour goes

off the gas: rolling the throttle closed to cause the engine to become a brake

on the gas: rolling on more throttle to cause the engine to develop more power

pillion pad: a small seat attached to the rear fender of a motorcycle to provide seating for a passenger

poker run: a motorcycle event in which participants stop at marked checkpoints to draw playing cards that by the end of the run determine a poker hand

rake: slope; the inclination of the steering head leaning back from vertical

rolling on the throttle: giving the bike more power by rolling the valve that controls the amount of vaporized fuel charge delivered to the cylinders

roost: accelerating with so much power that the rear tire throws dirt behind it, preferably into the face of a following rider; generally, showing up or embarrassing anot rider

round section tire: a tire that when inflated on the rim forms a round cross section with the width equal to the height

scooter: a tongue-in-cheek reference to a large motorcycle, generally used only among knowledgeable riders

Shoei: a brand of helmet

sidestand: an arm attached to a motorcycle that swings out from the left side to support the bike at rest; kickstand

skid lid: a safety helmet

slick plastic arrows: directional traffic control arrows made of smooth white plastic that are glued to the surface of the road

speed wobble: a sudden instability of a motorcycle at speed in which the front end of the bike darts from side to side uncontrollably

stoppers: brakes

stoppie: when braking on the front wheel causes the rear of the bike to rise off the pavement

superslab: a generic term for any multilane, high speed, limited access highway, including a freeway, tollway, motorway, parkway, or superhighway

tank slapper: a speed wobble so severe that the handlebars bang alternately against the sides of the fuel tank

target fixation: when a rider's eyes focus on a point in the distance or a line on the road, causing him or her to inadvertently steer the bike toward that area rather than in the intended path

tarmac: British term for what Americans call asphalt

time hack: an informal measurement of time, such as verbally counting out seconds to determine following distance to sight distance

tire cross section: the shape (profile) of the cross section of an inflated tire mounted on the wheel rim; what you would see if you could slice through the tire from side to side without letting the air escape

tire profile: the lateral curvature of the tread of an inflated tire, usually expressed as a comparison of height to width

trail: the distance along the ground from the steering axis to the center of the contact patch; on a common street bike this distance is about 4 to 6 inches

trailing brake: applying the rear brake as a motorcycle leans over into a corner

trailing throttle: closing the throttle as the bike decelerates to apply engine braking

tucking: a front wheel suddenly turning itself too sharply toward a turn with the bike leaned over

warp speed: any speed that is obviously in excess of the posted limit. "Warp 10" would hint at 100 mph, without admitting the actual speed.

wheelie: when a driver rolls on the throttle quickly enough to lift the front wheel of a bike off the pavement

white lining: driving on the broken white line that separates traffic lanes; usually done by motorcyclists as they drive between cars in heavy traffic

x-trap: a place in the road where railroad tracks or cable car tracks cross, forming the shape of the letter x and creating a slit in which the narrow tire of a motorcycle can get caught or wedged

Index

255